The Stories Behind Every Song

R.E.M.
Inside Out

CARLTON
BOOKS

The Stories Behind Every Song

R.E.M.
Inside Out

Craig Rosen

Copyright © Carlton Books Limited 1997, 2005

2 3 4 5 6 7 8 9 10

This edition first published in 2005 by Carlton Books Limited
20 Mortimer Street
London W1T 3JW

ISBN 184442 449 9

Project Editors: Lorraine Dickey, Lucian Randall
Copy Editor: Mike Flynn
Senior Art Editor: Diane Klein
Design: Tony Truscott
Picture Research: Lorna Ainger/Sarah Edwards
Production: Sarah Schuman

Printed in Dubai

DEDICATION
In memory of my friend Baird Mitchell
(1961-1988)

AUTHOR'S ACKNOWLEDGEMENTS

The quotes in this book that are not attributed to a specific writer or
publication are from interviews I conducted with the members of R.E.M.
in 1985, 1987, 1990, 1994, 1996, 2001, 2003 and 2004.

All the other quotes are attributed to the sources where the material
was pulled from. I'd like to thank all the authors, and radio show hosts
and producers whose interviews I culled from for the purposes of filling
in gaps in this book. In addition, on occasion, I consulted other books
on R.E.M. including: Marcus Gray's *It Crawled From The South: An
R.E.M. Companion*, Tony Fletcher's *Remarks: The Story Of R.E.M.*,
Jim Greer's *R.E.M.: Behind The Mask*, David Bowler and Bryan Dray's
R.E.M.: From Chronic Town To Monster, *R.E.M.: The* Rolling Stone *Files*
by the editors of *Rolling Stone*, Rodger Lyle Brown's *Party Out Of
Bounds* and Johnny Black's *Reveal: The Story of R.E.M.* Each of these
books is worth pursuing for any serious R.E.M. fan. In addition, be on
the lookout for Anthony DeCurtis' forthcoming R.E.M. bio.

Thanks to Dave DiMartino for recommending me and Lorraine Dickey
for agreeing that I was the man for the job;to Lorna Russell for pushing
for an update, to Chuck Crisafulli for the advice, Bertis Downs, Brian
bumbery, Nikki Herceg, and Karen Moss for their help and cooperation;
and Peter Buck and Mitch Easter for agreeing to be interviewed
specifically for this book. Thanks to fellow R.E.M. fan Rick Gershon
for providing me with copies of his clipping collection; Joel Oberstein;
Howard Stein and Lyndsey Parker at LAUNCH; Barbara and Harry
Rosen; Lorna Ainger, Terry Burrows, and Lucian Randall at Carlton
Books; and Michael, Peter, Mike, and Bill for the music and memories.
Special thanks to Patti, Tyler, and Chloe for
their love, support, and patience.

Additional thanks for help with pictures go to Laura Levine, Sandra-Lee
Phipps, Weaver D and Karen Weiss.

CONTENTS

When I first got the call from a friend informing me that a publisher was searching for someone to write a "stories behind the songs" book on R.E.M., I was immediately interested. Having recently completed my first tome, *The Billboard Book Of Number One Albums*, which profiled all of the American chart-topping albums from 1956 through 1995, it would be a welcome relief. Instead of writing about everything from the Beatles, Nirvana, and R.E.M. to the Singing Nun, the soundtrack of *The King And I,* and SSgt. Barry Sadler, I could write about something I specifically knew, followed, and cared about deeply.

Unlike New York's rock critic elite and various other hipsters, I completely missed the boat on the Hib-Tone single of 'Radio Free Europe,' and would spend months searching for it years later. However, I did discover R.E.M. fairly early on. In the summer of 1982, I received a copy of *Chronic Town* at the office of my college newspaper. Shortly thereafter I saw the band open for the English Beat at the Country Club in Reseda, California. From then on, I was hooked. The release of each new R.E.M. album was a monumental event. When an R.E.M. tour stopped in Southern California, the L.A. date alone would not suffice. My friends and I would also make pilgrimages to Santa Barbara, Orange County, and San Diego to catch all the West Coast dates. We knew that these were

Michael Stipe on the *Monster* tour: "No real turds in the punch bowl."

special days. R.E.M. was too good to remain a cult band forever. The band would soon graduate to arenas and the tours would become less frequent.

The fact that our hunch came true was bittersweet. Sure we could tell the naysayers that "we told you so," and celebrate the fact that something we believed in was being appreciated by the masses, but some of that early magic was gone. Nothing stays the same forever and R.E.M. was no exception.

Popularity, however, didn't mean that R.E.M.'s music became any less meaningful, as the band evolved from the mysterious little folk-rock group into arena rockers and back into a Baroque ensemble only to plug in again and rock the world. *New Adventures In Hi-Fi*, found a nice balance between the band's rocking and more introspective sides, while *Up, Reveal* and *Around The Sun* saw R.E.M. reinvented as a trio at the dawn of the 21st

I could safely call R.E.M. my favorite band. Over the years I've had other faves—Paul McCartney and Wings, Aerosmith, the Clash, the Buzzcocks, the Psychedelic Furs, and the Replacements—but none has maintained as consistent a body of work as Athens, Georgia's favourite sons. Sure the band has had an occasional misstep, but as Stipe once told me, "there has yet to be a real turd in the punch bowl, in terms of records."

Century and beyond.. As Peter Buck once said, "When we finish making records, hopefully, it will be just like a pilgrim's progress or something of where we've been, and where we've headed in the side trips. I don't know if you will be able to hear the albums and read it like a book and understand our lives and what we've done and all that kind of stuff, but I think there will be a clear portrait of us meandering where we go, and I like that idea."

INTRODUCTION

This book is designed to provide insight into that meandering, but by no means is it the be-all and end-all. As the members of R.E.M. pointed out during early interviews, the band's songs evoke emotions but are purposely vague so that the listener can find their own meanings. This, in fact, may be the secret to R.E.M.'s success and ironically may be the reason why some of the band's songs are so meaningful.

commercial zenith is somewhat distressing. Could the music world be taking R.E.M. for granted? Was R.E.M.'s tremendous success in the first part of the '90s a fluke?

Whatever the case, there's no doubt in my mind that R.E.M. remains a band worthy of our continued attention. While the band has changed in sound and numbers, its material continues to ring true with emotion and sincerity

R.E.M. pictured around 1984—"They're real, they mean it."

As clichéd as it may sound, R.E.M.'s music is an essential part of the soundtrack to my life. Over the years, I found meaning in their songs before I would discover what they were specifically written about. I found comfort after the death of a friend and my grandmother in the songs on *Reckoning*, years before I learned that the death of Stipe's friend Carol Levy had inspired the album track 'Camera.' When my mother died right around the time the first edition of this book was published, I returned to *Automatic For The People* and found new meaning and solace in its songs.

Other R.E.M. songs bring back memories of dating the woman who is now my wife, travel, a friend's suicide, weddings (including my own), work, and my son and daughter. When I listen to R.E.M.'s music, those memories, both good and bad, come flooding back to me.

The point behind all of this is that while this book will offer you some insights into the inspiration and recording of R.E.M. songs, you should by no means forget about what that song means to you   that is just as real and as important as any facts and theories contained here.

As the band celebrates its 25th anniversary, R.E.M. has gone from underground critics' faves to mainstream favorites to one of the world's highest-paid bands. The fact that the sales performance and critical response to its post-Bill Berry efforts is lackluster compared to the band's early '90s

that's missing from much of today's pop.

I hope this book inspires readers to pull their old R.E.M. albums off the shelf, dust them off, and give them another spin. You'll find, as I did, that these albums are just as vital today as they were when they were released. While working on this book, I may have grown tired from the fatigue of writing, but I was surprised that I found the band's music constantly refreshing.

As Michael Stipe once said, quoting the liner notes on an album by gospel group the Revelaires in the B-side rarity 'Voice Of Harold,' "they're real, they mean it—a must." The same is true of R.E.M and the band's entire catalog of recordings. Now, go listen.

HIB-TONE SINGLE

Radio Free Europe

It sounded murky. Cover art was reproduced poorly, and it suffered from improper distribution. Despite the flaws, 'Radio Free Europe' was the most important American indie rock single of the 1980s, heralding the arrival of an Athens, Georgia-based quartet called R.E.M.

In the year before the single was recorded, R.E.M. had established itself in the college town of Athens, Georgia, as a hot up-and-coming live act. It was on April 5, 1980, that the band played its first live performance at an abandoned church on Oconee Street, which also served as home to singer Michael Stipe and guitarist Peter Buck. Bassist Mike Mills and drummer Bill Berry rounded out the band, which showed a unique dynamic from the beginning. Mills and

Berry were schooled musicians who met in the ninth grade and had played together in several bands, while record store clerk Buck and art student Stipe were musically inexperienced. Buck hadn't picked up a guitar until 1978, while Stipe had a brief stint in a band in St. Louis that he would prefer to forget.

Despite the relative inexperience of half of the band, by the time R.E.M. contacted producer Mitch Easter, himself a veteran of a pop group called the Sneakers, the quartet was already an impressive unit, having discarded its earliest material in favor of new songs. Its first attempt to record demos at an Athens club called Tyrone's left the band unsatisfied. It was Peter Holsapple, a member of the dB's, who recommended that they contact Easter. Mitch Easter's

The church on Oconee Street, the site of R.E.M.'s first live performance.

studio—known as the Drive-In—was set up in his parent's garage in Winston-Salem, North Carolina. "I had seen their name on a poster, but I had never seen them or anything," Easter said. "So when they came into the studio, it was the first time I ever laid eyes on them or heard them. It was just kind of out of the blue."

When R.E.M. arrived at the Drive-In on April 14, 1981, Easter was pleasantly surprised. "They came over the night before the session and we sat around and talked. It was one of those fun kind of things where you are talking to people that you can talk to. They were like rock guys that I was familiar with," Easter said. "It was just real easy to talk to these guys who I had never met before and it was great. They went over and did their stuff and I was just struck by how kind of traditional it was, and I mean that in a totally positive kind of way. I was a fan of what was happening in the '80s, but the quality control wasn't really that good. In the new wave, the spirit was great, but not everyone was that good. They were sort of apart from that. They were part of the new wave

Mitch Easter of Let's Active and friend at the Drive-In studio.

scene commercially, you might say, but in their songwriting they really harked back to '60s bands. They really made me think of a Fab Four kind of vibe, a '60s rock combo kind of thing they had going, which somehow kind of cheered me up."

One of the songs R.E.M. recorded during that first session was 'Radio Free Europe,' which immediately appealed to Easter. "I thought it was great," he said. "I thought it was a really catchy song. It seemed like all the '60s rock combos that were catchy. They didn't mess around, they got right to the point. And that's what I thought was great about that song."

Musically, the sound was instantly appealing, propelled by Berry's insistent drumming and Mills's melodic bass lines, while Buck's ringing arpeggios added flavor. "You got it right away. It had some cool stuff like the bass line, and the sort of connector part before the chorus was real good," Easter said.

Yet the most distinct part of the song was Stipe's throaty singing, undeniably passionate, but for the most part indecipherable. "The image of 'Radio Free Europe' or whatever [Michael] was getting at there didn't even matter, because it was a good phrase, something we all knew," said Easter. Yet the fact that Stipe's vocals were difficult to understand would become an issue that would haunt the band throughout its career. Easter, however, didn't have a problem with the way Stipe sung. "I was always utterly mystified at all the attention that was put on that, because there are so many records that you can't tell what they are saying. I thought, 'Why is it such a big deal with this

guy? He's not the first?' Obviously, 'Louie, Louie' comes to mind. I thought that was in the grand tradition of things. It didn't even get my attention particularly, I just thought he had a good voice."

Mills was also blown away by Stipe's vocals. "I'll never forget the time when we wrote the music to 'Radio Free Europe' and I heard the melody that Michael had put over it. Where? How? Why? When?," Mills said to Jon Storey and Stuart Batsford in the British fanzine *Bucketful Of Brains*. "To this day, I don't know what I did," Stipe responded. "All you guys' jaws dropped… and I'm saying, 'What'd I do? What'd I do?'"

Years later, Stipe admitted to Andy Gill that he intentionally slurred his words. "I purposely did not want any of the lyrics understood," he said. "The main reason for that was that I hadn't written any of the words yet. So I just kind of blabbered over the whole single." Nonetheless, Stipe told Eric Flaum of *Goldmine* that he was impressed with the results. "We just sat around for a day and threw out all of this stuff," he said. "Never having been in a studio before, it was pretty amazing."

Although the words may have been obscured by Stipe's vocals, there was a definite inspiration behind the single. "Michael and I were talking about weird commercials and we remembered the spot they used to run for Radio Free Europe where they had that Czech disc jockey talking and then he introduced 'de Drivter… On Broadvay,'" Buck told Jeff Nesin of *Creem* in 1984. "When I was a kid I thought that stuff was perfectly natural, but as I got older I thought, 'Isn't that strange—America is spreading cultural imperialism through pop music.' We should send money so that they can listen to the Drifters. Now, I'd rather have them listen to the Drifters than have cruise missiles, but we thought that was really strange. So the song was related to that. To uncomprehending outsiders listening to rock'n'roll and not having a clue as to anything about it. I can't imagine someone behind the Iron Curtain figuring out what 'On Broadway' means. So it's an evocation of that without referring to the commercial."

Stipe, himself, was also somewhat of an enigma. "Michael was wearing these sunglasses, which made me think that he looked like Ian Hunter [the one-time lead singer

with Mott The Hoople]," Easter recalled. It turned out that Stipe had an eye infection, which required him to wear sunglasses. Stipe chose to record his vocals in a spot where he could not be seen by his bandmates and Easter. "I don't think he was really freaked out, but I think he was like a lot of people," Easter said. "I don't think he wanted to be looked at."

Initially, 'Radio Free Europe' and the two other tracks recorded during the first session at Easter's Drive-In studio weren't intended for commercial release. Instead, the band used the recordings as a demo tape for use as a calling card to drum up interest for a planned trip to New York City.

R.E.M. sent off 400 cassettes, featuring cover art made from photocopies, and stickered with the label "Danger: Do

Not Open." About a hundred of the tapes also included a dub version of 'Radio Free Europe,' which would later turn up on bootlegs.

A few months later, an Athens law student named Jonny Hibbert expressed interest in releasing a single by the band on Hib-Tone, his start-up label, in exchange for the publishing rights to 'Radio Free Europe' and 'Sitting Still.' The band agreed, and the songs were initially published by Hibbert's Dorothy Jane Music, despite the reservations of the band's friend, Bertis Downs, who was acting as their attorney.

The band wanted to go with the recording of 'Radio Free Europe' it had cut with Easter, but Hibbert insisted that it needed to be remixed. "When Jonny Hibbert came back up

Even in their early days R.E.M. had "a Fab Four kind of vibe," according to Mitch Easter.

to remix it, I thought, 'What for?,'" Easter recalled. "I thought it sounded O.K. and didn't know a whole lot and I didn't have a whole lot of equipment to change things with. But he came up any way and we spent hours remixing it, and it sounded pretty much the same."

When the single came back from the pressing plant, the band was not pleased. "Basically, I don't know what went wrong," Buck said years later. "The tapes are pretty clear, but the record itself doesn't sound very good. Rather than wait for us, he put it out. The guy didn't have any money, so I can't blame him. But when I heard it, I thought, 'This sucks.' At that point, I thought, 'Maybe this is the only thing we are ever going to do and it doesn't suit me.'" Buck took out his frustrations on a copy of the single. "I had a big pile of singles and I broke one and I nailed it to the wall."

Buck has a theory as to what had happened. "I know it's not the mix, because the mix is really good," he explained. "I know it's not the master, I've heard that and that was good, so I guess it's the pressing. That was the only part we weren't there for, because we were on the road."

Easter has a slightly different take. "It did seem to me that it wasn't mastered very well, or it wasn't pressed at a very good pressing plant, because the tape did have more life in it than that pressing did," he said.

Nonetheless, the single was released. The mostly black-and-white primitive cover art was as mysterious as Stipe's lyrics. "We just wanted something kind of different," Buck told *Bucketful Of Brains*. "Everyone at the time seemed to be putting out records with those Sex Pistols graphics, you know, the cut up letters. We were trying to combine different aspects of rock'n'roll, so there's this kind of weird arty front cover—even though the reproduction wasn't done all that well. And a kind of moody back cover photo." Buck says the front cover is "…just a smear. I think Michael took a picture of something when he was sneezing." The band is pictured on the back cover, but none of the members are looking at the camera. The credits read: "peter-g, michael-v, bill-d, mike-b."

To almost everyone's surprise, 'Radio Free Europe' became a critical success. "The single was only marginally available," Buck told Jon Young of *Trouser Press*. In fact, the first 1,000 copies didn't even have an address listed on the sleeve. "It did well for an independent record, but only in three cities: Atlanta, Athens, and New York. Sales totaled 5,000. It sold 4,000 initially and then it went out of print for eight months."

However, those copies ended up in the right hands. 'Radio Free Europe' was named the single of the year in the prestigious *Village Voice* Jazz & Pop poll, which surveyed more than 200 music critics. Despite all of the problems, R.E.M. had arrived.

Sitting Still

While 'Radio Free Europe' showcased R.E.M.'s more propulsive rock side, the flipside, 'Sitting Still' displayed their folk influences. "I was surprised at how sort of delicate and almost folky it was," Easter said. "I was expecting some kind of rock band and I was surprised when they came out with this folk-rock kind of number. I liked it, because my dad had always liked folk-rock kind of stuff and I had always heard it around the house and always liked it, but it wasn't what I expected, because these were the years of Klaus Nomi and stuff like that. I just thought, 'Wow, what a pleasant little song.'"

It was Buck's folk rock-flavored guitar riffs that would earn the band comparisons to such '60s California-based groups as the Beau Brummels and the Byrds.

The Byrds comparison, in particular, would stick with the band for years, much to their annoyance. "I'm a huge fan, I'm not sure that the rest of the guys in the band are," Buck explained years later. "I think you can probably tell some of the influence from my guitar playing, but not in any other way. It was an easy tag for people to grab on to and we did it ourselves by describing ourselves as a folk-rock band. But it just got to be a drag that in every review someone would say, 'They sound like the Byrds.' Point a Byrds album out that we sound like. There's a few elements of style that are similar and I did learn a huge amount from them, and I love their records, but no one else in the band really listens to them and I'm not the only songwriter."

Perhaps in an attempt not to limit themselves to folk-rock, the band included what some have described as a "polka" version of 'Sitting Still,' as a joke, on the demo tape that featured 'Radio Free Europe.'

Like 'Radio Free Europe,' and much of the band's early works, the subject matter of 'Sitting Still' was, for the most part, a mystery. "I remember Michael said it had something to do with his sister, who was a teacher," Easter revealed. More specifically, the song is said to be inspired by Stipe's sister Cyndy, who taught deaf children. Stipe repeatedly sings in the chorus, "I can hear you," but by the song's end he asks, "Can you hear me?," which is perhaps a challenge to listeners to decipher his slurred singing.

One line in the song in particular has been hilariously misinterpreted by fans as "We could gather/throw up beer." A decade after the release of the Hib-Tone single, even Stipe claimed to be baffled by the song. "I can remember the first two lines," he told Jeff Giles in a 1991 interview for *Rolling Stone*. "'Up to par and Katie bar'—'Katie bar the door' is a Southern expression. 'Up to par and Katie bar the kitchen door, but not me in.'" When pushed for more Stipe admitted, "I don't remember, I really don't. I haven't sung that song in five years. I mean sung the real words. I've syllabilized it. Is that a word? When we sing it in concert, I wing it. I don't know the words. I know the sounds. I can approximate them."

'Radio Free Europe' and 'Sitting Still' would resurface on *Murmur* two years later, when some listeners were still looking for hidden meanings in Stipe's lyrics. Others, however, had given up and were just enjoying the grooves.

althougth the members of R.E.M. were less than pleased with the experiences that surrounded the release of 'Radio Free Europe' on Hib-Tone, the band planned to follow up the single with an EP partially funded by David Healey who, like Hib-Tone's Jonny Hibbert, was a young entrepreneur.

Healey, an art student from Princeton, New Jersey, moved to Athens during the summer of 1981 in the hopes of launching a record label, tentatively called Dasht Hopes, with the members of R.E.M.

Initially, the band wasn't sure it would work with Easter again. "I had to fight to get that session," the producer recalled. "This place in Atlanta had popped up and they were doing a lot of work for the other new wave bands like Pylon and stuff like that. They were going to record there. I remember seeing the band in Greensboro, and talking to [the band's manager] Jefferson [Holt] and giving him this big pitch— I didn't think that the 45 represented the sound we could get. I wanted them to come back, because I liked them."

Eventually, Holt and the band realized that the return to the Drive-In, which charged a mere $250 a day, was the right choice. For three days in October 1981, the band went back to Easter's studio. "It was really great," Easter recalled. "They were a little more confident at that point from playing and having the single do well. It felt like the perfect situation."

"We didn't even have a record deal at the time. We just drove up and made the record," Buck recalled. "We were a work in progress. The first 12 songs in our set were gone within three months of us starting out."

While the band had discarded a dozen songs, it did have six keepers worthy of recording. Five of them would end up making the EP. Two others—'Ages Of You' and 'Shaking Through'—would be recorded and appear on subsequent releases. "We were just kind of finding our feet as songwriters," Buck explained. "All of those songs we wrote in the space of a year."

The decision to record an EP rather than a full album seemed logical at the time. "We just felt we weren't really

The latter song, which remains unreleased, featured Stipe reading a short sex story called 'Jazz Lips,' about an African-American jazz musician and his Swedish girlfriend, from the pages of a '50s men's magazine. "Doing tape loops and that totally appealed to Michael, who definitely had the art-school sensibility back then. He took lines out of that story and recited them in this beatnik sort of way, and there was feedback and other sounds on it. It was just something we did for fun. They were really into all that kind of manipulation. That old-time studio stuff of chopping up the tape and all that. It was probably the best session that I did with them in a way, because they felt so free and they were really into all that stuff."

CHRONIC TOWN

there yet, as far as songwriting goes, to make a full album," Buck recalled. "All of our peer group in Athens would write 12 songs and make an album. Everyone was saying, 'You should make an album,' but I didn't think we were ready to make a full album. I thought the EP was a great way to get us out and get us around and we could write some more songs. It turned out to be true, because we wrote a lot of good material in the next few months that ended up on *Murmur*."

With the band's confidence riding high, and with no pressure from a record company, R.E.M. and Easter were free to experiment during the sessions. "The band was ready to do cool stuff and stretch out a little bit," Easter recalled. "I was really into tape loops back then, so we worked some tape loops into 'Wolves' and this other kind of art noise thing called 'Jazz Lips.'"

During the *Chronic Town* sessions, R.E.M. were willing to try out experiments.

Buck confirmed that the band was ready to experiment during the sessions. "I was basically asking Mitch, 'What's this?' One day I asked what a tape loop was so he made a tape loop and we made a track and it took, like, an hour."

Stipe, too, was a novice in the studio. "The first year-and-a-half we were a band and playing, I didn't know the difference between the bass guitar and the guitar," he said in a radio interview. "And then someone finally told me that the bass guitar has four strings on it. Then it took me another year to figure out that the bass guitar was the one that was doing the low sounds."

Perhaps that naiveté led the band to experiment in the studio and outdoors, as Easter occasionally chose to move the proceedings outside. "Because my studio was in a place where you could go outside and do things, I said, 'Hey it's nice outside, let's do this outside.' It was just goofiness," Easter recalled. "It was just a way to make the session less formal and make the band feel like they were skipping school. It was really just for fun. We got some great things that way."

The furious pace of the sessions was almost as rapid as the tempo of R.E.M.'s songs at the time. "I think we only worked two or three days," Buck recalled. "It was a really fast thing. It was the first time we went into the studio where we could hear the end result kind of sounding like the way we wanted it to sound."

That sound was an accurate depiction of where R.E.M. was at the time. "*Chronic Town*, like all of our records, fits exactly where we were at that moment and we rushed right through it," Stipe told Timothy White on a Westwood One Radio special. "And that's exactly what we were doing live at the time. We were so terrified to be on stage, we would catapult our way through every single song. We would finish an hour-and-a-half set in 40 minutes."

While R.E.M. continued to work with Healey in preparation for the release of *Chronic Town*, they hadn't given up hope of landing a recording deal with an established label.

Ian Copeland, who ran a booking agency called F.B.I., had befriended Mills and Berry back in their day in Maçon. Ian's brother, Miles, headed I.R.S. Records, an A&M Records-distributed label that had such (then) cutting-edge acts as the Go-Go's, Wall Of Voodoo, and the Buzzcocks on their roster. Miles also managed The Police, a trio that featured another Copeland sibling, Stewart, on drums.

While Ian Copeland had passed Miles a tape and put in a good word for R.E.M., Mark Williams, another fan of the band, passed their demo tape to I.R.S.'s young VP, Jay Boberg. The tip from Williams, an Atlanta DJ and college rep for A&M Records, was enough to intrigue Boberg.

However, Boberg wasn't the only young executive interested in the band. Jim Fouratt, a New York club promoter who had been instrumental in booking Athens acts in the Big Apple, had established a production company with producer Kurt Monkacsi, who had ties to RCA Records. The band recorded seven songs with Monkacsi, at RCA studios in New York on February 1 and 2, 1982.

R.E.M. had established interest from the other parties, but found no one ready to commit. Undaunted, the band returned to Drive-In in the middle of February to polish off *Chronic Town*, before sending the tapes to Sterling Sound in New York in March to be properly mastered.

Boberg, however, had not forgotten about the band. On March 12, he caught R.E.M. at the Beat Exchange, a seedy club located just off Bourbon Street in New Orleans. By most accounts, it was a terrible night. Nonetheless, Boberg was

impressed and vowed to sign the band.

R.E.M. was also pleased, as it seemed that I.R.S. would be an ideal home for the band. "They had the Buzzcocks at the time, the Cramps, the Fall, and Wall of Voodoo," Buck told David Fricke. "They were doing a lot of the kinds of records I was listening to. And it was the perfect label for us." It also made sense for I.R.S. to pick up the already recorded 'Chronic Town' EP, rather than have the band go back into the studio. "I.R.S. was doing EPs on everyone at first," Easter noted, "so they had the perfect thing ready to go."

Exactly who should receive credit for signing R.E.M. remains a subject of debate to this day. Ian Copeland maintains that Miles signed R.E.M. to I.R.S. as part of trade of sorts that the two brothers hammered out. "He had this all-girl group called The Bangs and I didn't really want to handle them so I did a deal with him, 'I'll do The Bangs if you sign R.E.M.,'" he told Jim Irvin in *Mojo*. "And The Bangs turned out to be The Bangles and R.E.M. were very beneficial for I.R.S., so it was a good deal all the way around."

Whatever the case, R.E.M. signed with I.R.S. on May 31, 1982. While the band was thrilled, Miles Copeland had other things on his mind at the time. "It was a big day for us, but Miles Copeland walked straight past us because the Lords Of The New Church had just arrived," Berry told Tom Doyle in *Q*.

David Healey's hopes of starting his own label were dashed, but R.E.M. still had some unfinished business to take care of with Hibbert, who still owned the publishing rights to 'Radio Free Europe' and 'Sitting Still.' After some persuading, Hibbert, who was strapped for cash, eventually sold back the rights to the songs to the band. By then, R.E.M. had established their own company, Night Garden Music, which published the five songs on *Chronic Town*.

On August 24, 1982, the EP was released on I.R.S. Records in the US. Overseas, however, the EP would remain unreleased until it was included on the CD of *Dead Letter Office* in 1987.

The EP's cover sported a photo of a gargoyle years before the carved stone figures would become popular characters in Walt Disney's interpretation of *The Hunchback Of Notre Dame*. The photo of the gargoyle was also to be featured on the label of the first 10,000 copies of the EP, but I.R.S. soon ditched the plan, because it was too expensive.

As with the Hib-Tone 'Radio Free Europe' sleeve, the band chose to make the credits as vague as possible. Back was the first names-only approach, but on *Chronic Town*,

R.E.M. didn't even bother to include the one letter description of the band members responsibilities, but it did help people match the names to the photo on the back cover. Although the EP sports the credit "a dasht hopes production," Healey is simply listed as "ex producer."

The songs are listed dead-center, with those titles with the fewest characters appearing first, resulting in a pyramid-type design. Whether the songs are listed in the correct running order is debatable, since there is no side one or side two – instead the sides are identified as "poster torn" and "chronic town." (On *Dead Letter Office* the songs were sequenced with the "chronic town" side first, and that's the model we've followed here.)

Another mystery, of course, was what exactly is 'Chronic Town?' More than a decade later, the hip-hop nation would adopt the term "chronic" as slang for particularly strong marijuana. But it's doubtful that's what the members of R.E.M. had in mind at the time. As Berry explained, 'Chronic Town' "is a city in the state of mind." With the EP filled with "wolves," "boxcars," and odd hobbies such as "gardening at night," and fueled by the undeniably catchy guitar hooks and intriguing vocals, R.E.M. took you there.

Chronic Town's "Ex producer" David Healy, left, with Bill Berry in 1982.

Wolves, Lower

The first taste of R.E.M.'s recorded work following the release of the 'Radio Free Europe' single didn't disappoint. With an insistent Buck guitar riff, a fast-paced Berry drumbeat, and a Stipe howl, R.E.M. returned in fine form.

The initial recording of 'Wolves, Lower,' however, wasn't quite up to scratch. "We recorded it when we did the original batch of songs for the EP, but it was as fast as hell," Easter recalled. The fast version even got mastered for vinyl, but then the band had second thoughts about the track. "For

The slower version, however, was an Easter favorite. "I just loved it. To me, it was their masterpiece at the time," he said. "It had a lot of good recording highlights."

Among the high points was a portion of the vocal track recorded outside the Drive-In Studio. The decision to record outdoors was prompted by Easter's desire to be different. "It was really weird, but by the time I started the studio I was 26, and I felt like I was 100," he said. "I felt like I had been around this stuff forever. I felt like I was way behind and it was

Out set Riding Hood, so obliging and sweet,
And she met a great Wolf in the wood,
Who began most politely the maiden to greet,
as tender a voice as he could.

He asked to what house she was going, and why;
Red Riding Hood answered him all:
He said, "Give my love to your Gran; will try
"At my earliest leisure to call."

For 'Wolves, Lower,' R.E.M turned to such childhood classics as *Little Red Riding Hood*.

time to catch up, but I also knew it was kind of impossible to catch up, so I thought my approach would be to be incredibly cavalier about the process. I was going to not do the stuff they always told you do."

Of course, one of the things any professional producer is not supposed to do is record a studio album out of the studio, but, to Easter and R.E.M., it didn't matter. In fact, the natural sounds surrounding the studio would add atmosphere to the recording.

"We had really loud insect noises there in good weather," Easter explained. "I think we just did the chorus part out there. I think I used a noise gate, so it turned off between vocals. There's actually crickets buzzing underneath the voices, which you don't really hear, but I think subliminally it must do something. You could hear it if you listened to the multi-track tape, but in the finished thing it's not too obvious."

As was the case with much of R.E.M.'s material, Stipe's lyrics aren't easily understood, but the line about "wolves at the door" brings back visions of such childhood classics as *The Three Little Pigs* and *Little Red Riding Hood*.

whatever reason, they decided to give it another try, which was a good thing because it really was like the speed of light," Easter added. "When you hear that version now it sounds silly."

Although there wasn't a single released from *Chronic Town*, I.R.S. Records gave listeners a taste of R.E.M. by including 'Wolves, Lower' with the Lords Of The New

Church's 'Russian Roulette' on a free flexi-disc included in the December 1982 issue of *Trouser Press* magazine.

The band also made its very first video for the track. The clip, directed by Valerie Faris and Jonathan Dayton, who would later work on *The Cutting Edge* series, was shot in Hollywood, California. The video featured Stipe lip-syncing, something which inspired him to disavow the practice for several years in future clips. "I agreed to lip sync," Stipe explained in a radio interview. "You're very familiar with it I'm sure. It's where they play a song and you stand there and pretend that you are singing and your mouth moves and you put a lot of emotion into it, and I couldn't hack that."

'Wolves, Lower' was originally titled simply 'Wolves,' but was expanded, reportedly because Stipe had inexplicably wanted to put a comma in the title. However, the song reverted back to the original one-word title, leaving out the comma when it appeared on the UK 12-inch of '(Don't Go Back To) Rockville.'

Gardening At Night

An important milestone in the history of R.E.M., this song inspired the name of the band's music publishing company, Night Gardening Music. However, that name wasn't the band's first choice. "Their publishing company was going to be called Murmur," Easter recalled, "but they couldn't get it, so they settled for Night Gardening."

Still, the name was appropriate, as 'Gardening At Night' marked a turning point in the band's songwriting. "Right around the time we wrote 'Gardening At Night' our songwriting started getting better," Buck explained. "We wrote that and 'Just A Touch' the same week."

As is the case with several of its songs, R.E.M. had a number of different versions of 'Gardening At Night.' "I think I got Michael in trouble with his friends over that song," Easter said. "He had two ways to sing that song. The sort of soft way and the other hard way, which was more like the 'Radio Free Europe' voice. I encouraged him to use that soft voice, because I thought it was a different angle. They had other songs on the record that were more aggressive and I thought his voice sounded good that way."

Easter's pick, however, didn't sit well with some of the R.E.M. faithful. "When tapes went back to Athens, it was considered to be wimpy by some people, but I still think it was the right thing for him to sing in that sort of falsetto soft voice."

If fans had not already checked out a bootleg of the other version, they had their chance to hear the alternate take on an official release. I.R.S. decided to include 'Gardening At Night (Different Vocal Mix)' on the 1988 "best of" collection, *Eponymous*.

"The one that ended up on the compilation that I.R.S. put out, that is the vocal I really like," Buck said. "On that one he

Producer Mitch Easter opted to go with Michael Stipe's softer voice on 'Gardening At Night.'

is singing in more of a full-throated voice. He went back and for some reason said, 'I really want to sing it this way.' None of us liked it, but Michael really loved it.

"A couple of years later when we were doing that compilation, he said, 'God what version is that? I said, 'That's the original,' and he said, 'God, why didn't we use it? I prefer that one, but the other one is fine too.'"

On the instrumental front, Buck used Easter's electric sitar on the track. "That was typical of that session," Easter

---

Peter Buck and Michael Stipe contemplate 'Gardening At Night.'

---

said. "They were really interested in using some different instruments. I had a lot of guitars and instruments around. I was sort of building up my supply of oddball things and I liked to bring them out at the sessions and say, 'See what you can do with this.' I think Pete also used my electric 12-string on that song."

What, exactly, does 'Gardening At Night' mean? "It's basically a metaphor for the uselessness of everything. But if you didn't get that I'm not surprised, it's kind of a confused song," Buck told John Platt in *Bucketful Of Brains*. "Actually there was an old guy in my neighborhood who would be out gardening at 2 a.m. in his suit and tie. I'd see him when I was out trying to get beer at the Magic Mart or somewhere. I told Michael about the guy and he wrote the song."

Carnival Of Sorts (Box Cars)

This song is the title track of sorts of *Chronic Town*, as the song's lyrics feature the words "chronic town." It was also the first of many R.E.M. songs to have a reference to trains. For many of R.E.M.'s early tours, 'Carnival Of Sorts (Box Cars)' served as a show-closer.

"That was always like the last encore song," Buck said. "I'm not sure what the influences were. It's got all those chords, but speeded up and kind of rocking."

As was the case with 'Gardening At Night,' a few different versions of the song exist. "I remember we did one that had that Casio [keyboard] and one didn't," Buck explained. Easter confirmed that the song's introduction was played on a Casio. "It was like one of those you can get for $30 at a department store," he said. "We used this old tape recorder microphone to mike that thing up to make it sound sort of bad and distant."

Other than the keyboard and Stipe's usual obscure lyrics, 'Carnival Of Sorts (Box Cars)' was pretty straightforward. "That was a big favorite of fans live," Easter added. "People always asked for it."

The song's lyric, "poster torn," also served as the title of one side of the EP.

1,000,000

This is the hardest rocker on *Chronic Town* and features some of Stipe's most passionate, but indecipherable, vocals. Again, it is a fairly straightforward song.

"I don't remember any kind of funny recording stuff, except the drum part intro with the toms," Easter recalled. "Later, when we attempted that art-school stuff with tape loops, I remember making a loop out of that drum pattern and cutting it so it had an odd number of beats in it and we made that loop the foundation of that 'Jazz Lips' thing they did."

Part of '1,000,000' also ended up in the 1983 science fiction film *Strange Invaders*. "In the scene, it's real great, this guy comes in and turns on the radio and we're on," Buck said in a UK radio interview, "and he feeds his dog a can of beer and the dog laps it up. I thought, 'How appropriate.'"

Stumble

'Stumble,' the final track on the EP, perhaps benefited—or suffered, depending on your point of view—the most from the band's art-school ambitions, with its weird beats, spoken-word mid-section, and use of tape loops.

"The drums remind me of a Pylon song," Buck said. "Bill had been playing with Love Tractor, so there was the kind of disco-thing in there too. We were learning how to write songs and it was less traditional than any of our other early stuff. It has these weird kind of broken chords and weird beats. In a way we were just kind of figuring out how to write songs. We certainly didn't have a lot of chance to go back and reflect on them."

Easter had a rosier memory of the tune. "I really like it," he said. "To me that had the quintessential R.E.M. vibe at the time. It had the slowed down ska beat and the thin sounding, repetitious non-full chord guitar part, and a bass line that moved under it. I thought the way they did that was really clever and cool. I liked that I lot.

"I thought it was great that Pete Buck just didn't play chords all the time," Easter added. "He played these sort of melody things that were sort of raga-ish, and the bass sort of made the chord changes happen underneath it. Plus it had the sing-song kind of melody that I thought they did really well back then."

The song's middle section lent itself to greater experimentation. "Of course that was the perfect opportunity to use more tape loops," Easter added. "I think that was a song that they quickly thought was really stupid, but I thought it was really fun to record."

The producer was also fond of Stipe's lyrical device. "I liked that line, 'We stumble through the A-P-T.'—I guess meaning 'apartment.' That was really happening."

With its moody and mysterious sounds, catchy guitar riffs, and passionate but mostly indecipherable vocals, *Murmur* was the perfect marriage of R.E.M.'s rock instincts and the experimental drive of producers Mitch Easter and Don Dixon. Yet it was a collaboration that almost didn't happen.

Even after *Chronic Town* garnered critical raves, the powers that be at I.R.S. Records weren't certain that Easter was the right producer for R.E.M.'s full-length debut. Instead, they suggested the band work in Atlanta with Stephen Hague, whose credits would later include work with the Human League, Orchestral Manoeuvres In The Dark, and New Order. Hague had the band play 'Catapult' nearly 50 times to a click track. Later, the producer took the tapes to Boston to overdub some synthesizers. By most accounts, the band was deeply disillusioned by Hague's plan to polish its sound. More than a dozen years later, however, Buck said it wasn't as serious as some would have you believe.

"It wasn't such a bad experience," he explained. "I like Stephen and he's made some great records, but he wanted to work in a way that we weren't interested in working. I.R.S. wanted to try it out and we were like, 'Sure, we'll try that.'"

Years earlier, however, Buck complained about the sessions. "When we eventually did *Murmur*, every song on it was a first take," he told David Fricke. "But Hague had us do songs 35 times. And then he'd put together an edit of say, the

---

Dream on: R.E.M. captured during the *Murmur* era. From left, Stipe, Berry, Mills, and Buck.

---

chorus from the 13th with the bridge from the 29th. It got to the point where I didn't know what we were doing. Two days in the studio and we didn't even finish one song."

Unhappy with Hague's production style, the band convinced I.R.S. to give Easter and Dixon a shot. At Reflection Sound Studios in Charlotte, North Carolina, the band cut a demo take of 'Pilgrimage' with Easter and Dixon.

But I.R.S. was no more impressed with the Easter-Dixon demo than the band was with Hague. "The result was that the label didn't like either," Easter recalled. "At that point, the band was really headstrong. They said, 'Too bad, we're doing it this way,' and I think that's because the other session had really been miserable for them."

Although Buck's memory about the Hague session has brightened over the years, he does recall that the band became worried about I.R.S., a record company whose expectations had grown having experienced its first taste of massive commercial success with the Go-Go's 1981 album *Beauty And The Beat*.

"At first the people at I.R.S. said, 'Don't worry, you won't have to do anything. You don't have to have a hit single.' But when we got around to do *Murmur*, the Go-Go's had a hit, and the people at I.R.S. were saying, 'You need to have a big producer. You need to have a hit record.' It really bummed us out. We took a $7,000 advance instead of getting like $200,000 from a major label so we could do what we wanted

MURMUR

to, then they were saying, 'You have to use this producer. We don't want you to record it in the South. We want you to record it in L.A. You have to have a disco song.' We didn't pay attention to any of it. It was like basically, 'You can fuck off!' It was a little depressing that all of a sudden they had to get involved. In a way it kind of made us more guarded.

"We trusted Mitch and Don a lot, but we also had the fear that the record company was going to make them make us do something we didn't want to do," Buck continued. "So when we got around to *Murmur*, we were always asking, 'Why are we doing this? Whose idea is this?' But to Mitch and Don's favor, they didn't try to make us do something we didn't want to do. Their job was to protect us and they did, but at the time we didn't really know it."

Easter and Dixon also felt the wrath of the record company while recording *Murmur*. "During the course of the *Murmur* sessions, Jay Boberg from I.R.S. came out to the session and gave Don Dixon this big speech about having a hit," Easter recalled. "I don't think those guys were in a hurry to make a record in Los Angeles or New York or any other big industry center. The band was real weary about that, because they didn't want to get turned into something they didn't feel good about."

R.E.M. did have a good feeling about making the move from Easter's Drive-In Studio in Winston-Salem, North Carolina, to the larger Reflection Sound Studios, located approximately 80 miles south in Charlotte. "We liked the vibe at Reflection," Buck explained. "They usually record gospel artists there. We also needed more space than the Drive-In would allow for different instruments to be brought in for the album. There are no distractions in Charlotte, no places to go for parties or nightclubbing to interrupt what we are doing in the studio." I.R.S. gave R.E.M. a budget of $15,000 to record the album, while Easter and Dixon split a $2,000 advance for their services.

The decision to move to Reflection also had a lot to do with I.R.S.'s insistence that the band record its debut album at a studio with a 24-track board. At that time, Easter's Drive-In was only a 16-track. The move to Reflection also led Easter to ask Dixon, who was not credited but helped out with some mixes on *Chronic Town*, to come on board as a co-producer. "It was too intimidating to go there myself, so I asked him to get involved so I wouldn't feel totally swamped by that place. Don was an old friend I had known since 1970 and he had a lot more experience."

After the sessions with Hague, the members of R.E.M.

From left, Jay Boberg of I.R.S., Mike Mills, and R.E.M. manager Jefferson Holt.

were gun-shy about embracing new technology in the studio. "They heard all these tacky records that were coming out then. They were really appalled by modern keyboard sounds," Easter recalled. "But all old-timey stuff was OK, so we were able to use pianos and organs, even electric pianos, but that was our limit, that and guitars were sort of our palate. They were really worried that if Don or I suggested some kind of effect or something that they would end up sounding kind of goofy and dated, but what they didn't realize is that Dixon and I had impeccable taste."

It took the members of R.E.M. a while to get over the session with Hague. "In particular, Bill had gotten that bullshit about doing 2 million takes so he would play utterly like a robot," Easter added. "We had to keep telling him that everything those other guys told him was crap, because he was good. That was the kind of thing that Don Dixon and I were trying to rebel against. That whole miserable way of making records that had set in the '70s and the '80s."

It took a pep talk from Easter and Dixon to get the band back on track. "Once we really kind of yelled at them to not go in there to make a demo, but to make a record and experiment like they used to," Easter recalled. "Once we got that out of the way, I thought it got going really good."

The production by Easter and Dixon was a great influence on the sound of the album, but Buck said that he pretty much had the album plotted out in his head before the band entered the studio. "I knew which songs were going to be on the record and had a good idea of what order they were going to be in," Buck explained. "Mitch and Don did a great job. They had never really heard many of the songs before. Some of them were brand new. We would go in and record them. I had pretty much in mind what I wanted. An acoustic guitar, a load of electric guitars, a soft electric guitar, and a 12-string, and Mitch and Don would find ways to make it all sound interesting. We didn't know enough to know what we were doing. The arrangement ideas were all ours, but then Mitch would say, 'Why don't you record a 12-string like this and mike the strings, as opposed to miking the amp.' A lot of what kind of makes that record sound the way it does was making all the weird instrumental ideas we had work together."

Even before *Chronic Town* came out, R.E.M. had written six new tracks for its first full album. "So often bands make one good record and then for the second they write all the songs in like six days just before recording them," Buck said in *Bucketful Of Brains*. "We figured we wouldn't have any more time off between that time and recording, so we sat down and wrote a bunch of songs that we could work up on the road."

Armed with a full repertoire of quality songs, the band set its sights high on *Murmur*. "The idea was to make a strong record with no filler, like *Aftermath* by the Stones, where every song is different but it sounds like a group effort," Buck told Jon Young in *Trouser Press* shortly after the album's release.

While Buck may have had a grand plan, Stipe was still a novice who didn't know the difference between sharp and flat. "For the first two albums that we made, when I was singing the guys would say I was out of pitch and I just kind of nodded," he said on a radio interview. "Then I would say, 'What do I need to do?,' They'd say, 'You're a little flat, and then I would go out and sing it again and they would say, 'You're a little sharp now.' "

As for Stipe's mysterious lyrics, he admitted that much of it was just sounds rather than words. "The first couple of albums, there was really nothing to write. Often there weren't real words, it was just a lot of sound."

Even if Stipe was singing a bunch of gibberish, his voice packed a powerful emotional punch while the band worked up instantly memorable hooks. The band's decision to title the album *Murmur* wasn't based on Stipe's singing style, but on his claim that it "is one of the six easiest words in the English language to say." He told Tim Sommer, "I think it comes right after mama, which is probably why it was picked. It's got nice implications, I guess."

The band's decision to feature kudzu, a strange vine that grows in the South, on the cover of *Murmur*, also had some rather nice implications. It gave a hint of the band's Athens, Georgia, homebase—and looked mysterious. For those who had never visited the South, the cover photo looked like a picture of another planet.

While R.E.M. didn't sound quite out of this world on *Murmur*, their music was out of step in a time where alternative rock fans were embracing British synthpop and Michael Jackson was the biggest pop star on the planet. That, ultimately, may have been part of the band's initial appeal, as R.E.M. somehow managed to sound simultaneously familiar, with elements of classic rock, yet fresh and new.

"On the whole record there's little touches of '80s digital reverb on it, but not a whole lot," Easter recalled. "The whole thing has this sort of pillowy sound, which to me is real '70s. In a way it was the last of the '70s records. It's got that sort of dead kind of drum sound. We did the drums in a drum booth and by then drum booths were completely out of fashion, but I remember Bill wanted to record in a drum booth. He always thought that was cool."

After the sessions, Easter played an advanced tape of the album to his bandmates in his own group, Let's Active. All were impressed. "I thought the final result was really cool and that it still sounds odd and distinctive. I was pleased with it, although when we got finished, I had no idea if it was the right thing or not."

Months later, when *Murmur* was named album of the year by such publications as *Rolling Stone*, the band was pleased, if not flabbergasted. "I was flattered, but there are records of ours I like better," Buck said. "*Murmur* probably has the most impact, because it was our first big record. It probably meant a little more then, because there wasn't a whole lot of stuff on major labels that was like that. I like almost all of them more, to tell the truth. I like the songs better on just about every album… At the time, I thought *Reckoning* was much better than *Murmur*."

Still, Buck got a kick out of the fact that *Murmur* was more highly praised than such commercial blockbusters as Michael Jackson's *Thriller*. "I figured out that Michael Jackson sold 137 times as many records as we did," he told *Rock* magazine. "You can't do anything but laugh at us beating out Michael Jackson for album of the year."

Radio Free Europe

Since most of the world missed the Hib-Tone single, R.E.M. decided not only to remake 'Radio Free Europe' on its first full-length album, but to make it the opening track. It was a good decision as it is a quintessential R.E.M. song with Mills's melodic bass playing, Buck's sweet Rickenbacker riffing, Berry's steadfast drumming, and Stipe's impassioned vocals ringing pure and true.

Buck, however, feels the band made a mistake by remaking the track. "I think we shouldn't have put 'Radio Free Europe' on the record," he said. "I don't think we captured it the way we did on the single and I just think we were past it at that point, even though it was a cool song. I don't think it hit us the way it did. At that point it was a year-and-half old, which doesn't seem like anything, but it was like ancient history

Howard Finster's Paradise Garden was featured in the 'Radio Free Europe' video.

to us. But [the record company] really wanted it on, and we were like, 'Yeah, it's a good song, so why not.'"

There is still debate about what is the definitive version. When I.R.S. Records compiled the 1988 "best of" collection *Eponymous*, the label went with the Hib-Tone version, perhaps just to give fans a chance to hear the original. "To me the version on the album was more pro, but it was a little bit too sedate," Easter said. "I kind of wish there had been a version between the two."

Aside from the tempo, there were other changes. The *Murmur* version of 'Radio Free Europe' featured a strange buzzing introduction. To accomplish the effect, Dixon linked a bass to an amplifier and filtered it through a noise gate, so the listener hears the buzzing sound, but not the bass. "The idea was kind of tied to the song, like somebody was trying to tune in a shortwave radio," Dixon told Tommy Tomlinson in the *Charlotte Observer*.

"Everybody knew it was a real catchy simple song, and it made sense to release it again to a wider audience," Easter explained. "There were a lot of reasons for re-recording it. Between the first session and *Murmur* the band got better. I think you can tell. Even between *Chronic Town* and *Murmur* there is something a little more solid about it. They probably felt they could do it better. A lot of their early stuff was real fast. They ended up doing it quite a bit slower."

The version on *Murmur* is considerably less frantic than the Hib-Tone take, but it has a new found power in its clarity.

Although the single stalled at No. 78 in the US, it fared better during the "Rate-A-Record" segment on *American Bandstand*. The song was awarded the uncommonly high score of 95. A video clip for the song, directed by Arthur Pierson, featured the band walking through folk artist Howard Finster's Paradise Garden in Summerville, Georgia. A raucous live version of 'Radio Free Europe,' recorded on November 19, 1992, in Athens, Georgia, at a benefit for Greenpeace, was included on the 'Strange Currencies' CD single.

Pilgrimage

After the ill-fated demo sessions with Stephen Hague, R.E.M. returned to Reflection Sound Studios in December 1982 to record a demo with Easter and Dixon. "For our first demo for *Murmur* we drove up to Charlotte and recorded and mixed 'Pilgrimage' with Mitch and Don and we said, 'That's what the record should sound like,'" Buck recalled. "So the record company said, 'Go ahead, do what you want to do.'"

Instead of re-recording the track for *Murmur*, the band and Easter and Dixon decided to use the demo on the album. "That's the only take we ever did and the only mix we ever did, that's why I'm so pleased with it," Easter recalled.

However, Easter remembers a less than enthusiastic response from I.R.S. about the demo. "They didn't really reject, but they didn't take to it either," he recalled. "They were just lukewarm about it, but the band just went ahead. The band agreed it was a good mix and everything, so we never did any more to it. I love the fact we did it in a day and that's the one."

The track begins with a haunting and distant Stipe vocal and features an undeniably catchy chorus highlighted by Mills's and Berry's backing vocals. Berry's percussive effects also add a nice touch. 'Pilgrimage' would serve as a soundtrack of sorts to fans who followed the band around from gig to gig.

Laughing

With its layered guitar strums and Stipe's sweet singing, 'Laughing' is another one of *Murmur*'s heavenly, but most mysterious treats, as most of the vocals are hard to decipher. Ironically, one of the few lyrics decipherable in the song happens to be "misconstrued."

On a few occasions, Stipe attempted to set the record straight on the song's lyrics. "The first line is about Laocoon, a freak mythological figure

Photographs like this served as part of Michael Stipe's inspiration for 'Laughing.'

who had two sons. All three were devoured by serpents," he told John Platt in *Bucketful Of Brains*. "It was a popular theme in Renaissance painting. It's also like the photo you see of the women in Nazi Germany. You know, the woman with the shaved head clutching her baby running from all these people who are laughing at her. But that's a real expansive definition of the song. There's also John Brath's novel *End Of The Road* where a statue of Laocoon features heavily. Oh! Did I change the gender in the song from a man to a woman?"

Even Buck was a bit confused by the song. "I know Michael told me it's about that statue, Laocoon, but I don't

know what it means," he told David Howard in *Contrast*. To make matters worse, Stipe once claimed that the song was "a rewriting of *The Scarlet Letter*."

While Stipe's lyrics, even with any kind of explanation, remain for the most part a mystery, the instrumental approach to the song was fairly straightforward. "A whole bunch of us played acoustic guitars on that," Easter recalled. "We did this sort of protest sit-in thing with four people on acoustic guitars. It was me, Don Dixon, Pete Buck, and Mike Mills. Then we tracked it again, so there are eight acoustic guitars on it."

Talk About The Passion

'Talk About The Passion' is the only song that R.E.M. didn't have completely written before entering Reflection Sound Studios to record *Murmur*. "They didn't really have it together," Easter recalled. "They had been playing it some, but they didn't have an arrangement. It was kind of rambling and went on forever. We kind of worked the arrangement out right then, and then recorded it. That was fun to do."

On the track, which Berry has called a favorite, Easter played guitar. "That was sort of the beginning of us using a lot of acoustic guitar," Easter recalled. "That whole album has

The fact that Easter and Dixon were free to pick up a guitar and play along helped make the recordings a success. "The reason why these were great sessions is that they were pretty ego-free," Easter recalled. "Everybody just wanted to make a good recording. I played acoustic on a number of songs and sometimes we did it live."

Easter and Dixon weren't the only guest players. To add to the song's bittersweet atmosphere, the band hired a cello player, who was not listed in the album's credits. "We hired this lady from the symphony orchestra," Buck told John

Michael Stipe, left, and guest guitarist Mitch Easter during a 1983 live date.

Platt in *Bucketful Of Brains*. "We paid her $25. We told her roughly what we wanted and she was dumbfounded that we weren't going to give her a score. But she was great in the end."

While the song's emotionalism shined through the sweet melody and vocal, few picked up on the intent of Stipe's lyrics. "The song was about apathy," he told Robert Hilburn of the *Los Angeles Times* in 1985. "When I wrote it, I was thinking about all the hunger in the world, which sounds like a cliché now, but this was a year and a half ago."

A 1988 video clip, taped when the song was released as a single from *Eponymous*, made Stipe's intent perfectly clear. The video featured images of homeless people juxtaposed with a warship. At the end of the clip, a message was flashed on the screen: "In 1987 the cost of one destroyer-class warship was 910 million dollars."

a lot of acoustic on it playing the same thing as the electric and it really worked well on that song." 'Talk About The Passion' also features Buck's first guitar solo, which was taught to him by Mills, the bassist.

Moral Kiosk

Following in the wake of the relatively sedate 'Laughing' and 'Talk About The Passion,' this song upped the ante on *Murmur*, hinting at a return to the more rocking approach the band favored on *Chronic Town*. On the track, Buck's guitar has a more angular sound, while Berry adds some interesting

percussive effects that bring the listener in and out of the song's chant-like chorus. Another highlight is a Stipe yodel.

"That was a good song," Easter recalled. "We got into this thing where Pete Buck used this little Ampeg amp of mine for the whole record, except on 'Pilgrimage,' where he used this even littler amp the studio had. We got into this thing of miking the amp from way back. You could really hear that on 'Moral Kiosk' and it sounded great."

As for the lyrics, Mills attempted to offer a dictionary-like definition. "Well, if you take what a kiosk is—a column and

place where they post notices that say this is what you should do tonight or tomorrow—a moral kiosk, I guess, is either a place to tell you what you should do morally or a place to hide yourself from decisions you have to make," he explained on the syndicated radio show *Rockline*.

Perfect Circle

Quite frankly, 'Perfect Circle' is one of the most beautiful songs R.E.M. have ever recorded. It was also an early sign that the band had great potential to write moving ballads. The song developed from a Buck observation that was possibly filtered through Stipe, while Berry came up with the music.

"People don't have to know the story or the genesis of the song to get what it means to us," Buck told David Fricke. "For example, the most moving moment I've had in the last couple of years was at the end of one of our tours. I hadn't slept in days. I was tired as I could possibly be and we were doing a concert that night for a live radio show. And I was standing in the City Gardens in Trenton, New Jersey, at the back door and it was just getting dark. These kids were playing touch football, the last game before dark came, and for some reason I was so moved I cried for 20 minutes. It sounds so trivial. But that's more or less what 'Perfect Circle' on *Murmur* is about. I told Michael to try and capture that feeling. There's no football in there, no kids, not twilight, but it's all there."

As Stipe later pointed out, the reason why Buck's vision isn't expressed in the lyrics is because he didn't use it. In fact, Stipe wasn't sure which sport the kids that moved Buck to tears were playing. "Peter always tells this story abut how 'Perfect Circle' was inspired by a bunch of young boys playing baseball," he told Andy Gill. "To me it was about my ex-girlfriend." He called the song one of his "real gut-spillers" in an interview with the then 10,000 Maniacs vocalist Natalie Merchant in *Musician* magazine. With the lyric, "pull your dress on and stay real close," it does seem like the song has more to do with a woman than football or baseball, but most of the other lyrics are vague.

Berry composed the song while in his kitchen playing with a little Casio keyboard. "It just came out and it sounded pretty cool," he told Timothy White in an interview for Westwood One Radio Networks. However, the track turned out to be challenging to play live. "I couldn't play drums and piano at the same time, so I had this little toy Casio, which is

Michael Stipe called the ballad 'Perfect Circle' one of his "real gut-spillers."

what I wrote it on, and we would inevitably spill beer into it and stuff and the tempo would change and it wouldn't work. So it kind of scared us off for a while," he added.

In the studio, the band utilized a different approach. "It was just this little snippet that they used to play live with a Casio with a rhythm box in it," Easter recalled, "but we decided to make it bigger and use the real pianos." Just as the band frequently used more than one guitar on *Murmur*, they opted for two pianos on 'Perfect Circle.' "It was Bill and Mike playing at the same time on these two different pianos that Reflection had," Easter added. "One was a real nice piano.

The other was an old upright piano. The combination of the two together was a really nice sound. That's definitely the basis of that song."

In addition, Dixon played bass on the track. "I put some backwards guitar on there and we went back and put the acoustics on it," Easter recalled.

Catapult

'Catapult' was the song that R.E.M. initially recorded with Stephen Hague, who tried to professionalize the band's sound with the use of a click track and overdubbed synthesizer, and for that reason, it is forever tainted in the minds of the band's members.

"That was a problematic song, because that was the song that they did with Stephen Hague," Easter confirmed. "They hated that version of it so much that they were truly freaked out about it. We recorded it again, but I don't think they ever liked it. I really liked the song, but I don't think they like our version either, although it wasn't as offensive to them."

The fact that the band's opinion of the song didn't change over time was disappointing to Easter. "I remember Pete Buck saying that it had a terrible mix in an interview, but I don't know what he was talking about. I just think that their opinion of that song got ruined by their bad experience."

'Perfect Circle' was Buck's first favorite R.E.M. song and one he continues to feel good about. "I really love that song, even though I'm not even sure I play on the recording," he said during a radio interview. "I can appreciate it more as a fan than a musician. I really love that song. I still have a real warm feeling for it."

On at least one occasion, Buck noted that 'Catapult' showed off a country influence that would become more apparent on *Reckoning*'s '(Don't Go Back To) Rockville.' "A lot of country guitar playing is really neat," Buck told Jon Young in *Trouser Press*. "It's melodic and pithy and not chord-

Michael Stipe with his sister Lynda in a scene from Laura Levine's *Just Like A Movie*.

oriented, without being jerk-off guitar solos. I stick things in all the time that are real country. That's a country lick right before the chorus in 'Catapult.'"

With its thumping bass line and uplifting vocal that highlights the joys of childhood, 'Catapult' is an early R.E.M. standout, even if the band didn't like it. "I thought it was one of their really good catchy songs," Easter said. "I thought it could have been a single. It is really easy to digest and that, 'We were little girls, we were little boys' is so good and memorable."

As an introduction to the song in concert once, Stipe said, "I used to hurt myself a lot when I was little." As Buck pointed out, childhood is a subject that Stipe has addressed frequently in his lyrics. "Michael is really interested in that subject, maybe because he had a weird childhood himself, a kind of time and innocence lost," Buck told Lynne Aldridge. "Without getting too heavy, basically you look on things differently as a child to what you do now, and when you try to put yourself back in that position [it] only makes it seem more distant."

Buck also pointed out that Stipe is very close to his family. "Michael had a very strong family life," he told a British radio interviewer. "He has two sisters and he sees his family a lot. The family in that time was real important to him and that comes through in the lyrics, but it's not as if this is 1967 and we want to go back to the days of innocent children, because it's not going to happen in 1984."

A live version of the song appeared on the '(Don't Go Back To) Rockville' single and the expanded 1992 edition of *Murmur*.

Sitting Still

'Radio Free Europe' wasn't the only oldie to turn up on *Murmur*. Unlike that song, however, the band didn't re-record 'Sitting Still,' the B-side of the Hib-Tone single, for *Murmur*. "It's the same one they did in my garage," Easter confirmed. "We just mixed it again at Reflection and we slowed the tape down a little bit, so it comes off a little differently. I think we redid a couple of out-of-tune backing vocal bits, but it's the same one."

"That take is the same that is on the Hib-Tone single,"

Buck agreed. "I think Mike re-did the bass, but the basic track is the same." According to the track sheet from the sessions, something called "today's bass sounds" were added on February 1983, so Buck's memory is correct. On the Hib-Tone version, Stipe's vocal was re-recorded in May 1981, after the initial session on April 15 of that year. A track of "Blue Cheer guitar" replaced the "flange bass." Buck still has fond memories of writing the song: "I remember writing that sitting in that house on Barber Street that we lived in."

9-9

This explosive and discordant rocker, which is appropriately sequenced as the ninth track on *Murmur*, is the one song that threw a wrench into the theories that R.E.M. was nothing more than a group of Byrds copyists.

"Right away they were seen as being really melodic, which at the time was a bit of a negative with some people," Mitch Easter explained. "It was probably written as the song that was going to be the opposite of that. It's kind of not like anything else on the record. They were into bands like Gang Of Four and stuff, back then, and it was probably meant to be more than that type of song."

'9-9' also has the distinction of being the R.E.M. song that is the most difficult to decipher, but that was their intent. "We purposely recorded it so you would never be able to decipher any of the words except the very last phrase, which is 'conversation fear,' which is what the song is about," Stipe told Steve Pond in *Rolling Stone*.

The song opens with a spoken Stipe intro, over a bed of guitar and bass noodling. "Michael,

if there is a space when he doesn't do anything, he gets antsy, he talks," Buck explained to a British radio interviewer. "I'm not sure what he's saying on that one."

To give the song its mysterious sound, Easter and Dixon employed an innovative studio technique. "We kind of mixed it a different way," Easter recalled. "We ran the whole song back into the studio through some speakers and re-miked it to make it sound kind of different."

On the track '9-9,' R.E.M. tipped their hat to British post-punk band Gang Of Four.

The band first attempted to record the song during the *Chronic Town* sessions, but it was never finished. "It was the same concept," Easter recalled. "Maybe the words weren't ready, or maybe they didn't have the arrangement together or something. It's kind of a weird song, it has kind of a funny beat to it and it is all angular and strange."

Initially, the song almost didn't make *Murmur* either, but the band reconsidered after a request from I.R.S. Records president, Jay Boberg. "We would never have put '9-9' on the first record if he hadn't said, 'I really like that song, would you please record it for me?' That was a cool thing to say, because it obviously wasn't going to be a single."

A live version of '9-9,' recorded in mono in Paris, France, on April 20, 1984, turned up as the B-side of the '(Don't Go Back To) Rockville' British 12-inch single. Unfortunately the recording fades out before the song is over. The full live version, however, is included on the 1992 expanded edition of *Murmur*.

Shaking Through

Like '9-9,' 'Shaking Through' also dated back to the *Chronic Town* sessions. In fact, the band completed a demo for the track, which, save for Stipe's vocal, isn't terribly different from the version that appears on *Murmur*.

Despite the fact that it made it on to the album, neither Buck nor Easter are particularly big fans of the song. "They could just crank songs like that out all the time," Easter said. "They had a million of them it seems to me. I was never a

huge fan of that one. It was a little too complacent sounding to me. It didn't grab me the way others did."

The *Murmur* version clocks in at four minutes and 29 seconds, making it the second-longest song on the album. "It's such a long song," Buck complained. "It seemed like it was eight minutes long." ('Talk About The Passion,' the longest song on the album, runs for four-and-a-half minutes.)

The *Murmur* version includes a 25-second untitled instrumental interlude, a device that the band would use on *Reckoning*, between 'Camera' and '(Don't Go Back To) Rockville.'

Although the co-producer and guitarist didn't necessarily like 'Shaking Through,' the fans didn't complain. Highlights of the recording include a majestic piano, a catchy guitar part, and a wonderfully warm Stipe vocal.

We Walk

With its nursery rhyme-like lyrics, sugary guitar picking, and odd studio effects, 'We Walk' is possibly the weirdest and most endearing song on *Murmur*. As Stipe once noted in a live performance, "This is a song that your mom and dad would like." It was also one of the most difficult to record.

"It was a hard one to get right," Easter recalled. "They couldn't get a good groove happening on that." To get the right beat, Easter returned to his old tricks of using tape loops. "Bill actually played it, but then we looped it, that made it dead steady and that's what it needed. It needed to be sort of mechanical, because it has that *Get Smart* guitar part, so that had to be all straight for the song not to sound loose and like nothing."

Yet even after the tape-looped drum track and the guitars, something was still missing. To complete the song, Easter and Dixon concocted one of R.E.M.'s most notorious studio experiments.

"We had a mike set up in the hallway, in the staircase

hallway near this rec room, which was under the control room, and that's where Michael would sing and there was a pool table near there," Easter recalled. "Once the microphone was on and we could hear the pool game coming through the mike, and because it was some distance away, it sounded cool. It had that sort of reverbish sound. We just put the tape machine into record and recorded a few minutes of these pool balls."

The duo then added the recording to 'We Walk.' "For some reason, the sound of the slowed-down pool balls colliding made that song make sense," Easter added. "God knows why. But it was one of those things we liked to do back then."

As for the lyrics, Stipe said they were inspired by an old acquaintance. "I used to know a girl who lived on the second floor of this house and every time she walked up the stairs, she would say, 'Up the stairs, into the hall,' she didn't get a credit, but I did say thank you."

West Of The Fields

The album closer, 'West Of The Fields,' is one of those rare R.E.M. songs that was a collaboration with someone outside the band. In this case, it was Stipe's Athens pal Neil Bogan. "Michael wrote it about a trip to New Orleans and Neil helped fill in the lyrics," Buck explained.

Easter describes the frantic rocker as "kind of a cool dramatic song. We used an organ on it and the organ really

tied it together. It came together immediately after we added the organ."

Years later, Buck was less than complimentary about the way he wrote the song. "In those days, if it didn't have three different bridges and a separate A and B section before the chorus, it just wasn't any good," he told Vic Garbarini in *Guitar World*. "Maybe it's because I wasn't a great player, but I felt I had to put in all those extra chords. 'West Of The Fields' is a perfect example—there must be 15 chords in that song. So we wanted no lead guitar, and no heavy punk—just a fast, weird folk-rock record with tons of overdubs."

R.E.M. in the fields of kudzu. From left, Berry, Mills, Stipe, and Buck.

for all rock acts with any sort of success on their first album, the second album is a time of *Reckoning*. They've had all their lives to prepare for their first album, but if that takes off, the band goes on the road on a virtual non-stop tour and is somehow supposed to write material for their follow-up while the world waits for an album that will prove the debut was no fluke.

That scenario suited R.E.M. well. While critics were falling over themselves praising *Murmur*, the band was on the road, trying to win over the real people, who had came to see what all the fuss was about. And there was plenty of fuss. *Rolling Stone* named the band best new group and *Murmur* the best album of 1983. The *Village Voice* named it the second best album of the year in its annual critics poll, while *Rolling Stone*'s sister publication, *Record*, named *Murmur* the top debut album and third best album of 1983. The praise was music to the ears of the band and co-producer Mitch Easter.

The powers that be at I.R.S. Records may have been a bit alarmed, however, when they read initial press reports about the album that quoted Easter. "At the time, I was saying this is going to be their *Led Zeppelin II*. The reason I said that, in those years, if you said that, you would make everyone mad," Easter said. "But the other reason was that I thought there were parallels, because *Led Zeppelin II* was done when the band was on the way up and they recorded it on tour."

Although *Reckoning* wasn't recorded while the band was on tour, it was squeezed in between tours. "We toured ten months of the year in those days," recalled Buck. "We toured and toured all through '83, from whenever we finished *Murmur*." It was during a break in touring that the band rehearsed for two weeks, writing some new material at the old Electric Ballroom in Athens, before taking the show on the road again to test the new material out in front of audiences.

When the band was ready to enter the studio in

RECKONING

"It was a great kind of vindication," recalled Easter. "It is great to have people tell you what you did was good, especially in face of less than total support from I.R.S. I don't recall anyone saying, 'Hey great job, we're going to go all the way with this one.' What I seem to remember is silence. Then the thing came out and it's record of the year in *Rolling Stone*. I never expected anything, but it was cool. It was this wonderful sort of surprise."

Although *Murmur*, which sold in the US for a special introductory new artist price of $6.98, wasn't a massive commercial success—it peaked at No. 36 on the American charts—the critical praise did provide the band with a certain amount of freedom. "It was a good thing," Easter recalled, "because we knew the record company wouldn't probably worry about us doing the next record, since the first one went well, they would probably trust us and it would be OK."

Murmur **turned R.E.M. into a force to reckon with.**
From left, Buck, Mills, Stipe, and Berry.

December 1983, it once again decided on Reflection Sound Studios in Charlotte, North Carolina, with Easter and Dixon again behind the mixing board. The band recorded on December 8–10, took a one-day break, and started up again on December 12–15. After the holidays the band finished the job in sessions running January 10–16. "We did *Reckoning* in 11 days, recorded and mixed it," Stipe told *Discoveries*' Jim Fanning and Russell Miller. "I don't think any of us slept that whole time… and you can really kind of tell on the record." Stipe told Tom Sheehan in *Melody Maker* that "if there was any conscious thought behind *Reckoning* it was just not to make *Murmur* part two."

"We went in the studio and didn't use all our time," Buck recalled. "We worked really fast. In a way, it was a reaction to having this kind of layered, meticulous first record. The second one tended to rock a bit more. We still had Mitch and Don helping, so they managed to get a fair amount of production expertise in, probably against our will. I think we were just trying to knock it out and go." The band recorded six songs in the first two days, most in two or three takes.

"They had taken a couple of weeks out from touring to go

bash out the album," Easter noted. "It was in that good sort of jaunty spirit that they did *Reckoning*." The sessions were so productive that the band also managed to record additional material that didn't make the album, such as its covers of Pylon's 'Crazy,' the Velvet Underground's 'Pale Blue Eyes,' R.E.M. original oldie 'Ages Of You,' and the soundtrack cut 'Wind Out,' all of which appeared as B-sides and later on the odds-and-ends compilation *Dead Letter Office*.

The decision to record fast was also, in some ways, a reaction to the overwhelming critical praise the band received for *Murmur*. Stipe would later compare the band's plight to Nirvana's. "*In Utero* is for all intents and purposes Nirvana's sophomore jinx record," he told Vic Garbarini. "And they did exactly what we did on ours, *Reckoning*, which was to record it quickly and with as few overdubs as possible. And that was totally about us reacting to *Murmur* being picked over Michael Jackson's *Thriller* as the album of the year. I mean, we were nobodies!"

As a result of the pace, the sessions were considerably looser than those for the first album. "On *Murmur* the band was thinking, 'We're in the studio to make our album,' whereas *Reckoning* was done in this real confident way," Easter recalled. "The band knew that they knew how to make records and they were just going to do one. It was very businesslike. There were no emotional worries really and it stayed that way throughout the whole session. We just went and did it."

Despite the album's title, Easter said it didn't seem as if the band were looking at the second album as their day of *Reckoning*. "It strikes me that Michael just likes words and he liked the sound of that one," he said. "I don't think he was thinking of it thematically… at that point. I don't think they were feeling make or break. Maybe they were worried about the sophomore jinx, but they didn't act worried. They mainly just acted confident and with good reason, because everyone loved them then."

Buck, however, saw things differently. "A second album is always a day of *Reckoning* for a rock band," he told *Rock Magazine*. As a result, R.E.M. made the album a bit more diverse than *Murmur*. "We wanted to show people we're not a band that can only do one thing. There's a country song, a funeral chant, ballads, rocket rockers, and some incoherent stuff. We didn't follow up *Murmur* with the record everyone expected."

34 Interestingly enough, *Reckoning* was initially set to go by

another name. An I.R.S. Records press release, issued while the band was finishing work on the album, listed the tentative title as *Second Guess*.

At least instrumentally, however, R.E.M. weren't second-guessing themselves. "They were playing well and the basic tracks were good and solid," Easter explained. "Some things were recorded live that weren't live on *Murmur*. On *Murmur*, we went back and re-did bass a lot of times. On *Reckoning*, the bass tracks were pretty much all live with the drums. The whole thing was a little more confident and could stand in a more straightforward manner."

"It was also a case of what the songs called for," Easter added, "and the songs sounded a little more like live tracks, but there was still piano on some." Overall, *Reckoning* is "a little less of a studio album than *Murmur* and has more of a live feel," he explained.

While the band had grown more confident instrumentally, Stipe was still having trouble adjusting to the spotlight. "Michael had such a bad experience on that tour—he was still bloodcurdlingly shy—and he still didn't really know what he was doing, and by this point he was afraid to ask," Dixon told Tommy Tomlinson of the *Charlotte Observer*. "I spent a lot of time, just me and him, doing vocals on that record." Dixon also told *Mojo*'s Dave DiMartino that Stipe had "a bit of an identity crisis" during the making of *Reckoning*.

It was during the period of the *Reckoning* sessions, however, that Stipe won his battle with shyness. "It took years to get over that, though," he told Bill Flanagan. "It went from shyness as a child to this really loud, extreme, extroverted personality at the end of high school, which then flip-flopped back into extreme shyness. That was a particularly long and intense period that I was only brought out of around *Reckoning*."

During the sessions, Stipe showed his eccentric behavior, once again recording his vocals in the stairwell of the studio where he could not be seen. He became obsessed by memorabilia at the studio from the PTL Club, a religious group that included the infamous Tammy Faye Bakker. In between takes, he munched on garlic, having been turned on to the leek for its supposed healing powers.

Although Stipe was coming out of his shell and the band may have laid off the studio effects on *Reckoning*, it certainly didn't let up on the mystery on the album's sleeve and liner. The cover was a bizarre painting of a two-headed snake by the Reverend Howard Finster, whose folk art-filled garden

R.E.M. at Bill Miller's Whirlygig farm, where *Left Of Reckoning* was shot.

was featured in the 'Radio Free Europe' video clip. The credit for Easter and Dixon, who were paid an advance fee of $3,000 for their work, read "machinists," rather than "producers." In what was becoming an R.E.M. tradition, there was no "side one" and "side two" on *Reckoning*. Instead the sides were labeled "L" and "R," for "left" and "right," respectively.

With the release of *Reckoning*, R.E.M. also opted to play with the preconceived notions of rock video. Although the band taped a traditional rock video for 'So. Central Rain' at Reflection Sound Studios, it also opted to commission James Herbert, a professor of art at the University of Georgia in Athens, to shoot an additional clip at Bill Miller's Whirlygig farm, near Gainesville, Georgia. Herbert, who was more comfortable shooting short films than four-minute rock videos, ended up making a film to accompany the album's whole first side, appropriately titled *Left Of Reckoning*. Buck

called the piece, which didn't feature the band playing their instruments, "a weird image thing... It didn't do our careers loads of good," he told Sandy Robertson, "cause it didn't have naked women in it."

Perhaps the most perplexing thing about *Reckoning* was the notice on the album's spine: "file under water." This was a play on the messages that appeared on some records in the '50s and '60s, which were designed to help record clerks stock titles in the appropriate section. "The record deals with a lot of water imagery, travel and passage and going from here to there," Buck explained. "And there is a lot of sad elements in there." Stipe took that theme even further. "The real title of the record is *File Under Water*," Stipe told Barney Hoskyns. In the US, both titles appeared on the spine, and there was no title on the cover, except for the sticker on the shrinkwrap that included the *Reckoning* title and informed potential buyers it was "the second album from R.E.M." In the UK, however, the *Reckoning* title appeared on the cover.

Whatever the title, R.E.M. met their day of *Reckoning* head on, with their integrity intact and their audience growing, while they continued to rack up reams of praise.

Harborcoat

With a quick series of rapid-fire drum beats and an anthem-like guitar riff, R.E.M. kicked off album number two in grand style. The sweet, melodic, uplifting sound is there in all its glory, with Stipe's passionate vocals, echoed wonderfully, and slightly off kilter, by Mills and Berry. Yet those hoping that the vocal murk of *Murmur* would give way to more clarity on *Reckoning* had to be disappointed, at least initially.

Co-producer Easter is still perplexed by the meaning of 'Harborcoat.' "I always wondered what 'Harborcoat' is supposed to mean and do to this day. I don't know what the song was about," he said.

Although you would never guess it, even with an unofficial lyric sheet from the Internet, Stipe claimed the song is "a rewriting of the Anne Frank diaries" in an interview with Harold DeMuir, adding, "If you want definition, read the dictionary." By the way, there is no dictionary definition for "harborcoat," although there is one for 'Hairshirt,' a future song, included on *Green*, and also titled after an apparent article of clothing.

In another interview, Stipe said 'Harborcoat' and *Murmur*'s 'Laughing' "were violent and brutal," to Bill Flanagan, "but they're both so internal and folded in on themselves that no one would ever pick up on that except as a general gut feeling."

When Stipe would later make similar claims about 'The One I Love,' it seemed valid, given the song's lyrical twist and the raging shouts of "fire." 'Harborcoat,' at least to these ears, sounds uplifting with the heartfelt sentiment, "a handshake is worthy, if it's all that you got." The only part of the song that seems remotely "brutal" is the line about "metal shoes on wood" pushing "through our back."

Whatever the subject matter, 'Harborcoat' was effective as an album-opener and in showcasing an R.E.M. secret weapon. "Bill and I are singing almost as much as Michael," Mills revealed on *Rockline*. The mix of voices is mesmerizing, but it wasn't interesting enough to keep two of the three interested in performing the song, as both Mills and Berry have admitted that they don't particularly care for 'Harborcoat.' "It's not that I dislike the song, it just sounds real thin live," Berry told Flanagan. Mills was "sick to death of it."

7 Chinese Bros.

This song is as mysterious as 'Harborcoat,' but at least there is a reference point. The song's title, as well as the lyric about "swallowing the ocean," were lifted from the children's book *Five Chinese Brothers* by Claire Huchet Bishop and Kurt Wiese, published in 1938. In the story, each of the five brothers has a unique talent. One of the brothers can "swallow the sea." "I think it was suggested by something he saw," Easter confirmed. "I think he saw a phrase that was like that and turned it into the song."

Although Stipe may have used the children's book as a starting point, there is very little else in the song related to *Five Chinese Brothers*. In fact, the haunting lyric, "she will return," could possibly be a reference to the band's late friend Carol Levy, whose death inspired the song 'Camera.'

Stipe may have added two to *The Five Chinese Brothers*, but they still were "swallowing the ocean."

Initially, Stipe had a hard time putting down his vocals on '7 Chinese Bros.,' so Dixon suggested that he attempt the song again. "He did two takes and couldn't get the vocals, so he just walked in, grabbed this album off the shelf and was

looking at the liner notes and said, 'Run the tape' and did it in one take," Buck told John Platt in *Bucketful Of Brains*. That version was released as the B-side 'Voice Of Harold,' and subsequently turned up on *Dead Letter Office*. It was only after cutting 'Voice Of Harold' that Stipe found the inspiration to lay down a suitable vocal track on '7 Chinese Bros.'

Still, Stipe was never quite satisfied with the track. "There was a bit of a fight with Michael over the mix," Easter recalled. "It wasn't like an ugly fight, but he never thought the mix was right. He always thought the drums were too loud."

Even if Stipe was never fully satisfied with the song, '7 Chinese Bros.' was embraced by fans. "That was another classic modal-sounding R.E.M. song where the guitar had this familiar and yet slightly odd quality about it," Easter said. "It had that sort of simple but real memorable guitar line that they were real good at."

So. Central Rain

On October 6, 1983, R.E.M. made their national television debut on NBC-TV's *Late Night With David Letterman*. The band was featured performing its "hit," 'Radio Free Europe,' but the demand for the band was such that they got to play a second track. Rather than play another *Murmur* song, R.E.M. informed Letterman that it would be playing a song "too new" to have a name. That song was 'So. Central Rain.'

Even then, R.E.M. was bucking tradition. When bands perform in front of millions of TV viewers, they generally perform songs from their latest album in an effort to promote their new product. By playing a song that wouldn't be in the stores for months, R.E.M. created a record company nightmare by spurring demand for a record that didn't exist. (More than a decade later, the band would once again buck the system by performing 'The Wake-Up Bomb' on the *MTV Music Video Awards* more than a year before it would be released on *New Adventures In Hi-Fi*.)

The preview of the song on the Letterman program effectively showed that R.E.M. had reached a new level of emotional depth. Even if it was hard to figure out why Stipe was "sorry," you could feel his pain, especially with the bloodcurdling screams that came at the song's emotional climax.

'So. Central Rain' was written while the band was in sunny Los Angeles on tour in support of *Murmur*. Buck was attempting to reach his parents on the telephone when Georgia was in the midst of a massive storm that severely flooded some areas. "The weather report was, 'South central rain, all the phone lines are down,'" Buck recalled. "It's a kind of a being away from home song without having the Holiday Inn and groupies in it. Actually that was before we had enough money to stay in a Holiday Inn and we never got groupies."

Even before it was titled, the band frequently performed the song on the tour in support of *Murmur*. "We came up with the music first and I didn't hear Michael sing it until we were almost on stage with it," Buck recalled. "The first time I actually heard the lyrics, it really moved me." In fact, Buck nearly wept, recognizing his own experience was reflected in the song's lyrics.

Despite his love for the song, Buck has mixed feelings about the recording. "I'm not sure if that is exactly the arrangement or mix that it should have been," he said. "That was one of the ones about a month after it came out I kind of wished that we re-recorded it as a single and did a different version."

The version that was included on *Reckoning* was enhanced by some studio wizardry. Initially, the band and Easter and Dixon weren't happy with the song's intro. "Don Dixon did this edit, which put that little guitar bit at the beginning of the song, which to me was just sheer genius," Easter explained. "We weren't real happy with the way the song started. The arrangement was OK, but it just started right in. And Don thought of doing that. It's actually part of the chorus. I thought that was so good. It worked very well." (On the Letterman performance that predated the *Reckoning* sessions by a few months, the band performed the song without the guitar intro.)

The production duo also experimented with Berry's drum track. "Bill played every other snare beat," Easter recalled. "When we got finished, we thought 'It needs something,' so we had him hit beats in other spots, just by coincidence there was some reverb on that channel, so you get this alternating reverb beat and non-reverb beat. I thought that worked very well. That one got a bit of studio chopping that helped it a lot."

In keeping with Stipe's vow not to lip-sync, a video clip, directed by Howard Libov, was shot at the end of the sessions at Reflection. Although the members of the band mimed playing their instruments, Stipe sang live. "We just ran the multitrack right into the video machine, and Michael sang it live… and he actually delivered, which was great," Easter said.

The video revealed an intimate portrait of Stipe singing a highly emotional song, his eyes closed, and hands on the headphones. Easter said it proved that he wasn't afraid of singing in front of people or the camera. "He did do his vocals in the hallway during the *Murmur* and *Reckoning* sessions where no one could see him, but I don't know if he was hiding or not," Easter explained. "I've worked at Reflection with other people who didn't like to sing out in that big room, so I think it is kind of a natural singer thing to be in a smaller area. And, he sang for real in that video with cameras on him, so he obviously was not afraid to sing in front of people."

David Letterman gave R.E.M. the chance to play a song "too new to be named."

While some of the lyrics in the song were quite clear, especially Stipe's cry of "sorry," others were obscured in typical Stipe fashion. "I never purposely tried to make any song indecipherable or slur the words," Stipe told Andy Gill. "I've been accused of that. I just sing a song the way I think it should be sung. Something like 'So. Central Rain' to me is so clear. I couldn't use better diction and been able to sing the song."

For the single release, the song's title was altered slightly, becoming 'S. Central Rain (I'm Sorry).' If fans didn't catch all of the song's lyrics on *Reckoning*, R.E.M. gave them another chance when it released a sparse guitar and vocal version, recorded by VARA Radio in Utrecht, Holland, on September 14, 1987. The song was included in 'Time After Time Etc.,' a medley that featured the band's interpretation of Peter Gabriel's 'Red Rain' on the flipside of the 'Finest Worksong' 12-inch and CD single.

The title 'So. Central Rain,' inspired a play, named after the song, written and directed by Jamie Baker, which ran in Burbank, California. *South Central Rain*, as Baker called it, was the sequel to another one of his plays, *Don't Go Back To Rockville*, which also took its name from a *Reckoning* song.

Pretty Persuasion

"This is a Mamas and Papas song. Not really. Well it's got two singers, [but] it doesn't have a tambourine," Stipe once said while introducing 'Pretty Persuasion' in concert. Although R.E.M. was known to perform the Mamas and the Papas's 'California Dreaming' in its live set, 'Pretty Persuasion' is an R.E.M. original, featuring the vocal harmonies of Michael Stipe and Mike Mills, and it doesn't sound much like anything by Mama Cass and company. In fact, the song reminded Easter of another veteran rock act. "I always thought that the guitar intro sounded a lot like 'Couldn't I Just Tell You' by

Todd Rundgren," he said. "I imagine that there was some inspiration there."

'Pretty Persuasion' was an oldie, at least in the R.E.M. catalog. It dated back to 1981, before *Murmur* was recorded. During the *Murmur* sessions, on February 17, 1983, the band recorded a live version, directly to two-track, which was released as a bonus track on the 1992 expanded version of *Reckoning*. "That was really fun," Easter said of the two-track recording. "People were talking about doing it again and I was one of them. I thought it should be on the record. I think they were really tired of that song when they did it for the album, but they kind of knew they had to, because people liked it so much. I thought it was a great song. It was a little tougher, and yet it was really catchy."

Stipe provided some interesting dance steps during performances of 'Pretty Persuasion.'

After the band completed a new recording for *Reckoning*, Easter came upon a revelation. "The thing that is funny is that the multitrack official version that we did sounds almost identical to the live two-track version that was done before." A close examination of the two versions reveals that the vocals are quite different, but the instrumentation remains fairly consistent.

In the band's early live performances, 'Pretty Persuasion' was a particularly memorable number, as Stipe provided some interesting dance steps during the frantic mid-section.

Time After Time (Annelise)

With its shimmering guitars and tribal drumming, the raga-like 'Time After Time' is one of the few R.E.M. songs that shows the definite influence of the Velvet Underground, perhaps the favorite band of the members of R.E.M. collectively. "It's slow and in D," explained Buck. "We got a really good kind of Rain Parade feel to it. Talking about a lot of this stuff is like going back to high school."

Easter also remembers the song fondly. "That's really a pretty song," he said. "It was really fun to do that. It was kind of like 'Perfect Circle.' It was fun to build it up. Although it is just guitars, I thought the way it added up is really nice." To add some extra atmosphere to the track, Easter banged a metal pipe against a steel chair leg.

As for the "Annelise" the song is parenthetically titled after, that remains a mystery. "I'm pretty sure I know what that's about and who that's about, but I'm not going to tell you," said Peter Buck.

Once again, the mix of this song was a bit troublesome, as Stipe thought his shouts of "hey, hey, hey" after the instrumental break were too loud. "We liked the mix of the song a whole lot, so we decided we were just going to do the bit with the 'heys' and edit it in, and it took us about six hours," Easter recalled.

Although that work proved tedious, it may have been well worth it in the end, as 'Time After Time (Annelise)' is a beautiful, atmospheric gem that provides a nice closing to side "L." The band saw fit to feature it as the lead song on 'Time After Time Etc.,' a live medley that included a cover of Peter Gabriel's 'Red Rain' and 'So. Central Rain,' which was released on the B-side of 'Finest Worksong.'

Second Guessing

This upbeat song, which kicks off side "R," was almost the album's title track. It's also another song that Mills was never crazy about performing live.

One journalist thought Stipe was directing the lyric, "who will be your book this season" at his band mate Buck, who is an avid reader. "I would never direct something like that towards Peter," Stipe told Bill Flanagan. Who exactly Stipe was addressing remains a mystery, but it could have been the critics who took him to task for his indecipherable singing, as Stipe asks, why are you "trying to second-guess me?"

Letter Never Sent

The letter is a recurring theme in the R.E.M. story. It served as a central image in this song, the B-side collection *Dead Letter Office*, and *New Adventure In Hi-Fi*'s 'E-Bow The Letter.' Living up to the song's title, Stipe has been known on occasion to write letters that he never mails. "He sometimes writes letters like that, believe it or not," Buck explained to Tom Doyle in *Q*. "His postcards especially are like scripts to some weird movie that you're only getting the middle part of."

As Stipe once explained, he preferred to write his early lyrics, especially the personal songs like 'Letter Never Sent,' with some distance. "I approach my lyrics from the third person instead of the first person, which gives it a slight detachment," he told David Fricke. "It's kind of a protection—

I would no more care to cut my gut open and display it to the 200,000 people who are going to buy the record."

Like a quick note on a postcard, the music of 'Letter Never Sent' was composed at a fast pace. "Strangely enough, that's the song which probably took the least time to write," Mills told Lynne Aldridge. "Peter had the guitar lines and we worked out everything from that."

"I think it took about as long to write as it did to play," Buck explained. "If we can work out a song in about 20 minutes, we love it."

"Rock'n'roll by definition should come from the heart. You've got to work the truth and honesty into the music," Mills added. However, the bassist said in a subsequent interview that he also didn't enjoy playing this song live.

Camera

Although there was no credit on the band photo featured on the 'Radio Free Europe' Hib-Tone single, the photograph was taken by Carol Levy, whom Stipe met one night when he smeared lip gloss all over her face at an out-of-control Halloween party. Once a member of Boat Of, a short-lived noise group that included Stipe, Levy was an important part of the Athens scene and a staunch R.E.M. supporter.

In a strange tragic twist, the night that R.E.M. celebrated the release of *Murmur*, its first full-album, Levy was killed in a car accident on her way back to Athens after traveling to Atlanta to catch a screening of Susan Seidelman's *Smithereens*, a film that starred punk legend Richard Hell.

The death of photographer Carol Levy inspired the track 'Camera.'

Although she is not mentioned by name, and there are no car wrecks in the song, 'Camera' is a slow and moving ballad written in memory of Stipe's close friend Levy. "If you didn't know that you would still know what the song is about," Buck explained. "We just happened to know her. It was just a real intense experience writing and recording that one. We had never done anything like that before. We were like a dance band almost. We played so people could drink beer and dance and meet people of the opposite sex. When we did something really slow like that it was kind of a weird experience, especially with the subject matter, which was still relatively fresh at the time. I remember that as being a really intense day when we recorded that."

Easter also picked up on the emotion surrounding the song. "The first thing we did one day was to get a vocal down on that song," he recalled. "We took a few takes on it. It was kind of hard to sing. Normally, Michael was extremely fast with vocals, but with that one it took more time to get one we liked. I remember not being totally satisfied with the pitch in some parts, but Michael told us that was as good as it was going to get. He would not sing it any more."

Stipe, likely overcome with the emotion from singing a song about the death of his friend, probably just couldn't bear

to sing the song any more.

In a throwback of sorts to *Murmur*, the band created additional atmosphere for the track with some unconventional instrumentation. "That was Michael playing the wok, holding it against his chest, full of water, then slopping it around," Buck told *Rock Magazine*. "It's amazing. The first day of recording we cut seven songs without overdubs and vocals, yet we spent a whole day recording Michael banging away on a wok."

In what was becoming an R.E.M. trademark, the band chose to break up the space between 'Camera' and '(Don't Go Back To) Rockville' with a 20-second untitled interlude.

Buck said the piece was just some studio business that the band decided to include on the album. "They always say something, 'Test the mikes, play something.' You don't want to go through the song and ruin it, so you just start making noise," he explained on *Rockline*. "It just so happens we all kind of made noise that fit together with that funk thing."

"I guess that is just to let people know that it's not quite so mystifying in the studio and making records," Stipe explained. "That was just something we did while we were recording the album. We decided we liked it. It also in some way correlated with the song 'Camera' and provided some kind of bridge between 'Camera' and 'Rockville,' because they are really different songs."

(Don't Go Back To) Rockville

'(Don't Go Back To) Rockville' is another song about a girlfriend, but it's not as tragic or somber as 'Camera.' The girl in question in the song is Ingrid Schorr, who was nearly a member of Oh-OK, a band featuring Stipe's younger sister

lawyer liked the song so much that one night in the studio we decided that we would record it just for him, not to use at all," Berry told John Platt in *Bucketful Of Brains*. "We thought, 'Let's give it a real country twang,' and it came out really

'(Don't Go Back To) Rockville' was Mike Mills' musical plea to Ingrid Schorr.

good. So we added a few parts to it, like the piano and the screeching tremolo guitar. We thought it was good, but even then we almost didn't put it on the album as we thought it wasn't really representative of us. But then we thought, 'What the hell,' so we did. Rockville is in Maryland by the way, a real factory town, not anywhere you would want to visit."

Buck, in particular, seemed to enjoy the band's stab at country music. "We were all joking that we should put on fake beards and cowboy hats and have the picture sleeve single shot with us in a pick-up truck and see if we could get on country radio," he said during a British radio interview. "There's a country station in Athens that plays it, but probably the DJ knows us."

Even before R.E.M. decided to take the country road on '(Don't Go Back To) Rockville,' Stipe was claiming to be influenced by the musical genre. "No one's picked up on our country thing, either," he told Jon Young in a 1983 interview in *Trouser Press*. "My vocals are influenced by early country singers, mostly women: Patsy Cline, Skeeter Davis, Kitty Wells, and Wanda Jackson."

Lynda and future Magnapop singer Linda Hopper. The trio rehearsed together, but Schorr was ultimately replaced by Lynda Stipe's boyfriend, David Pierce.

When Schorr considered leaving Athens, Mills was moved enough to write this song. Initially, however, the song was quite different from the version that ended up on *Reckoning*. "We used to do it a lot faster, like how Buddy Holly would do it, if you can imagine that," Buck told a British radio interviewer.

The band had shelved the song for two years, until it decided to cut it as a gift of sorts for Bertis Downs. "Our

Easter, however, said R.E.M.'s country connection was funneled through late '60s rock. "I think it was country by way of the Lovin' Spoonful—country by way of longhaired rock bands," he said. "I didn't see those guys walking around with their George Jones records at that point. They might have had them at home, but I wasn't aware of it."

Whatever the case, '(Don't Go Back To) Rockville' is a standout track. "In an alternative universe," Buck quipped, the song "might have been a hit single."

Little America

This album-closing rocker can be interpreted many different ways. In performance, Stipe occasionally prefaced the song with the 'Pledge Of Allegiance,' before announcing, "I think I'm Rambo!" He has also been known to alter the song's lyrics, replacing "Another Greenville, another Magic Mart" with "another Reagan, another Bush" followed by the sound of a bomb exploding.

As Buck once pointed out, he is no fan of patriotism. "I'm really ill about it," he told a British radio interviewer. "I really despise Reagan. He's worse, as far as foreign policy goes, than Eisenhower was. He's the most backward thinking jerk, he's not a very intelligent man, and basically, the whole unseen premise of his presidency is that if you are not a white American, you are not an American at all."

Aside from the political agenda, expressed with the lyric, "rally round your leaders," 'Little America' also served as an R.E.M. road song of sorts, as the band opted to name the tour supporting *Reckoning* after the song. "Certainly, in some twisted way, it is a road song, but it's not 'on the road rock'n'roll,'" Buck told a British radio interviewer.

The song includes the immortal lyric, "Jefferson, I think we're lost," a reference to former R.E.M. manager Jefferson Holt. "It comes from driving in our van with our manager," Buck told John Bitzer in *Music Connection*. "Since he's driving, he can't drink while the rest of us can. So we're stopping to go to the bathroom every 10 minutes and constantly yelling directions at him. He says, 'I know where I am, I'm not lost.' [And we say], 'Jefferson, we're not anywhere near the God damn city, the hotel's not out there.' I got so mad one night, I started the road map on fire in the van. But it's also a comment on America—'Where the fuck are we?' None of us are really too pleased about who's running the country, where our money's going, and the straightforward tendency to dissolve any idea of civil liberties by 'Our Man in Charge.'"

Following the bitter split between R.E.M. and Holt in 1996, it seems unlikely that the band will ever perform this song again.

Former manager Jefferson Holt, left, with R.E.M. during happier times.

talking With The Taxman About Poetry, the 1986 album by British punk-folk troubadour and friend of R.E.M. Billy Bragg, was subtitled The Difficult Third Album. The back cover featured Bragg slogging through the London snow, guitar case in hand. Had R.E.M. been more straightforward and literal, that subtitle and photo—with the members of R.E.M. in Bragg's shoes—would have been appropriate for Fables Of The Reconstruction, the band's difficult third album, recorded in snowy London during February and March of 1985.

"You can't really describe London in February," Buck explained. "If it didn't snow, there was sleet or rain. I hate to complain, but I had to walk almost a mile carrying my guitar to the tube and then take a 40-minute tube ride out to where we were, then walk another half-a-mile, sometimes with the wind blowing. When you get to the studio, the last thing you want to do is play guitar. You want to sit down and have a

---

R.E.M. were on "the verge of a nervous breakdown" during the sessions for their "difficult" third album.

Coke or a beer or something." But it wasn't just the weather that was getting R.E.M. down. Despite the tremendous critical acclaim and growing cult following the band garnered with Murmur and Reckoning, R.E.M. found themselves at a crossroads of sorts. "At the time, I don't think any of us were really happy," Buck recalled. "It was just to the point where it seemed like everything was picking up and we felt like things were out of control a little bit. We hadn't made up our minds that we were going to be in a big band. In a lot of ways we were trying to figure out what we were doing."

Stipe had similar concerns. "Records always reflect the mindset of a band at the time," he told Eric Flaum in Goldmine, "and during Reconstruction we were all on the verge of a nervous breakdown. And we weren't sure if we really liked each other or not, and that was really reflected in the record."

That confusion, dread, and despair is quite apparent in the grooves of the album. What isn't apparent is exactly what the album is called. The cover had the words Fables Of The, printed on one side, and Reconstruction Of The, on the other, leaving it unclear what the correct title was, although Fables

Of The Reconstruction is used most often. "I maintain that the name of the record is *Reconstruction Of The Fables*, because everybody has decided it's *Fables*… and that really bothers me," Stipe told Andy Gill. "The cyclical title, to me, really defined the whole identity that the band was taking on at the time. It seemed to make a lot of sense to me at the time."

It was a phone conversation Stipe had with his father that inspired the title. "He said the word reconstruction," Stipe said on *Rockline*. "I think we were talking about carpentry, which is a hobby of mine." When Buck called Stipe on the claim, telling him not to "exaggerate," Stipe explained further: "OK, I want to be a carpenter," he clarified. "[My father] said this word reconstruction. It really struck me at the moment, I don't know why, but I dropped the telephone and hung up on him and decided to name the record that. It's as simple as that. It doesn't have very much to do with Southern politics and all that."

On another occasion, however, Stipe had a different take on things. "Fables brings up the whole thing about story-telling, and that kinda ties in with lost heritage, the tradition of a story being passed down from generation to generation,"

The latter explanation could have been on Stipe's mind when he came up with the off-handed remark in *Rolling Stone* about what the then-forthcoming *Fables* sounded like: "It reminds me of two oranges being stuck together with a nail." Years later, Stipe would explain that he made the comment after a full day's work and it was just a flip answer.

Although the fruit and nail analogy was a stretch, R.E.M. was looking to change its sound. With Mitch Easter's band Let's Active beginning to make a name for itself, R.E.M. had to decide on a new producer for the crucial third album. Among those considered was Beach Boys collaborator Van Dyke Parks. "We talked to him after *Reckoning*," Buck confirmed. "I really like him, but I don't know the guy at all. He's quite a provocateur and an interesting guy, but we just got the feeling he wasn't involved on that level. We just got the feeling that what he would like to have done was get paid a lot of money to do string arrangements. He was really nice. He said, 'If you want strings on your record, I'll do it. Why the hell not, but I don't know if you need me.'"

The band did, however, want to work with strings. To guide them through such experimentation, they called on the

FABLES
OF THE
RECONSTRUCTION

he told Gill. "A lot of people have picked up on the reconstruction politics thing after the Civil War, especially since we're supposed to be a Southern band—and that was not unintentional. The whole reconstruction politics thing was a pack of shit, and it's kinda like politics today. So in a way that's a valid interpretation. For me, though, I was thinking much more in the way of reconstruction of something, tearing it apart and putting it together."

services of veteran producer Joe Boyd, known for his work with Richard Thompson, Fairport Convention, Nick Drake, and the Incredible String Band. "I really liked him as a producer and a person," Buck said. "I loved his past work."

Initially, Boyd had to turn the offer down, having already committed to produce an album by Canadian singer Mary Margaret O'Hara and the major label debut by 10,000 Maniacs. After O'Hara canceled, Boyd contacted R.E.M.,

45

Veteran producer Joe Boyd guided R.E.M. through *Fables Of The Reconstruction*.

hopeful he could still work with the band. Three weeks after the band conducted some demo sessions with Boyd in Athens, the members of R.E.M. flew to London to begin working on *Fables* at Livingston Studios.

However, it may have been too soon. "We had just got off an eight-and-a-half month tour," Buck told John Platt in *Bucketful Of Brains*. "We rehearsed for eight or nine days [and] wrote these 15 songs... having no idea what we were doing."

In the studio, the band had a plan in mind, even if it was what Boyd didn't want to hear. "There was a lot of 'pull the voice back!' when we were mixing," Boyd told Jim Irvin in *Mojo*. "Same with the guitar. With a lot of groups, everyone wants their bit louder. With R.E.M. everyone wanted it quieter. It made it very difficult for me to get a vivid image in my mind, an idea mix."

Boyd's desire to find the right mix wore on the band. "He has this idea that there is the perfect mix for each song, and he'll work and work and work to get the mix, and it drove me up the fucking wall," Stipe told Gill. "But in the end, I'm really glad he was so meticulous."

Consistent with Boyd's background, Buck says that *Fables* is "the record where the folk influences started being kind of apparent. It was there from the beginning, but this is the one where some of the structures were more folky. It was also a weird psychedelic record in kind of a way."

If circumstances hadn't prevented it from happening, it could have been an even weirder album. "In a way that record, the third record, is the one that should have been a two-record set," Buck explained. "We just had reams and reams of really weird material, and we should have stuck it all on and not worried about it. There was really a whole album worth of stuff that we just should have shoved on there and had it be a 20-song album and really confuse everyone.

"We had one song called 'Theme For Two Steps Onward,' which was a really good song. We actually did horn overdubs on it, but it didn't have a finished vocal. Michael said, 'Let's put it on the next record. I just don't feel like I did the lyrics right.' But when we went to look for it to work on it, we couldn't find the tape and we didn't know how to play it."

Even in its released, single-disc incarnation, *Fables Of The Reconstruction* turned out to be a bizarre gem of an album, even if the members of the band initially didn't like it. Berry, at one point, went as far as saying that the album "sucked." "I hate the last record more than anybody else in the band," he told Clea Simon, following the release of *Lifes Rich Pageant*. "People have said to us, 'God, we're really glad you put out a really great record this time 'cause we can tell you now we didn't like the last one.' And I agree with them. It was a little lame."

Today, however, Buck has reconsidered *Fables*. "I think the record is really strong, the songs are really good... really odd and creepy," Buck said. "I think people were kind of confused because there is like a Stax-Motown thing on there and feedback guitar and folk ballads. Maybe it was a little too much."

Boyd also has regrets. "I always felt frustrated that I didn't get a better record," he told Irvin. "There was a raw energy about the first two albums that this one lacked a little bit."

However, like fine wine, *Fables* seems to get better with age. And the members of R.E.M. who initially dismissed the album are starting to look at it in a different light. "A lot of people come up to me and say, 'I wasn't sure at first, but now I think it's one of their best records,'" Boyd told *Mojo*. "Even Michael has said that to me. He now thinks it's a great record. So that pleases me."

Feeling Gravitys Pull

For those who bought into the theory that Peter Buck was nothing more than a Byrds copyist who only played jangly guitar, the opening of *Fables Of The Reconstruction* may have come as quite a shock, effectively rewriting R.E.M.'s own myth. On 'Feeling Gravitys Pull,' Buck's guitar was more jagged than jangly, owing more to '80s British post-punk acts such as Gang Of Four, than to some '60s throwback.

Those who were listening closely, however, knew that the discordant sounding track wasn't out of character, as R.E.M. had explored the use of similar sounds on *Murmur*'s '9-9.'

There From Here' include no such punctuation.

In 'Feeling Gravitys Pull,' Stipe paints a nice lyrical picture by dropping the name of an acclaimed American surrealist artist/photographer in the line "it's a Man Ray kind of sky." The lyric "time and distance are out of place here" could be a comment on how the band collectively felt "out of place" during the sessions held in London. Whatever the case, Stipe told 10,000 Maniacs singer and close friend Natalie Merchant that the song was one of his "real gut-spillers" in *Musician* magazine.

In 'Feeling Gravitys Pull,' Michael Stipe name-dropped American surrealist Man Ray.

Yet on 'Feeling Gravitys Pull,' R.E.M. weren't content to merely borrow a guitar sound. The song is swathed in moody strings. Buck explained that there is "certainly a little hello" to Gang Of Four in the song, "but it's also really seasick and weird. I like the fact that it is a real queasy song."

The song, which Buck has called one of his favorites, effectively captured the band's mood at the time. "As weird as that album can get, that's how I felt every day," he told *Melody Maker*. "The thing that sums it up is that bit at the end, where the strings come in and it goes down, 'neargh.' I probably looked like that too."

Although his singing is fairly audible, there is very little you can glean from Stipe's lyrics. The gravity subject matter of the song would reappear on *Lifes Rich Pageant*'s 'Fall On Me.' Another element that would resurface on the next album would be Stipe's apparent dislike for apostrophes, as both 'Feeling Gravitys Pull' and 'Cant Get

Maps And Legends

In the wake of the howl of 'Feeling Gravitys Pull,' 'Maps And Legends' sounds utterly tame and is a lot more in the traditional R.E.M. mode. The guitars shimmer and Stipe

croons sweetly, effectively supported by Mills and Berry's haunting backing vocals.

'Maps And Legends' is the first of several songs on

Fables Of The Reconstruction that were inspired by Stipe's friendships with the eccentric elderly residents of Athens and its surrounding areas.

"A lot of that song has to do with the people who I go around and visit," Stipe told Jim Ladd. "One man lives outside of Athens. His name is Reverend Ruth. He has this huge garden and he has concrete sculptures and a huge globe that hangs from a tree, [and] all these concrete paintings

he has made of Egypt and Assyria and kind of biblical places he has visited. He taught geography when he was a younger man. He and his wife will take you into their house and he will sit down at one of those little K-mart organs and start playing and his wife stands with her hand on the stove and starts singing. It's about the most beautiful thing you have ever heard in your life. She has a voice that surpasses everything recorded."

In concert, Stipe has sent the song out to another of his old friends. "There was this man named Elijah Pierce. He used to live in Columbus, Ohio. He had a barbershop and

when he wasn't cutting hair, he was carving wood. He died last year. The Columbus Museum of Art bought up all his little pieces of wood and now he's famous. This song is for him."

At another date, Stipe dedicated 'Maps And Legends' to *Reckoning* cover artist, the Reverend Howard Finster, whom he called "a man of vision and feeling—a fine example to all."

Despite the song's title, Stipe revealed that 'Maps And Legends' actually has more to do with his acquaintances

Reckoning cover artist Howard Finster, according to Stipe, "a fine example to all."

than, well, maps and legends. "There's a lot of people like maps," he told Henry Jackson. "You look at them and you can lay them out on a table and read them and run your finger over them. You can find their little stories, their little squares and circles. Some are filled in, some are not. Some have lines connecting them and it's real pretty, nice and mysterious, but you can't make heads or tails out of it. So then, when you're done with that, you go down to the key and it tells you what the circle means. And then you look at the map and it starts to make sense. There are a lot of people like that."

Aside from his friends, Stipe could also be referring to his own songs when he sings that "maybe these maps and legends have been misunderstood."

A live acoustic version of the song, recorded on May 24, 1987, at the Texas Records benefit at McCabe's Guitar Shop in Santa Monica, was included as the B-side of 'The One I Love' single, and subsequently included on the expanded edition of *Fables*, released in 1992.

Driver 8

The band's first train song had been 'Carnival Of Sorts (Box Cars)'. 'Driver 8', more literal than its predecessor, is an R.E.M. classic that features a number of the band's trademark sounds—a melodic bass line, catchy guitar riff, and passionate and throaty Stipe vocal. "It's kind of the quintessential R.E.M. song," Buck confirmed, "those chord changes and the riffs and everything."

In fact, Buck would use the E minor, A minor combination of chords again in such future R.E.M. standouts as 'The One I Love,' 'Losing My Religion,' and 'Bang And Blame.' "I can't

Stipe, Berry, Mills, and Buck take a break in front of a train—the kind that inspired 'Driver 8.'

5099
5099
SOUTHERN RAILWAY
SR
SERVES THE SOUTH
LOOK AHEAD-LOOK SOUTH

think of any band I like that hasn't used them. The Beatles, Elvis Costello, Neil Young pretty much used them on every song," he told Vic Garbarini.

'Driver 8,' which was performed on the *Reckoning* tour, went through several different incarnations before the band stumbled upon the recorded version. "There was an acoustic version that was acoustic guitar, banjo, and vocals that was really cool," Buck recalled. That interpretation of the song, taped while the band was on the L.A. stop of the Little America tour, was previewed on *The Cutting Edge*, an I.R.S. Records television program that aired on MTV. In the studio and on the road, a version with "really heavy" guitar was attempted, but also didn't make the cut.

Trains made a logical topic for R.E.M. "We all live near the train tracks, so we hear trains all the time," Buck said in a British radio interview. Stipe explained that the train imagery was "a romanticism… that is somehow associated with that

mythological America that never really existed except in people's minds" in an interview with Andy Gill.

In the song, an overworked engineer is urged to "take a break" by a conductor who says that they will reach their "destination," but they are "still a ways away." By the end of the song, the destination still hasn't been reached. The engineer and the conductor still haven't found what they are looking for.

Fittingly, the song features a snatch of a harmonica mimicking the sound of a train whistle, and the video, directed by Stipe and James Herbert, is primarily comprised of footage of trains.

A live version of the song, recorded in Seattle, Washington, on June 27, 1984, first appeared as the B-side of the 'Wendell Gee' British 12-inch single, and was subsequently included on the expanded edition of *Fables* that was released in 1992.

Life And How To Live It

In this fairly upbeat rocker, some fans may have thought Stipe was giving them listening tips with the lyric, "If you tire of one side, the other serves you best."

However, the song, featuring Stipe, Mills, and Berry's three-part harmonies, is about another one of the eccentrics that Stipe had run into. "That's actually about a man who lived in Athens and had a house that was divided into two different apartments and he had decorated each apartment different from the other," Stipe told Ladd. "He would just live in one for a while and then move to the other. He had this kind of schizophrenic lifestyle. He would change from one to the

other. And he had completely separate closets with completely different kinds of clothes in each one. When he died they went back into his house to clean it out and found thousands of copies of a book he had written but never given out to anyone called *Life And How To Live It*. It was his own philosophy about life and how to live it."

Those not privy to Stipe's explanation may have thought he was giving such advice in the song and are probably still scratching their heads. An arty video clip for the song, featuring the band performing, was directed by Jackie Slayton and James Herbert.

Old Man Kensey

As the title suggests, this song is yet another about the characters in Mr. Stipe's neighborhood. However, Stipe didn't write the lyrics to this song himself. 'Old Man Kensey' is one of those rare R.E.M. tracks that has a writing credit attributed to someone outside of the band. "Michael writes all the lyrics, but occasionally one of us will give him help," Buck explained. "I think he was just around with people and got someone to help him."

In the case of 'Old Man Kensey,' it was Athens scenester

and Limbo District member Jerry Ayers, who also co-wrote 'Windout' with the band and '52 Girls' with the B-52's. "Jerry's an older guy, not like he's ancient, but he's a little older than me," Buck added. "He had been like a Warhol superstar drag guy in the '60s. He's a really smart guy and I like to hang around with him."

Stipe once explained the story of Kensey in concert before performing the song. "He was a guy who played dead in a coffin and had a friend drive him down to the Piggly

Wiggly [market]. His friend would beckon a woman to check out Kensey and when she leaned over, he'd pop his eyes open and holler, 'Boo!'"

Buck once described Kensey, who supposedly lives in Summerville, Georgia, as "a dog kidnapper" who would collect ransom money and "go out and get drunk. He's out to lunch."

If anyone doubted that such a character actually exists, Stipe pointed to photographic proof. "If you look at the inside sleeve of *Reckoning* and the picture of Howard Finster, there is a figure in the background sitting on the couch," he said during a British radio interview. "That's Kensey." There is such

'Old Man Kensey' co-writer Jerry Ayers—"a smart guy" who Buck likes to hang around with.

a photo of Finster, but it is nearly impossible to make out another figure in the photo.

The song, which Buck describes as "almost a children's story," opens with an ominous bass line courtesy of Mills. The bassist is also behind the ghostly backing vocals that add to the mood. The "dog kidnapper" story is evident in the lyrics about Kensey's desire to be a "dog catcher." In the song, Kensey is also "gonna be a clown."

51

Cant Get There From Here

Just when *Fables* threatened to sink from the weight of odd characters and moody songs, R.E.M. kick up their heels with this atypical funk workout. "I think that we were listening to a whole lot of soul records and that kind of popped up," Buck

said on *Rockline*. "We played it live a couple of times in Athens doing these surprise shows and we figured, it is not really the type of thing that we are known for, but everyone liked it. It's kind of self-mocking. We are these white guys who have grown up with black music and can't really approach it, like, say if I was Al Green. It's like a tongue-in-cheek tribute to Ray Charles, James Brown, and all the great Georgia music giants." In fact, in the song's lyrics, Stipe mentions "Brother Ray," which is likely to be a reference to Ray Charles.

The light-hearted 'Cant Get There From Here' would pave the way for such similarly lightweight, but uplifting, songs as

'Stand' and 'Shiny Happy People,' as well as the future funk'n'soul-influenced track 'Radio Song.' "It was kind of like 'We Walk,'" Stipe said on *Rockline*. "We never intended for it to be on a record, but it sounded OK."

In the song—which features Jim Dvorak on trumpet, Peter Thomas on tenor saxophone, and David Bitelli on tenor and baritone saxophone—Stipe recommends that those in need of "inspiration" visit Philomath, a small town located between Lexington and Crawfordville, Georgia. Buck confirmed that the town is "real but fictional-sounding" in a British radio interview. Stipe also swore he had never visited the town. The liner notes of the 1988 "best of" collection *Eponymous* revealed that the small city once had its own post office.

R.E.M. paid tribute to soul legends like Ray Charles in 'Cant Get There From Here.'

Aside from being the band's foray into funk, 'Cant Get There From Here' also revealed a few other things. For one, Stipe sings in several different ranges in the track, ranging from the deep voice in the verses to the falsetto scream that rings in the chorus. "I figured out that I had all these different voices in me, and maybe one of the first songs I tried using more than one or two of those voices at a time was on 'Can't Get There From Here,'" he told Julie Panebianco.

Playing the soul man/preacher to the hilt, Stipe proclaims "Gentlemen testify" several times in the song. He used a similar device in the band's cover of Archie Bell And The Drells's 'Tighten Up,' which was originally released as a flexi-disc in *Bucketful Of Brains*, and subsequently included on the 1992 expanded edition of *Reckoning*.

The video clip for 'Cant Get There From Here,' directed by Stipe, Aguar Bros. Films, and Hartley Schilling, also had a few revelations. It managed to capture the band's sense of humor and, for the first time, showed a few of Stipe's mysterious words on the screen. "I guess that was just kind of a way for me to contradict my own rules," he explained on *Rockline*. "I directed and did the video myself, I even did that lettering, but if you notice, only some of the lyrics are on there."

Apart from the lyrics, the clip also featured the band in a mock drive-in setting in Mills's '66 turquoise T-Bird and Berry's lavender and white '64 Ford Galaxy. "We just try to do things that are entertaining to us," Buck told *The Bob*. "'Cant Get There' was a silly song, so we figured we'd have to be really silly: 'Let's do it at a drive-in, and use all the cool cars we own.' So we did that."

Green Grow The Rushes

This delicate and pretty tune is the first of three R.E.M. songs that deal with American oppression of the people of Central America. Unfortunately, the meaning of 'Green Grow The Rushes,' like *Life Rich Pageant*'s 'The Flowers Of Guatemala' and *Document*'s 'Welcome To The Occupation,' largely fell on deaf ears.

"I thought 'Green Grow The Rushes' was the most radical song ever put on vinyl and no one ever approached me about it," Stipe told Bill Flanagan in *Musician*. "About two years later a complete stranger came up and said, 'That's the most intense song about foreign policy I ever heard,' and I hugged him."

In interviews, Stipe revealed that the song is about guestworkers, "particularly Hispanic guestworkers in America," he told Harold DeMuir. "In fact, that song brings in pieces of the whole history of guestworking in how our country was settled, but it wasn't obvious enough and people really never caught on to it."

As was the case with much of R.E.M.'s early material, Stipe's lyrics only offered a few clues as to what the song was about, rather than a complete picture. He does mention "surplus cheaper hands," and in an ingenious twist of a lyric from the patriotic standard 'America The Beautiful,' Stipe changes "the amber waves of grain" into the "amber waves of gain." Stipe was proud enough of the phrase to write it on a T-shirt, which he wore on stage during several dates of the *Reconstruction* tour.

In concert, he revealed that 'Green Grows The Rushes' was inspired by an old folk song. "When American soldiers went marching into Mexico they sang it."

Kohoutek

Like 'Cant Get There From Here,' this song features Stipe singing in a few voices. Aside from his familiar singing style, he begins the song in a near falsetto, a technique that he uses on occasion throughout the song.

He also chose to put himself in the song—in the third person. Although the back of the album lists the song's title as 'Kohoutek,' the album's inner sleeve has the title misspelled 'Kahoetek.' The song hinges on the lyric, "like Kohoutek, you were gone," which makes a bit more sense after you learn that it is named after a comet sighted in March 1973 by the Czech astronomer Dr. Lubos Kohoutek.

Buck felt the song wasn't that memorable. "I barely remember writing it or doing it," he said. "We only played it live a few times. I don't remember recording it. I swear we only played it live about three times, but I bought a bootleg that has it on it. I think it fits in the body of the record, but it doesn't stand out for me."

Stipe evoked images of the comet Kohoutek in the R.E.M. song of the same name.

Auctioneer (Another Engine)

This song is the one all-out rocker on *Fables Of The Reconstruction*. It was written, appropriately enough, on the road. "I remember having that in the encores," Buck recalled. "We had a few new things that we did on the *Reckoning* tour. We did 'Theme From Two Steps Onward,' that, and 'Hyena.'"

The fast-tempo song opens sedately before breaking into full-out rage, with Stipe singing of an auctioneer putting "another engine" on the blocks. Buried deep in the mix, you can hear what appears to be an auctioneer's "barter holler." With Stipe holding a long note, Buck adds an effective, and stinging guitar riff, making the track one of the band's most explosive recordings to date.

From left, Stipe, Buck, Berry, and Mills rocked out on 'Auctioneer (Another Engine).'

Good Advices

After the kick of 'Auctioneer,' the soothing 'Good Advices' is as comforting as an old shoe, as R.E.M. returns to its familiar folk-rock style.

As the title suggests, Stipe sings about various bits of advice that he has encountered. As perhaps a sign of things to come, his singing is easily understandable, hinting that perhaps someone gave the singer some advice—enunciate.

Buck has mixed feelings about the song. "It was kind of like filler, but good filler," he explained to Anthony DeCurtis in

Rolling Stone. "It was a real nice song and it was done well. It's not one of the songs I'd pick out ten years from now to show what a good songwriter I was. It's got a nice mood to it. Sometimes you've to realize that not every song is going to be 'Like A Rolling Stone' or 'Satisfaction' or even 'So. Central Rain.' Some of them have smaller pleasures and smaller ideas and smaller feelings, and that's perfectly valid too."

When Buck was asked about good advice he had received, he told a UK interviewer to "Try not to die like a dog."

Wendell Gee

Despite his father's advice to the contrary, rock'n'roll didn't break Peter Buck's heart. This sweet folk-rock ballad, however, likely broke a few thousand. 'Wendell Gee' emerges as one of the most sympathetic and heartfelt characters in Stipe's eccentric-filled *Fables*.

A predecessor to 'I Believe,' 'Wendell Gee' features Buck picking banjo. "I really hated the track for a long time," Buck said during a British radio interview. "I must admit, I was wrong. I don't love it, but I like it."

Buck's initial disdain for the song made Stipe hesitant to approach his band mate. "When I got into the studio he was a wreck," Stipe said. "I was really afraid to go in because I knew he didn't like the song. I got there late in the evening and he had put down this incredible track that really took the whole song to another plateau."

Not unlike 'Old Man Kensey,' the band had sufficient background on the character that inspired the song. "There's a whole town and everyone's last name in it

"There wasn't even time to say goodbye." Wendell Gee's obituary, published in the *Athens Banner-Herald*.

Wendell Gee
Pendergrass

Wendell Gee, 69, of 695 John B. Brooks Road, died Saturday, Nov. 25, 1995.

A native of Jackson County, Mr. Gee was a son of the late Roy Gee Sr. and Emma Fowler Gee and widow of Jenny Gee. He operated Wendell Gee Used Cars in Pendergrass and was a member of Pendergrass Baptist Church. He was a U.S. Army veteran of World War II and was a member of the American Legion of the Georgia Sheriff's Association. He was preceded in death by a son, Randall Gee.

Funeral services will be at 2 p.m. Monday at Pendergrass Baptist Church with the Revs. Charles Jenks and Larry Elrod officiating. Burial will be in Pendergrass Cemetery.

Survivors include his wife, Lois Smith Gee; a daughter, Elaine Watson, Pendergrass; a stepdaughter, Rebecca Skinner, Jefferson; two sons, Ronnie Gee, Jefferson; and Ricky Gee, Pendergrass; a stepson, Patrick Garrett, Clermont; a brother, Roy Gee Jr., Pendergrass; 14 grandchildren; and three great-grandchildren.

The family will receive friends from 2-4 p.m. today and from 7-9 tonight at Jackson Funeral Home, Jefferson.

is Gee, apparently," Buck revealed in the British radio interview. "It's right near the train station. We always go to the train to drop off friends. There's a Wendell Gee's Used Cars, Gwen Gee's pool hall, Roy Gee's bail bonds—five different Gee stores all around and they are all weird things like pool halls, bailbondsmen and used cars. You just know they must be some kind of family."

With the line "there wasn't even time to say goodbye," Stipe hinted that Wendell Gee had passed away. However, Gee didn't die until nearly a decade later. His obituary, which appeared in the *Athens Banner-Herald* on November 26, 1995, confirmed some of Buck's story. Gee, who died at the age of 69, did operate Wendell Gee Used Cars in Pendergrass, Georgia. He was also the son of the late Roy Gee, a member of Pendergrass Baptist Church, the American Legion, and the Georgia Sheriff's Association. One thing the obituary failed to mention, however, was that Wendell Gee had been immortalized in song, and a bittersweet one at that.

LIFES RICH PAGEANT

following the depressing experience of making *Fables Of The Reconstruction*, R.E.M. needed a kick in their collective pants. While the band's evaluation of *Fables* has become somewhat brighter with time and distance, in the years immediately following the album's release no one was particularly happy with the record. To remedy the perceived problem, R.E.M. opted to make a change. The band decided to hire Don Gehman, best known for his work with American mainstream rocker John Cougar Mellencamp, to produce their next album.

After a demo session at John Keane's studio in Athens, Georgia, the band and Gehman reconvened at Mellencamp's Bellmont Mall recording studio in Bloomington, Indiana. The new facility had only been used for one prior album—Mellencamp's 1985 effort, *Scarecrow*. The pairing of still-underground R.E.M. with the established hit-making Gehman was mocked by some, with *Musician* magazine wondering if the harder-rocking approach should be called "R.O.C.K. in the R.E.M.," a reference to Mellencamp's hokey 1986 No. 2 American hit 'R.O.C.K. In The U.S.A.'

"It wasn't like we were trying to sound like John Cougar or anything, but we wanted to pick someone who had a different background than us, and he did," Buck explained. "He had a hit record background. Don's whole idea was to go

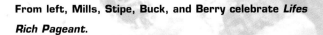

From left, Mills, Stipe, Buck, and Berry celebrate *Lifes Rich Pageant*.

for the gold—why put out a song that doesn't have a chance of being a top 10 single? I can understand that. In a lot of ways he really focused us. We just wanted to try something different. I think Don was good because he really did push us. In a way, he feels that the record wasn't what it should have been, because apparently John Mellencamp really wants to have hits and he will cut the record and rewrite them to make them clearer. I was like, 'I don't really care, I think this is the record we want to go with. I think it represents us really well.'"

It wasn't Mellencamp's record sales the band was striving for, but his sound, Buck explained. "I just like the sound of his records, the drum sound and the way the guitars intermesh," he told Robert Hilburn of the *Los Angeles Times*. "It's a real good rock'n'roll sound without being overly slick."

Gehman, who wasn't overwhelmed by *Fables Of The Reconstruction* or R.E.M.'s live performances, thought the band needed help. "I felt that R.E.M. were great songwriters and had a great mystique, but a lot of the power was lost—they weren't able to get things across in a real direct manner," he told Dave DiMartino in *Mojo*.

True to the band's goal of making a more traditional rock'n'roll record, much of the material on the album reminded those close to R.E.M. of the band's early work, in which energy was emphasized instead of moodiness. Buck attributed the renewed power of the band to the eight months on tour in support of *Fables*. Also, the members of R.E.M. took time to discuss their specific goals for the album. "We had never actually sat down before and talked about what we

57

wanted to do with the record, what we wanted it to sound like, where we wanted to go musically," Buck told Hilburn. "We did do that with this one."

Another factor in making the sessions a success was Gehman's work ethic. "He was really easygoing, and the one thing that impressed us is that he didn't like to work a long time," Berry told Clea Simon. "He'd work like six to eight hours and say, 'OK, that's it until tomorrow.' It's a real productive way of working because you don't get tired and therefore you don't make mistakes that you don't find until the next day."

The band also chose to augment its sound once again, but not with the lush string arrangements that swallowed *Fables*. Instead, it turned its sights on an old pump organ, which was dusted off and put to use on every track on the album, save for 'Swan Swan H.'

For *Lifes Rich Pageant*, R.E.M. producer Don Gehman, known for his work with John Mellencamp, was enlisted.

In working with Gehman, the band used new studio techniques that would affect its sound on future songs, such as *Monster*'s 'Let Me In.' "I learned a lot from him about how natural room reverb affects the kick drum and the guitar sound," Buck told Vic Garbarini in *Guitar World*. "Before then, I'd always just close-miked, because that's what we did live. Don would work for an hour on my guitar tone, mike it five different ways, then mix it down. I was like, 'Cool, I didn't know you could do that!'"

Stipe, who wrote most of the album's lyrics in the studio, also enjoyed the change, even if he didn't necessarily respond well to Gehman's criticism at times. "*Lifes Rich*

Pageant was the reconstruction of the deconstruction that *Fables* became," he told David Fricke in typical Stipe-speak. "Don Gehman came in with his really big drum sound and that opened some doors for us. He was also the first person to challenge me on my lyrics, just saying, 'What the fuck is this about?' I crossed my arms and walked out of the room. But I appreciated the challenge a lot. Don just said: 'What about what you're singing? What is this? Why do you want to put that out?'"

The result was a further refinement of Stipe's lyric writing and singing. "I wasn't real interested in the music being perfect," Gehman told DiMartino. "I was more interested in providing a little bit more clarity to Michael's voice, that was what I was really shooting for. And they were probably ready for it. It was my duty to prove the point that it could be done in a way that didn't lose any of the mystery and the mystique that they thought was so important to the band." Gehman's instincts proved to be correct. Even when Stipe's singing was easier to understand, the songs still managed to be enigmatic.

Another enigma was the album's title. In typical R.E.M. fashion, the band opted to mysteriously omit the apostrophe in "Life's" for no particular reason. The phrase, which certainly has a lighter feel than *Fables Of The Reconstruction*, was borrowed from the *Pink Panther* sequel *A Shot In The Dark*, a comedy starring Peter Sellers. The move showed that R.E.M. had a sense of humor, despite the ultra-serious tone of much of their music.

"There's a scene in one of the films where the inspector falls out of his car and into a pond... and someone says to him, 'Inspector Clouseau, you are all... you should get out of your clothes,' and Clouseau says, 'It's all part of life's rich pageant,'" Buck explained to Hilburn. The band started using the expression as a catch phrase whenever something went wrong. "If the sound system didn't work in Boise, for instance, we'd look at each other and say, 'Well, it's all part of life's rich pageant.'"

Working in Bloomington, which—like the band's home base of Athens—is a college town, proved to be conducive to the sessions. During the three weeks of sessions, the band stayed in scenic lakeside apartments. "Bloomington was a lot like Athens. There aren't many distractions." Mills told *Rolling Stone*. During the sessions, the band hung out with Mellencamp. "I like John," Buck told David Howard in *Contrast*. "He went out of his way to be nice to us. I met him

and he remembered my name and took us to parties." While the members of R.E.M. did go to bars at night to check out the local talent, for the most part, they focused on the task at hand. As a result, Mills said the album was not only "more accessible" than their previous albums, but was "the strongest, best album we've done." Mills even compared the album to the band's acclaimed first LP. "This one has a lot of mood, like *Murmur*," he told John Kordosh in *Creem*, "but this one has more strength and more power behind it."

"I like *Murmur* a lot," Buck said to Kordosh, "just because of the way it feels. But I think this one came out more like we wanted it to, song-wise and production-wise."

Berry was equally pleased with the album, which cost $100,000 to record, including equipment rentals, lodging, and plane tickets. "I'm happier than a pig in shit," he told Simon. "I just love the drum sound."

As was the case on their previous albums, R.E.M. once again chose to throw listeners a curve ball with the album's packaging. The track listing that appears on the back of the album cover is not the correct running order and omits each side's closing tracks—'Underneath The Bunker' and 'Superman'—which were added to the album late in the game. In another twist, Stipe, often criticized for his indecipherable lyrics, chose to excerpt a few lyrics from each song, and offer some explanations, on the back of the album cover. A note affixed to the shrinkwrap on the album informed potential buyers that the album was "new new new new new new new," quoted the "pistol hot cup of rhyme" lyric from 'Swan Swan H,' listed Gehman as the producer, and inexplicably ended with the words "Mammoth huge colossal understated." Perhaps the band was attempting to turn reviewers on to a few new adjectives, since "indecipherable" no longer fitted the bill. In the credits, manager Jefferson Holt was listed as "Ambassador: J.W. Holt," while attorney Bertis Downs was credited "Motivation: B.E. Downs IV." One side of the inner sleeve had an illustration of "Polynesian Boys Interlocking Sticks That Waves Can A Mass." Another head-scratcher.

Instead of the traditional side one and side two, this time R.E.M. offered its listeners a "Dinner Side" and "Supper Side." What fans received was a well-balanced aural meal that proved to be R.E.M.'s most accomplished and commercial platter to date. It also captured many of the different moods and topics that are—as Inspector Clouseau and Pete Buck might say—part of life's rich pageant.

Begin The Begin

From the onset of 'Begin The Begin,' with a crisp Buck guitar riff, the new-found power of Berry's drumming, and the clarity of Stipe's vocals, it's apparent that R.E.M. has emerged from *Fables Of The Reconstruction* rejuvenated and ready to rock.

In the song, in which Stipe challenges listeners to stand up against apathy and start over, the singer drops a few humorous self-effacing lines that mock his increasing role as a generational spokesmen. Fans may be looking to Stipe "for

reason," but he "can't think clearly," he "can't even rhyme." Stipe has been known to introduce the song in concert by saying it "is a song of great personal motivation, integrity and import. It was written especially for you."

Like such future R.E.M. songs as *Document*'s 'It's The End Of The World As We Know It (And I Feel Fine)' and *Automatic For The People*'s 'Man On The Moon,' 'Begin The Begin' has a few references to historical figures. In this instance, Stipe sings that he has to "begin again like Martin Luther Zen," a noble sentiment that conjures up images of the leader of the Protestant Reformation movement in

Germany and the slain American civil rights leader. A bit more puzzling is Stipe's reference to Miles Standish, followed by the words, "proud, congratulate me." Standish was an Englishman who was the leader of the Plymouth Colony, who died in 1656. (Stipe may have had a more contemporary Miles in mind—Miles Copeland, the head of I.R.S. Records.) As Stipe sings in the song prior to the Miles Standish line, he "looked for it," and he "found it." Perhaps Stipe is referring

---

In 'Begin The Begin' Stipe evoked images of Martin Luther King Jr. and Martin Luther.

---

to his more understandable and accessible sound, which would make Copeland "proud" and lead him to "congratulate" Stipe on his new-found clarity.

The song was composed on acoustic guitars in Stipe's living room. "We had 20 degree weather and we were huddled up in our jackets, trying to write songs for the album," Buck told Kordosh. "I had that one little riff and that was it. We just kind of sat and made it up and we went: 'Let's change this; let's make it so it never repeats.' The original version was about a minute longer and nothing is the same all the way through except the riff." The song was so complex that the band had trouble remembering it. "There were five different choruses, no bridge, no melody—see, it was really good," Buck added. "I was going, 'It should be eight minutes long and do each bit twice, all the way through.'" Instead, the band opted for a compact three minutes and 24 seconds, with Buck playing rhythm on a Robin guitar. Buck has said that the song has a little bit of a Wire influence, but "the connections are pretty tenuous," he told Bill Forman, "in that Michael will be doing something that he thinks sounds like Wire and I'll be playing something that sounds like Neil Young." Nonetheless, 'Begin The Begin' effectively sets the *Pageant* into motion. (A live version of 'Begin The Begin,' recorded at the November 19, 1992, Greenpeace benefit in Athens, Georgia, turned up as a bonus track on the 'Bang And Blame' CD single.)

These Days

Hot on the heels of 'Begin The Begin,' the frantic 'These Days' turns the heat up on the already percolating *Pageant*. In fact, the back-to-back pairing of these songs could very well be R.E.M.'s most compelling album-opening combination. With its clarion-call guitar figure and frenzied drum intro, 'These Days' stands as one of the most powerful anthems in the R.E.M. catalog.

"We certainly weren't thinking, 'We're going to write anthems,' but that did come out kind of huge," Buck said by way of explanation. "When we played it in front of 20,000 people the next year, it seemed to fit, but it wasn't a real conscious thing."

'These Days' comes as a bit of reassurance to those who may have been put off by Stipe's debunking of his own myth in 'Begin The Begin.' Early on, he threatens—in perhaps a precursor to Green's 'Turn You Inside-Out'—that he "will rearrange your scales." Yet later in the song he embraces fans, singing "we are… young despite the years," and "hope despite the times." If that weren't enough, Stipe tells the faithful that he wishes to meet "each one," because they have "many things in common." Despite such seemingly earnest sentiments, Stipe reveals he still has his tongue in his cheek. Several times in the song, he addresses the "happy throngs," and, at the song's close, Mills sings the barely audible line, "Take away the scattered bones of my meal." The kings have spoken.

Though Stipe's message may be mixed, Buck's new and improved economic guitar playing is quite clear, as Gehman taught him to be a bit more subtle. "The regular guitar is the main guitar and that's it," Buck told David Howard in *Contrast*. "Just through the beginning of the verses there's a 12-string that does the melody line. There's only two or three guitars playing at once. Don helped me question why I play at certain places."

Fall On Me

Prior to 'Losing My Religion,' 'Fall On Me' was R.E.M.'s most beautiful and stunning single. The fact that the song stalled at No. 94 on *Billboard*'s Hot 100, before falling off the charts, is tragic, as the mainstream missed a chance to hear this should-have-been hit. In a perfect world, it would have gone top 10.

Beginning with a striking Buck guitar lick, 'Fall On Me' employs R.E.M.'s pop instincts to their furthest extent, as the frequent use of Mills's sweet backing vocals give the song the feel of a lost '60s classic by the Mamas And The Papas.

In the song's lyrics, Stipe isn't California dreaming, but contemplating gravity and oppression. Initially, when the song was performed on the *Reconstruction* tour, 'Fall On Me' didn't quite come together. "I came up with the music," Buck recalled, "but we didn't really have a bridge for it and Michael kept changing the lyrics. We did it that whole tour in 1985 and when we went in the studio, Michael totally changed the melody as well as the lyrics and we came up with a different bridge for it. The genesis is the same, but it is pretty different if you listen back to the tapes in 1985, it's pretty different. We literally changed the bridge every night. We would go, well, 'Why don't we try to do this,' and poor Mike had to remember the chords and make up lyrics on the spot. But that was kind of cool, I love doing that kind of thing."

Stipe explained how 'Fall On Me,' the first song the band recorded as a demo with Gehman, evolved over time. "'Fall On Me' is still believed to be about acid rain," he told David Fricke. "Initially it was. But then I rewrote the song. If you listen to the second verse, there is a countermelody underneath it. That's the original melody to the song; that was the part about acid rain. In fact, the 'Fall On Me' that we all know and love is not about acid rain. It's a general oppression song about the fact that there are a lot of causes out there that need a song that says, 'Don't smash us.' And specifically, there are references to the Leaning Tower of Pisa and the guy dropping weights and feathers."

Despite his specific intentions in the lyrics, Stipe was happy to let listeners interpret 'Fall On Me'—which he once called "kind of a happy song"—in their own terms. "I pretty much intended it be taken by the listener, that song more than any other maybe, as exactly what the listener needs to hear out of it," he told Timothy White. "It's pretty much a song

Peter Buck provided a striking introduction to the should-have-been hit 'Fall On Me.'

about oppression and you can apply it in whatever way you wanted to and needed to."

To accompany that open-ended message, Stipe chose to make the video for the song quite different to the usual MTV fare. Stipe shot black-and-white footage of industrial wreckage, turned it upside down, surrounded it with fluorescent green borders, and superimposed the lyrics of the song—in bright pink block letters—on to the image. In keeping with the "no apostrophes" logic in the album's title, contractions such as "there's," "isn't," "let's," and "don't," appear without punctuation. The clip was completed for a thrifty $650.

"It was my idea, it was just something I saw and went out and shot it," Stipe explained on the syndicated radio program *Rockline*. "I made a film and put it out as a video. We're not in it, because we don't want to be. We have a really healthy dislike for everything that runs on MTV and none of us are actors, except for me of course. None of us are actors enough to get up and kind of dance around like everyone else does. It really kind of makes me sick. We just wanted to have a really beautiful fine film to go along with the music."

The fact that the words were included in the video is Stipe's response to those who wished the band would include a lyric sheet with the album. "Michael has a very subtle sense of humor and with this video," Buck told Kordosh. "It's a fuck you to the record company that says, 'Oh, lyric sheet with the records.' It's a fuck you to MTV and their videos.'" In one of the great ironies surrounding R.E.M., the band—who gave the music channel the finger and referred to it as "eMpTVee" in its fan club literature—would be lauded by the channel over the 'Losing My Religion' clip five years later.

Aside from the video, 'Fall On Me' was also heard as a musical backdrop in radio commercials in which Stipe endorsed local politicians. "It was kind of funny," Buck told

Roy Wilkinson. "I was driving around Atlanta visiting my mom and that comes on the Big 96 Rock, the big local dinosaur behemoth radio station, and there's one of our songs and Michael explaining why you should vote for this guy."

The 12-inch single of 'Fall On Me' was backed by the unlikely combination of the original instrumental 'Rotary Ten' and the band's cover of Aerosmith's 'Toys In The Attic.' A live version of 'Fall On Me,' recorded at the November 19, 1992 Greenpeace benefit in Athens, Georgia, turned up as a bonus track on the 'Crush With Eyeliner' CD single.

Cuyahoga

Like 'Fall On Me,' 'Cuyahoga' is another song that expresses concerns about man's negative effects on the environment yet still manages to be uplifting and optimistic. Instead of a Buck guitar riff, 'Cuyahoga' kicks off with a rumbling Mills bass line.

The song takes its name from the Cuyahoga River in Ohio, which flows through Cleveland into Lake Erie. As the back of the album cover reveals, "Cuyahoga = a dying river." Part of the river, on sacred Indian ground, became so polluted that it would burn if you threw a torch into it. "That's where the phrase, 'It didn't set the river on fire' came from," Buck explained on *Rockline*. "In 1910, 1915 they used to set the river on fire—I guess to clean it up."

The river, however, was just a starting point for the song's theme, which ran much deeper. "That's a metaphor for America and lost promises," Buck told Bill Forman. "This is where the Indians were and now look at it. It's one of the ugliest fucking rivers in the world."

Still, Stipe manages to turn the dire theme into hope for optimism, suggesting we "start a new country up." The chorus, with Stipe and Mills's voices interlocking, also manages to uplift. Composed mostly by Mills and Berry, 'Cuyahoga' remains close to the bassist's heart. "It's one of my favorites, at least to play live," he said on *Rockline*. "It's just the most fun for me."

Hyena

At least thematically, 'Hyena' is Stipe's pre 'It's The End Of The World...' vision of the apocalypse, as Stipe warns of the nuclear threat in this song that somehow manages to have a celebratory feel. The song opens with Stipe making some odd animal noises.

'Hyena' actually dates back to the *Fables Of The Reconstruction* sessions. "We had a lot of material for *Fables* and when we cut 'Hyena' and we listened back to it, we said, 'You know, that's twice as fast as it should be, so forget it,'" Buck recalled. The fog surrounding *Fables* had blurred the

band's vision. This fact became apparent when the band re-recorded 'Hyena' for *Lifes Rich Pageant* and found that it was too slow and opted to speed it up. "A lot of times we think we are doing the right thing, we make these decisions, but a couple of years later, things are different," Buck explained. "We played it live a lot and found a better arrangement for it. Michael had focused the lyrics better and vocally it made more sense as far as the notes hitting against the chords." Nonetheless, Mills has said that 'Hyena' is the song he "absolutely refuses to play" live.

Underneath The Bunker

'Underneath The Bunker' was a last-minute addition to *Lifes Rich Pageant*, designed, in part, to give the album a lighter feel. Like 'Hyena,' the song also dated back to the *Fables* sessions, but the original version was lost.

"When we did the very first version of 'Underneath The Bunker,' Bill had come back from some Greek restaurant and

said, 'I wrote this Greek thing.' And we did it really fast. It was more like a Greek oompah version."

On the version that turned up on *Lifes Rich Pageant*, Stipe's vocals are appropriately obscured to the point where it sounds as if he is singing over an intercom from an underground room.

The Flowers Of Guatemala

This delicate beauty of a song is Stipe's second—following 'Green Grow The Rushes' and preceding 'Welcome To The Occupation'—in his trilogy on the subject of oppression in Latin American countries. The song features a then-rare Buck guitar solo in the break and Mills on bass and keyboards. For added ambiance, Berry used glasses as a percussion effect.

'The Flowers Of Guatemala' has numerous references to amanita, which is a kind of poisonous fungi with white spores indigenous to Guatemala. Although the song's lyrics ultimately left some fans guessing what exactly the song was about, Buck said the band decided not to add additional verses to the song to give it a clearer picture. "I remember having a conversation with Michael about whether we needed to say in the third or fourth verse something like, 'Where have all the flowers gone, the flowers are on graves,' and we didn't think it was really necessary. I think people will figure that out—all they had to do was look at what was happening in Central America in 1986. At least they understood it was a kind of an elegiac song."

Apparently most fans got the message, or at least felt the vibe of the song, as Stipe remembered a powerful performance of the song at the Wang Center in Boston, Massachusetts. "We did two nights there and the second night we sang 'Flowers of Guatemala,'" he told David Fricke. "I looked into the audience and people were weeping openly. It was like, 'Oh, my God.' You could hear a pin drop. It was the most incredible feeling."

I Believe

"I bought a banjo and was trying to learn it," Buck explained on *Rockline*. "That was the first thing that I learned, and I thought, 'Gosh, this is going to be easy, I'm going to know all about the banjo in a week.' It turns out that is the only thing I've ever learned on the banjo."

On the day that the band cut the track, Stipe overheard Buck practicing his new skill. "He didn't know we were recording that," Stipe explained on *Rockline*. "I just told Don to turn on the tape and we recorded that, Peter playing it, and just stuck it on the record."

The fact that the banjo bit made the record was fine with Buck. "I kind of like those things. I like all of those albums that have little bits and pieces strung in between... I like it when you kind of don't know exactly what's what. Is this a song? Is this a piece? Is this the end of the other song?"

As the title would suggest, 'I Believe' is somewhat autobiographical as Stipe mentions he was "young and fever

Before Peter Buck added mandolin to his stringed arsenal, he had used a banjo. In its introduction, 'I Believe' showcases 13 seconds of Buck's banjo-picking skills—the result of a happy accident.

fell." "I had scarlet fever when I was two," he told Chris Heath. "I sang about it in 'I Believe.' I was hallucinating and I was being photographed in a Christmas sweater and it was very hot, and the photographer was coming in and out of focus like Jack Nicholson acid movies from the 1960s."

Aside from the childhood flashback, Stipe brings up the "what you want and what you need" concept that would also appear in *Document*'s 'Finest Worksong.' In concert, Stipe would preface 'I Believe' with an *a cappella* version of Mahalia Jackson's 'I Believe' or the traditional stomper 'Tired Of Singing Trouble,' which appeared as a bonus track on the 1993 expanded edition of *Lifes Rich Pageant*.

A note of minor interest: 'I Believe' was also the title of a song on the 1980 album *A Different Kind Of Tension* by the Buzzcocks, part of the roster of I.R.S. acts that led R.E.M. to decide that the label would be a suitable home.

What If We Give It Away?

This pleasant if somewhat indistinct song, along with 'Just A Touch,' was an R.E.M. oldie that was dusted off, revamped, and re-recorded for *Lifes Rich Pageant*. In its earliest incarnation the song was titled 'Get On Their Way.' In hindsight, Buck wishes that the band had given the song away, or at least left it off the album.

"There was other stuff that could have been on the record," he continued. "I don't know why that one got on. I think Don really liked it. I know some people at the record company said, 'That's cool.' But no one in the whole history of our band ever has mentioned that song. I think it is innocuous, but in a way it would be good if that wasn't on there. It was pretty much an old song, but I think Michael rewrote all the lyrics. It used to be in 3/4 time, if you can imagine that. At least half of it was in 3/4 time. You make records and a lot of times what you are doing seems to make sense, but you look back a couple of years and say, 'Why did we do that?'"

Just A Touch

This other previously unreleased R.E.M. oldie also changed considerably from when it was recorded years earlier. (The two-track take recorded during the *Reckoning* sessions was included later on the expanded edition of *Lifes Rich Pageant*.)

Stipe sings the *Lifes Rich Pageant* version like he has jumper cables attached to his ears, while the band plays with a ferocity that tops any

----

'Just A Touch' was inspired by the day Elvis Presley died—the day "when nobody laughed."

----

of their previous work. Buck thrashes his Robin guitar, Mills attacks the bass, organ, and piano, and Berry holds it all down with his steadfast drumming. The *Reckoning* session take, in comparison, sounds lethargic and thin.

"We wrote that in the summer of 1980," Buck explained. "When we were doing the *Fables* tour, we got tired of the songs we were doing, so we decided to pull one out of the past and we did it, and it actually sounded great."

In fact, 'Just A Touch' was the only song to be released by R.E.M. that was included on its first demo session, recorded on a four-track machine at Tyrone's in Athens, Georgia. The other songs—'Dangerous Times,' 'I Don't Want You Anymore,' 'A Different Girl,' 'Baby I,' 'Mystery to Me,' and 'Permanent Vacation'—are only available on bootlegs. 'Narrator,' another song from that period, turned up on a 1986 Hindu Love Gods single released by I.R.S., with Berry singing lead vocals.

Although it is not mentioned in the song's lyrics, 'Just A Touch' is about August 16, 1977, the day that Elvis Presley died. At the time, Stipe worked as a busboy in a restaurant in East St. Louis where an Elvis impersonator was the featured entertainment. Despite the fact that Elvis had died, the impersonator went on with the show as scheduled. As Stipe notes in the song's lyrics, it was a day when "nobody laughed." The death of Presley, who reappears in 'Man On The Moon' through Andy Kaufman's impersonation, has left Stipe's protagonist a bit confused. He's not sure if he should worship Popeye or Al Green, but he knows one thing for sure, he's so "Goddamn young."

Swan Swan H

With its folky story-telling tone and Civil War imagery, this song wouldn't have been out of place on *Fables Of The Reconstruction*. 'Swan Swan H' evolved out of an impromptu writing session spurred by a mishap.

"Our bus broke down in Wyoming," Buck recalled. "We had two shows at this college. They had two concert committees at this college and they each put on one show a year and they booked us and [middle-of-the road piano duo] Ferrante And Teicher on the same day, so Ferrante And

On the track 'Swan Swan H,' Stipe evoked ugly images of the Civil War.

Teicher had to play on our stage with all our equipment and we had to go on and play. It was really weird.

"That was in Laramie and we got to the bus and started driving and the bus broke down in Elk's Bow, Wyoming and we were there from like three in the morning to six in the evening. We wrote a bunch of stuff, but 'Swan Swan' was the only one that actually survived. We were probably sitting around drinking all day and the things we wrote later at night disappeared, but we started playing 'Swan Swan' almost immediately.

The song came together in about 20 minutes, Buck recalled. He described the song's style as "fake Irish" to Fred Mills and Todd Goss in *The Bob*. "That's where the Southern stuff comes from, you know, the child ballads, the Appalachian songs and stuff," he said.

Superman

This song is significant for two reasons. It marked the first time that a cover version appeared on an R.E.M. album, and Mike Mills's recording debut as a lead vocalist.

Along with 'Underneath The Bunker,' 'Superman' was a last-minute addition to the album, which may explain why the song titles were left off the back of the album cover. "It was going to be a B-side, but we thought that it sounded really good," Buck told Eric Flaum in *Goldmine*. "I had always hated it when I realized that the only songs I liked of some bands were the covers, but a song like that, practically no one in the world has ever heard it. We had the album all set without that and 'Underneath The Bunker' added on, and we thought, 'Why not? Nobody should complain if we add these on.'"

The song originally appeared on the self-titled album by a Texas quintet called the Clique that recorded for the White Whale label. R.E.M.'s version is fairly faithful to the original with the exception of the opening. The sound at the beginning of the track is from a Godzilla doll, not unlike the figurines that the band has historically placed on its amps during recording sessions and live performances. In Japanese, the doll says, "This is a special news report. Godzilla has been sighted in Tokyo Bay. The attack on it by the self-defense force has been useless. He is heading toward the city. Aaaaggghh!"

Before *Lifes Rich Pageant* was completed, Buck had promised that the cover version included on the album

In concert, Stipe has been known to introduce the song by saying, "This is a song about a war our country inflicted on itself a number of decades ago. It's about a period of our American history that was very, very ugly." The lyric "What noisy cats are we" was featured on one of the band's souvenir T-shirts, but Stipe said there was no deep meaning behind the lyrics. "People need to realize that there's potential for a great deal of nonsense involved," he told Jeff Giles in *Rolling Stone*. "That's a crucial element in pop songs."

A version of the song, recorded on January 29, 1986, at the Lucy Cobb Chapel in Athens, also turned up on the 1987 soundtrack to *Athens, Ga—Inside/Out*. The film documentary on the Athens music scene featured the band performing the song as well as a cover of the Everly Brothers' 'All I Have To Do Is Dream,' mistitled '(All I've Got To Do Is) Dream.'

"would be so obscure most people would not recognize it." Buck had discovered the song during his days at Wuxtry Records in Athens, where he worked as a manager. "They had piles of these shit singles and I'd go through and pick out things that looked interesting," he told Kordosh. "Picked out one—Professor Morrison's 'Lollipop Shop'—I figured it had to be a cock rock song, but it wasn't. So I got that and I got 'Superman,' and when I played that I couldn't believe it."

"I think it's a great song and I like the way we did it," he added. Buck added that he hoped the members of the Clique would be pleased, wherever they are. While 'Superman' was obscure, the Clique did have a few minor American hits, including the Tommy James-penned 'Sugar On Sunday,' which reached No. 22, and 'I'll Hold Out My Hand,' which reached No. 45. The band's self-titled album stalled at No. 177 in 1970.

When Clique producer/arranger and 'Superman' co-writer Gary Zekley got wind that R.E.M. had covered the song, he visited the band at a show in De Kalb, Illinois, and joined them on-stage while they performed the song, singing backing vocals and playing tambourine. Zekley, who was working as a computer-supply entrepreneur in Marina Del Rey, California, said he was proud R.E.M. recorded the song. "They did it the way I did it. They did the hell out of it. It speaks to me."

as those who have followed R.E.M. know, having a non-LP B-side is a band tradition that began with the release of the first I.R.S. single. Buck, a former record store clerk, was well aware of the concept of including previously unreleased material on the flipsides of singles. "I was really a fan of that," he said. "When our first record came out I said, 'I don't really care how it works, but we have to have a single and we have to have a non-album B-side,' so we had really good B-sides. It was before the B-side thing became a marketing idea."

Unfortunately for fans in the US, some of R.E.M.'s best B-sides were available only on costly British singles, imported from the UK.

In 1987, however, I.R.S. and the band provided a remedy to that situation by issuing *Dead Letter Office*, a collection that featured all of the band's B-sides to that point, neatly packaged, or as the back cover pointed out, "a virtuous compost—being a compendium of oddities collared, and B-sides compiled."

The compilation, broken up into a "post side" and "script side," even featured Buck's self-effacing liner notes and track-by-track comments. In addition, the CD featured the complete *Chronic Town* EP, available for the first time on compact disc. (This was also the first time that the EP had been available at all in the UK.)

Although the release of the compilation was a dream come true for R.E.M. fans, especially to newcomers who hadn't

DEAD LETTER OFFICE

bought all the singles on their initial release, Buck wasn't sure about releasing the album. "When we put out *Dead Letter Office*, I had some doubts about that... thinking maybe people would think we were trying to cash in, to sell records," he told John Platt in *Bucketful Of Brains*, "but I kinda like the idea of pulling together some of the bullshit and putting it out."

In the album's liner notes, Buck described the B-sides as "failed experiments, badly written songs, drunken jokes, and occasionally, a worthwhile song that doesn't fit the feel of an album."

R.E.M. risk the threat of being towed away, while contemplating the fate of dead letters.

He went on to add that *Dead Letter Office* features "at least one song from each category," but warned that the album shouldn't be taken too seriously. "Listening to this album should be like browsing through a junk shop," Buck wrote.

In junk shops, one can often find some discarded treasures. *Dead Letter Office* was no exception.

Crazy

This isn't the Patsy Cline country classic, but a cover of a song by R.E.M.'s early Athens scenesters, Pylon. In one of the first national magazine pieces on R.E.M., Stipe had attempted to distance the band from its Athens cohorts. "We're not a party band from Athens, we don't play New Wave music, and musically we don't have shit to do with the B-52's or any other band from this town," he told Buck's former college roommate Andrew Slater in *Rolling Stone*. "We just happen to live here."

Stipe, however, may have been exaggerating this point for dramatic effect, because they were undoubtedly all influenced by their Athens peers, even if it was more in spirit than in sound. "They liked their peers in Athens—Pylon, Love Tractor, and all that," Easter confirmed. "They really liked those bands and were friends with them too."

The influence of the band Pylon would reappear in such latter day R.E.M. songs as 'Drive,' and their innovative and energetic sound was something that R.E.M. had always envied. As Buck pointed out in the liner notes of *Dead Letter Office*, he had heard Pylon's version of 'Crazy,' which was issued as a single in 1981, on the radio on the day that *Chronic Town* was released. Buck "was suddenly depressed by how much better it was than our record," he confessed. As a tribute of sorts, R.E.M. had its way with the song during the *Fables Of The Reconstruction* sessions. It first appeared on the B-side of the UK single of 'Wendell Gee.' Pylon had to be proud.

With their cover of 'Crazy,' R.E.M. tipped their hat to early Athens scenesters Pylon.

There She Goes Again

R.E.M.'s initial recording of this Velvet Underground song was the flipside of the band's first I.R.S. single. The Lou Reed-led band is the one act that all of the members of R.E.M. cite as an influence. Buck was 14 when he bought his first Velvet Underground album—at a garage sale. "There are a lot of other bands that I appreciate," he said, "but they're the first band to really get me to sit up and be excited about rock'n'roll."

R.E.M.'s version was recorded live on to a two-track tape machine with Mitch Easter and Buck playing acoustic guitars and sharing a microphone. R.E.M.'s take is decidedly more folky and gentle than the Velvet Underground original, which appeared on the band's 1967 debut album *The Velvet Underground And Nico*.

The Velvet Underground, the one band that all the members of R.E.M. cite as an influence.

Burning Down

Although it never quite made it to a proper album, this song is an enjoyable R.E.M. oldie. "We recorded it for *Reckoning*," Buck recalled. "We wrote 'Burning Down' and we played it for around a month, and we didn't really like it, but we liked that one little riff. So we kept the riff and rewrote the song and called it 'Ages Of You' and then we threw them both away, but over the years we recorded them. In those days we worked really fast. We could record three songs a day and do all the overdubs."

In fact, both of these songs were set to appear on *Reckoning* at one time. "The original version of *Reckoning*, I think, had 12 songs on it, and those two would have been on there, but we didn't feel like they fit, so we just pulled them off and put them on B-sides," Buck explained. The songs were also pulled to make room for '(Don't Go Back To) Rockville.' 'Burning Down' was originally released as a bonus track on the 'Wendell Gee' double 7-inch single released in October 1985.

Voice Of Harold

'Voice Of Harold' is basically '7 Chinese Bros.' with different lyrics. It developed after no one was pleased with Stipe's original vocal takes on '7 Chinese Bros.' "I was trying to get him to relax without telling him what to do," Dixon told Tommy Tomlinson of the *Charlotte Observer*. "So I went upstairs into the attic to ostensibly change this damping plate up there. There was a stack of old gospel records up there, so I just grabbed one off the top of the stack. I tossed the record down and said, 'I hope this'll be inspiring.'"

Stipe scrawled "surfing for Jesus" on the record, which was *The Joy Of Knowing Jesus* by gospel group The Revelaires, and proceeded to sing the liner notes to the track of '7 Chinese Bros.' as a joke.

While the liner notes are for the most part nonsense in the context of the R.E.M. song, there is one phrase that sticks out—at one point Stipe sings, "They're real, they mean it!" That sentiment could also easily be applied to R.E.M. And it shines through even in this song, which is essentially an in-studio in-joke, but somehow managed to become much more.

As the liner notes to The Revelaires's album and *Dead Letter Office* say, "a must!"

Burning Hell

Those who say R.E.M. is some wimpy folk rock group have obviously never heard this heavy metal original. It's basically a joke, but it does show that the band can rock out if it wants. The *Fables Of The Reconstruction* outtake was written while the band was rehearsing at the Agoura Ballroom in Atlanta, in preparation for their 1984 fall tour.

"We had written a bunch of stuff," Buck recalled, "and we were playing it and Michael said, 'It has to have hell in the title.' He went downstairs and found some graffiti on the wall and one said, 'Hell is for children.' He was going to take that. I said, 'No, no, that's a Pat Benatar song, she played here and someone wrote that on the wall, don't fucking steal a song from her.' I thought 'Burning Hell' was a good title. I like AC/DC, but I couldn't help but feel a little

stupid when we did it. It was one of those things where we just cut it really fast and did it. I have no idea what it sounds like."

During a UK radio interview, Buck discussed the song at even greater length. "I was trying out this amp and it has a fuzzy button on it," he said. "You step on it and things start growing, so we just kind of wrote this heavy metal song so I could use my fuzzy button. I think I overdubbed, like, four guitar solos, and Michael just kind of screams and moans and yells."

"The words, if you can understand them, are hilarious," Mills added. Buck went so far as to nominate the lyric, "Women got skirts, men got pants, if you got the picnic, I've got the ants," as the band's best couplet ever.

White Tornado

This early track is the band's stab at a surf instrumental, and a fairly convincing one at that. "We wrote it the same day we wrote 'Radio Free Europe' and we wrote that song 'Romance' on the same day, too," Buck said. "We just used to knock them out like that. I think we recorded it like five times, never very seriously. Our very first demo session we did it and we did do it when we cut 'Radio Free Europe,' but we didn't put it on the single because we wanted a vocal on the B-side. It's the kind of thing that if we just had ten minutes at the end of the session we would throw it on and do some overdubs, just

to do it. It was a nice little B-side. When we did two sets, we used to open the second set with it."

Easter described the song as "a throwaway just for fun… Just about every band goes through their 'Let's play [a] surf song' phase. Neither Pete Buck nor Michael had a hell of a lot of experience. I think it was just one of those things you discover on the way to having your band and it did fit in with campiness of the time."

Although the song was recorded in 1981, it wasn't released until November 1986, as the B-side of 'Superman.'

Toys In The Attic

R.E.M. and veteran hard rockers Aerosmith aren't two groups that you would associate together. But they do have something in common. "We wrote a song about six years ago called 'Permanent Vacation,'" Buck said in 1987, shortly before Aerosmith released its album under that title. "But, I doubt very much that they stole it from us, because they never heard it."

Despite R.E.M.'s tendency to favor the more obscure acts, such as the Velvet Underground, for the source of its cover material, Buck admitted he was a fan of the band. "I like Aerosmith," he said. "I saw them in '73 and they were great. I have only good memories about those guys. I never saw them in the stadiums. I saw them open for the New York Dolls."

While Buck still owned a copy of Aerosmith's 1975 hard-rock classic *Toys In The Attic*, Stipe picked up a cassette of the album on the road. "We were at a truck stop where they had cassette cut-outs for 99 cents, and he bought like ten," Buck explained. "The things from the '70s that he liked were Blue Oyster Cult and that, so he said, 'Let's just do it,' so we sat down on the bus and figured it out."

Perhaps to throw fans for a loop, the band often included the song in its live set. "We invited Joe Perry to come down and play that song with us when we played it in Boston, but he said he was busy," Buck said.

R.E.M.'s version, recorded during the *Lifes Rich Pageant* sessions, is surprisingly hard-hitting for a band that Buck once described as "the least hard-edged of all the things I

listen to." R.E.M.'s take of 'Toys In The Attic' first appeared on the 'Fall On Me' 12-inch single.

Aerosmith's Steven Tyler: R.E.M. didn't seem likely to walk this way, but they did have 'Toys In The Attic.'

Windout

This rocking original was co-written with Athens scenester Jerry Ayers of Limbo District, who also collaborated with R.E.M. on 'Old Man Kensey.'

"I think he had this picture of us as this young jailbait boys rock band," Buck said. "So, he wrote 'Windout' and it was kind of like Kim Fowley and the Runaways. He gave us some salacious material that he thought we wouldn't understand, but we did like it. We recorded it, but it never felt like there was a record it fit on."

Although it didn't make it on to a proper R.E.M. album, the song was recorded and released more than once. 'Windout (with friends),' one of the bonus tracks on the expanded 1992 edition of *Reckoning*, featured Jefferson Holt and Bertis Downs on backing vocals. "While we were doing the sessions, Bertis and the other guy who is no longer with us recorded a version with them singing and screaming on it to kind of amuse us, and it was amusing," Buck said.

R.E.M. labelmates the Fleshtones also recorded the song on their 1985 live album *Speed Connection II*, with Buck guesting on guitar.

'Windout' made its first appearance on vinyl, however, on the 1984 soundtrack to *Bachelor Party*, which starred Tom Hanks and Tawny Kitaen. "I think it stinks," said Buck of the movie on a British radio interview. "I.R.S. did the soundtrack and in this business one hand washes the other. They let us get away with murder. They've never gave us any advice on how to make the records, the covers, the producers, anything. We just do what we want to and tell them this is it or nothing.

"When it came time to do the soundtrack, the Go-Go's didn't want to do it and I.R.S. said, 'Please, we want someone on this record who will sell it. Someone who people will go buy.' We gave them that track as kind of a favor, to show we had good faith in them, and all the things they've done for us weren't forgotten. I wish the movie was a bit better. I went to see it and it was embarrassing."

The guitarist went to see the movie at a theater in Athens where they sell beer. "The song was on for only five seconds, and I yelled out, 'Hey that's me. It's only for five seconds. I want my money back.'"

Ages Of You

When R.E.M. got tired of 'Burning Down,' they rewrote it as 'Ages Of You.' "It's just one four-note riff and we just keep trying to find a way to get it in a song," Buck explained. This track, like 'Burning Down,' was also recorded during the *Reckoning* sessions, but didn't make the album. "They were around and we kept thinking that we'd put them on an album," Buck told *the Bob*. "But as time goes by, the older

they get, the less likely it is that we'll put 'em out. So we decided that rather than not have them out at all, we'd put them on a single."

The song was originally issued as a bonus-track on the 'Wendell Gee' double 7-inch single, released in October 1985. A live version, recorded in early 1983, turned up on the 1986 I.R.S. benefit compilation album *Live! For Life*.

Pale Blue Eyes

One of Buck's favorite Lou Reed songs is 'Pale Blue Eyes.' Again, R.E.M.'s version is more folky than the Velvet Underground original, which appeared on the band's 1967 album *The Velvet Underground And Nico*.

"They loved the Velvet Underground," Mitch Easter recalled. "The thing about the Velvet Underground is that they are a perpetual influence on people."

For R.E.M.'s version, an outtake from the *Reckoning* sessions, Stipe altered the lyrics and Buck added an amateurish guitar solo. The R.E.M. version, clocking in at two-minutes and 49-seconds is nearly three minutes shorter than the Velvet Underground's original. Nonetheless, it still sounds classic. This was originally issued on the 12-inch of 'So. Central Rain.'

Rotary Ten

'Rotary Ten' is a *Lifes Rich Pageant*-era instrumental that is the first of several R.E.M. movie themes without a film. It wouldn't have sounded out of place in David Lynch's *Twin Peaks*, but it was recorded a decade too early.

"I write tons of instrumentals, because I sit around with the guitar and some things come up," Buck explained. "When we are doing demos, I'll say, 'I've got this instrumental. Let's just knock it out and see what happens.'"

Buck once described the inspiration for the song. "We wrote 'Rotary 10' for a movie that never occurred," he told David Howard in *Contrast*. "You can see someone walking down the street with a coat over his shoulder, with a seedy cymbal in the background going 'chu-ch-ch-chu.'"

'Rotary Ten,' which first turned up as the B-side of 'Superman,' would inspire the sequel, 'Rotary Eleven.' The existence of the first nine 'Rotaries' can't be confirmed.

Bandwagon

Shortly after this *Fables Of The Reconstruction* outtake was released as the B-side of 'Cant Get There From Here,' Buck told a British radio interviewer that he was concerned about how people so casually "wave a flag and [do] not tell you what it means." He said 'Bandwagon' was "vaguely about that" phenomenon.

It would seem that R.E.M.'s target was U2, whose frontman Bono paraded around the stage with a white flag during the band's 1993 tour in support of the album *War*.

More than a decade later, however, Buck has seemingly rethought the inspiration behind the song. "We are really good friends with U2," he said. "The song certainly isn't

about them. It just seemed to me that there is a big club everyone is to join if you listen to a certain kind of music, and we didn't want to belong. It's kind of a muddled little thing, that's why it's a B-side. It has the most chords of any song I've ever written, I think."

At one point 'Bandwagon' was called 'The Fruity Song.' It also went by another name. "When we first wrote it, we used

Some thought U2 was the target of 'Bandwagon,' but by 1993 any rift between the bands was history.

to call it 'The Clever Ditty,' because I think we consciously put in as many chord changes as we possibly could," Buck said in a British radio interview. "It sounds like the Lovin' Spoonful if they'd just discovered minor sevenths and ninths chords. It just goes on and on. It's actually got really good lyrics and good melody, it's just the chords are so funny, we can't play it without laughing, which is why it's such a bad take. Halfway through one of us really screws up the bridge."

Femme Fatale

This is the third Velvet Underground cover released by R.E.M. Although it was recorded live to two-track tape machine during the *Reckoning* sessions in the same hour that the band recorded 'Pale Blue Eyes,' it wasn't released until May 1986, when it appeared as a free flexi-disc with the magazine *The Bob*. It later came out on vinyl in March 1987 as the B-side of 'Superman.'

The fact that Stipe sang R.E.M.'s version in a soft, high voice made sense. The Velvet Underground original, included on that band's 1967 debut *The Velvet Underground And Nico*, was sung by German chanteuse Nico. It's worth noting that Big Star, another significant R.E.M. influence, also covered the track on the ill-fated *3rd: Sister Lovers* album. Big Star frontman Alex Chilton also chose to sing the song in a falsetto.

"You can kind of do your own Velvet Underground thing and it's great," Easter noted. "Velvet Underground songs really are endearing songs that are still cool."

Walter's Theme

This track is an instrumental, recorded live to two-track, which was inspired by one of the band's favorite dining establishments, Walter's Bar-B-Que. "We weren't ever actually doing a commercial for Walter, but we just started playing this little riff that sounded like Love Tractor and Michael just kind of improvised some stuff about Walter's," Buck explained. "In those days we could just stick that shit on B-sides."

When the song was initially released, as the B-side to 'So. Central Rain,' it was the untitled intro to the band's rendition of 'King Of The Road.'

Stipe, Berry, Buck, and Mills sample the food at Walter's Bar-B-Que in 1984.

King Of The Road

This cover version of the classic Roger Miller hit from 1965 was cut in the same take as 'Walter's Theme.' The recording, however, was not without its problems. "Every time we tried to cut it we were really drunk, so it always came out real raggedy," Buck told *The Bob*.

In his humorous liner notes to *Dead Letter Office*, Buck quipped that Miller should be able to sue the band for what it did to his song.

I n 1987, the world was going through some chaotic times, according to Buck, and that chaos was reflected in *Document*, R.E.M.'s fifth album. While the band's previous effort, *Lifes Rich Pageant*, had a lighthearted tongue-in-cheek title and some equally lightweight material, *Document*, as the title suggested, attempted to capture the world in a realistic light as the band saw it, and it wasn't a pretty sight. "*Document* was a very vitriolic statement," Stipe told Julie Panebianco.

Not only did the band choose to write about less obscure and more relevant topics, it also opted for more variety and a tougher sound. "I like this record better just as a record,

because I think the songs are better and I think it is more diverse," Buck explained. "I kind of like the hard-edge feel on this record, too. Of all the things I listen to, we are probably the least hard-edged... I think the harder edge is more of a reflection of the material and the fact that the record is about chaos."

The signs of chaos were evident right outside the famous Hollywood Boulevard hotel, where the band stayed while conducting interviews to promote *Document*. As Buck explained, "There were three winos that looked like they were dead," he said. "That really shows society is falling apart when people look like they are dead on the street and people walk right by them… You see winos on the street and look what our government is doing. It's chaotic all the way around."

On *Document*, the band also presented the material in a much more straightforward manner. "The songwriting is a little different, and lyrically more direct," Buck added. "There's a little bit less reliance on big choruses, which I've always tended to fall back on. If the song doesn't have a chorus that whacks you on the head, it's unsuccessful. But a lot of things I like don't have choruses. With a few songs on the record, we consciously didn't write choruses." Other songs, that sounded too much like R.E.M.'s previous work, were discarded altogether. As Stipe once explained, "We've tried to take our sound, explode the recognizable elements, pick up the pieces, and see how well they hammer together."

Hindu fighting—working with Warren Zevon, far left, influenced R.E.M. on *Document*.

There was also a change with the production. Don Gehman, who produced *Lifes Rich Pageant*, was unable to make the session for 'Romance,' a song the band recorded for the *Made In Heaven* soundtrack. In his place, he recommended Scott Litt, who had cut his teeth working with such acts as the dB's and Katrina and the Waves. The change in producers once again modified the band's sound.

"I don't see it as this huge move away," Buck said. "It's a refinement. Some of the things that people consider to be the keynote elements of our band aren't the way they used to be. The vocals are very clear and fairly direct. And the guitars are all kind of crunchy, not jangly. We are still songwriters and

are pretty loud here,' but we said it was OK, because we hadn't noticed it up to that point and it just seemed to fit the sound of the record," Mills said on *Rockline*.

Another change, at least in the credits, was the fact that the band chose to co-produce the album with Litt. "I think the reason that we got credit as co-producing is that we just got greedy in our old-age," Buck quipped. "I don't think we did anything any more on this record than we did on the last couple. We had the songs, arrangements, and ideas. We had a real specific idea of what we wanted to try to accomplish and we wanted to try to work with someone who was willing to work toward those goals."

However, Buck subsequently explained, along with the co-producing credit the band had to take on additional responsibilities. "I think we struggled with more of the mixes… that we co-produced. We had real specific ways that we wanted the songs to be. Before we would say, 'We're going to eat lunch and you guys start the mix.' This time we were there from the word go, so we were there when they were bringing up the kick drum and when they were starting a drum mix that takes two hours. That's the last thing I'm interested in, but I felt kind of obligated to be here for that. All in all, co-producing is rewarding and we will do it again. It just means we have to sacrifice a little bit of sleeping late."

R.E.M. also benefited from a number of outside projects, including a stint by Buck, Mills, and Berry moonlighting as Warren Zevon's backing band on his 1987 album *Sentimental Hygiene*. (The R.E.M. instrumentalists and Zevon subsequently recorded an album released in 1990 under the moniker Hindu Love Gods.) "With the outside projects you always tend to learn something," Buck explained. "Working with Warren taught the three of us—Mike, Bill, and I—a lot more

DOCUMENT

singers and musicians, rather than folk-rock singers and songwriters. It's just a different approach to what we do."

That different approach included moving Stipe's vocal track to a more prominent position in the mix. "We were mixing this record and about half way through the mix, we looked at each other and said, 'Wow, it seems like the vocals

about playing with discipline. Before it was like, we have to catch the energy, it didn't matter if we fucked up. Warren really is disciplined. He'll go in and do 30 takes of something to get the right one. Usually it was a real early take that we used, but we learned how to play consistently well and hope for the magic, rather than just play it two times and go

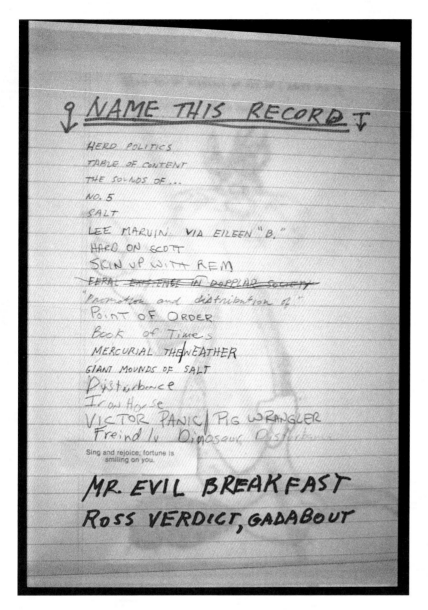

As evidence of R.E.M.'s rising stature, some of the Nashville industry insiders and session players were aware of the band. "They haven't had a rock band record there in a long time. So every once in a while some 40-year-old guy would come up and shake our hands and say, 'I think it's great you guys are recording in town. It's revitalizing the scene.' They're really trying to get rock bands from out of town and they haven't really had anyone since Dylan in the mid-'70s, one guy told me." (Actually, R.E.M. did play a small part in the attempt to revitalize the Nashville scene. On *Fervor*, the 1983 debut album by cow-punk band Jason And The Nashville Scorchers, Stipe co-wrote the song 'Both Sides Of The Line' and contributed backing vocals to, appropriately enough, 'Hot Nights In Georgia.')

At Sound Emporium, the band posted a note on the studio wall which read: "Name this record." Among the possibilities suggested were *Herd Politics*, *Table Of Content*, *The Sounds Of...*, *No. 5*, *Salt*, *Point Of Order*, and *Mr. Evil Breakfast*. Ultimately, *Document* seemed to make the most sense, but *No. 5* and *Table Of Content* found their way on to the album's artwork. "The reason why it

R.E.M. posted this note at Sound Emporium in an attempt to name the new album.

out and have a drink. That's why [*Document*] has more of a lively feel."

To record what would become *Document*, R.E.M. traveled to Sound Emporium studios in Nashville, where they spent approximately three-and-a-half weeks recording. "One of the things that is great when you are a band is to go to a different city to hang around for a while. We try to make it a point to go to a different town to record," Buck said. "We want it to be warm when we record, and it's got to a be a smallish town, so we don't get real caught up in going to see bands every night. Nashville was as good as any place. It was a nice studio. We had some friends there. Certainly the music scene isn't a big influence on us. You sit across the breakfast table from all these guys who are talking about publishing or a 10:15 a.m. session."

is called *Document* is that it is kind of a shortening of the word Documentary, which is a reference to film," Stipe said. "I think it is a very filmic album."

The title, it turned out, wasn't particularly original. In 1985 UK-based Aura Records issued an Alex Chilton compilation titled *Document*. Interestingly enough, R.E.M. is one of the acts cited in the album's liner notes for spearheading "the new American underground guitar boom" that had been influenced by Chilton. In addition, Buck and Mills had once listed Big Star's *Third*, and *#1 Record/Radio City* among their Desert Island Discs. "Sorry Alex," Buck said when asked about the album title. "I love Alex. We also used *Reckoning* and I had no idea that was the name of a Grateful Dead album. I've never even seen it."

Of course, R.E.M. album titles are usually not that simple.

Just as *Reckoning* bore the recommendation "File under water" on its spine, *Document* came with the warning "File under fire." "The whole album is about fire, about everything you think about fire as being cleansing, something that destroys everything in its path," Stipe told Bill Flanagan. "It's an element that's everywhere, the metaphorical and allegorical interpretations of fire are endless." As before, the band also chose to name each side of the album. On the back cover of the album, side one is listed as "Page," while side two is called "Leaf."

The band opted to mix the album in Los

Michael Stipe studies reference material for the track 'Exhuming McCarthy.'

Angeles, at Master Control. On May 24, 1987, after three and half weeks of mixing, Stipe and Buck previewed some material from *Document* in a rare acoustic set that was performed as part of a benefit concert for Texas Records at McCabe's Guitar Shop in Santa Monica, California. The set included 'The One I Love' (at that point known as 'This One Goes Out'), 'Finest Worksong,' 'Welcome To The Occupation,' and 'Disturbance At The Heron House.' "A friend of ours runs a record store and he was getting sued by somebody, or maybe he was suing someone," Buck explained. That friend, Michael Miester, was credited with taking the arty *Document* cover photo that captured Stipe engaging in one of his hobbies—photography.

In a strange coincidence, *Document* was released on the same day as *Bad*, Michael Jackson's hotly anticipated follow-up to his landmark *Thriller* album. "I went to a record store to see if they had our record in and every single person in line had the Michael Jackson album," Buck admitted. "That's OK, I don't think there is that much of a crossover. He will sell eight million to people who only are going to buy three records this year, and if they are going to buy three records, they're not going to buy ours. They're going to buy Michael Jackson, or Huey Lewis, or Bruce Springsteen, or whatever. So it's not like it's going to hurt us at all. He'll take up all the display space in front, but people will find our record. It's on the radio."

At the time, Buck was overjoyed at the initial success of

Document. "It shipped like 500,000, it's amazing," he said. (The success came in the wake of *Lifes Rich Pageant*, which had become the band's first gold album in America, with sales of more than 500,000.) Neither Buck, nor any one else would likely guess at the time that R.E.M. would become as common to the upper regions of the album chart as Jackson. In fact, *Document*, fueled by the fiery single 'The One I Love,' would reach the top 10 in America.

"I think this is the text-book example of true artist development," explained Jay Boberg, president of I.R.S. Records. "The band grows, and the audience grows under terms that the band, the audience, and the record company are all happy with." Boberg called R.E.M.'s long-awaited commercial breakthrough "a culmination of six years of work," and noted that the album was the label's biggest hit since the first two albums by the Go-Go's, which both reached the top 10 in America.

Even with the newly found mainstream success, R.E.M.'s faithful fans from its days as college radio staples continued to support the band. "It's almost like family," explained Bobby Haber, editor of the *College Media Journal*, which tracks college radio airplay. "You are real happy that your brother is a star, but no matter how successful he is, he is still family. I don't think that bond will ever be broken."

"In these days of harmless rock these guys are still a little dangerous," he added. "They have sort of an aura that makes them seem as underground now as they were in 1980."

Finest Worksong

With its insistent ringing guitars, hard-hitting drums, and impassioned vocals, 'Finest Worksong' is a call-to-arms album-opener not too dissimilar to *Lifes Rich Pageant*'s 'Begin The Begin.' "I never really thought about that, but it kind of has the same feel to it," Buck admitted. "It has the big

the reins," but warns that our needs and wants "have been confused."

Not only did 'Finest Worksong' serve as a potent first track, its title also inspired the name of the 40-city "Work Tour" in support of *Document*. "The tour is called the "Work Tour," because the album… has been tied in with the work ethic," Stipe explained. "If you think about the American work ethic, it can be a very ugly thing. A lot of the songs deal with a misunderstanding of work as kind of a replacement for feeling or a repression of feeling."

The work theme was also apparent in the artwork displayed on *Document*. The social realist paintings on the album's back cover and inner-sleeve dated back to the Great Depression in America, when President Franklin D. Roosevelt formed the Works Progress Administration, which put out-of-work citizens to work for the government. The work theme again surfaced in the Stipe-directed video clip for the song, which featured people swinging sledgehammers in perhaps a nod and a wink to the Peter Gabriel song that served as an inspiration.

At the time of the album's release, Buck spoke enthusiastically about possibly remixing the track. Eventually two remixes, one subtitled 'Other Mix,'

According to Peter Buck, 'Finest Worksong' was partially inspired by Peter Gabriel, right.

drum sound. I always thought it kind of sounded more like [Peter Gabriel's] 'Sledgehammer,' not exactly, but that's the way we think of things. Before we have titles for most of them, we say, 'That's the Gang Of Four song,' 'That's the one with all the chords in it,' or 'That's the stupid song.'"

There was little doubt where 'Finest Worksong' would turn up, Buck said. "The minute we wrote that, we pretty much knew that had to be side one, track one," he explained. In the opening spot, 'Finest Worksong' does indeed set the tone for the album, as Stipe effectively encourages the listener to rise up and take their "instinct by

the other the six-minute 'Lengthy Club Mix,' surfaced when 'Finest Worksong' was released as a single in March 1988. Both of the new mixes featured live horns, which were not included on the original album version. "When we first recorded it, we thought about using horns on it, but we couldn't quite get it together," Mills explained on *Rockline*. "We couldn't decide on what we wanted to do. When the opportunity came up to do a slightly different version, we said, 'Great,' so we got the Uptown Horns from New York and had a really nice couple of days putting horn sounds on it."

Welcome To The Occupation

'Welcome To The Occupation' was once described by Buck as "the most folky" and "probably the most traditional" R.E.M. song on *Document*—and for good reason. Stipe once said that the song was basically an extension of *Fables Of The Reconstruction*'s 'Green Grow The Rushes' and *Lifes Rich Pageant*'s 'Flowers Of Guatemala,' which to his dismay, few people understood. To make sure that 'Welcome To The Occupation' didn't suffer a similar fate, Stipe ghost-wrote the band biography that was distributed to journalists with *Document*. "It's no secret it's about our Central American policies," Buck explained. "But also 'Welcome To The Occupation' is about America, living in a country doing these things."

In Stipe's attempt to be brutal and to the point, he ended up offending Berry with the song's early lyrics. "There are some phrases and lines that we really cannot tolerate," Berry told Adrian Deevoy. "There was one in 'Welcome to the Occupation,' which originally said, 'Hang your freedom fighters' and I objected to that. I thought it was like kicking a dead horse. It seemed too politically blatant and I didn't like it. And, genius he is, he changed it to, 'Hang your freedom higher.'"

Stipe later clarified his intent. "I meant hang them like a picture, study them," he told Bill Flanagan. "I liked the dichotomy of the phrase, though I knew this was an incredibly brutal line." Berry agreed: "Believe me, I'm not pro-Contra, but that was just too blatant."

In keeping with the "File under fire" inscription on the album's spine, there are a few references to fire in the song's lyrics. The most telling is "fire on the hemisphere below," which can be taken a number of different ways. Introducing the song in concert, Stipe once said, "US out of euthanasia, US out of El Salvador. El Salvador prays for euthanasia."

Despite the ugly subject matter, 'Welcome To The Occupation' is a surprisingly sweet-sounding song that reaches a fitting climax with Stipe bellowing repeatedly, "Listen to me." This can also be taken as a plea aimed at those who had labeled his singing indecipherable. "I'm a little more comfortable with my voice these days but, to me, I've always been understandable," Stipe said. "It was just people not knowing how to listen. By now, perhaps they've figured out my phrasing. Not that it's incredibly hard, more like incredibly stupid."

Exhuming McCarthy

In the 1950s, Senator Joseph McCarthy, obsessed with the "Red Menace" of the Soviet Union, began to organize witch-hunt-like searches for Communist sympathizers in Hollywood. As a result, many people were black-listed, making it virtually impossible for them to find work. Approximately 30 years later, the members of R.E.M. felt that McCarthyism was making a comeback, as the Reagan administration had stirred up feelings of blind patriotism among the American public.

"I think that one of the things that Michael was writing about had to do with the whole flag-waving thing," Buck told Roy Wilkinson. "Though I like Bruce Springsteen, sometimes his songs get misrepresented as 'Ya Hoo America' stuff. That's so disgusting to see a crowd of people waving flags and think your country is great when in fact we're going through a dangerous period. People are hiding their heads in the sand and trying to make money."

The song includes references to the "me" decade phenomenon of executives taking seminars where they walk on coals to improve their "business acumen." Mills pipes in several times in the song singing "it's a sign of the times." That common phrase, slightly altered to *Sign O' The Times*, also served as the title of Prince's two-album set released in April 1987. Although R.E.M.'s use of the phrase could just be coincidental, Mills is a Prince fan and was known to wear a Prince T-shirt during some of R.E.M.'s live performances on the *Reckoning* tour. Years later the band mixed *Out Of Time* at Prince's Paisley Park studios.

During the sessions for *Document*, Stipe was photographed with two books on McCarthy—a biography and *A Conspiracy So Immense: The World According To Joe McCarthy*—in the control room of Sound Emporium.

Despite the heavy-weight subject matter, musically 'Exhuming McCarthy' is deceptively lightweight. The track

"Let us not assassinate this man further, Senator, you've done enough. Have you sense of decency, sir?"

"It's vampire-surf-guitar-funk," Buck said of the track. "I have no idea what that song came out of. When we first played it to him, Michael just started laughing and he laughed all the way through the song. He said, 'I'm going to have to work really hard to try to make this song not sound really, really jolly.' So the lyrics definitely aren't jolly. It's real sing-song in there. With the wrong melody, or a different and more upbeat lyric, that

Senator McCarthy's Communist witch-hunts were evoked in 'Exhuming McCarthy.'

begins with the sound of Stipe banging on the keys of his typewriter—his preferred device to compose lyrics on—before launching into one of the most catchy and strange R.E.M. songs to date. In the mid-section, the band opted to use an actual audio clip of McCarthy being attacked by US. Army lawyer Joseph N. Welch for his witch-hunt mentality:

song could have been so saccharin that you couldn't even get through that side of the record. You would have just thrown right up."

As per their decision to experiment with song structures, 'Exhuming McCarthy' "…doesn't really have a chorus." Buck added, "It has two verses in a row, which I kind of like."

Disturbance At The Heron House

The dire mood of *Document* continues with this song, which also doesn't have a chorus. Stipe's lyrics detail a meeting at a monument, which ultimately turns into a stampede as "the followers of chaos" are out of control. "It's a real Orwellian type of thing," Buck explained. But when asked if there was a real Heron House, even the guitarist was a bit baffled. "I'm not sure, I've never asked. That's the kind of thing I don't know about our lyrics. Is there a Heron House? I just kind of took it as a metaphor. There is a lot of bird imagery on this record, I don't know why, and also the animal thing is kind of like a George Orwell thing. But I guess I should ask, 'Is there a real Heron House?'"

With even his own band-mate somewhat puzzled by the song, Stipe, who once described the song as a "dire outlook on free will," was left frustrated. "I thought 'Disturbance At

The Heron House' was the most obvious song I'd ever written and not one person, not one, has worked out what in the hell it's about," he told Adrian Deevoy—without offering any further explanation.

Musically, Berry compared the song to a slowed-down version of 'Gardening At Night.' "It does have a little riff that is at the beginning of 'Gardening At Night' that is kind of similar," Buck confirmed. "I think when we wrote it I thought it was similar to Quicksilver Messenger Service or something, but it tended to get more and more rocked up as time went along."

A live acoustic version of 'Disturbance At The Heron House,' from the McCabe's Guitar Shop show, turned up on the 12-inch single of 'The One I Love,' and later on the 1993 expanded edition of *Document* released by I.R.S. outside of the US.

Strange

For the second consecutive album, R.E.M. opted to include a cover version. Rather than choose a song by an obscure American group, such as the Clique, the band chose to interpret the work of influential British post-punk unit Wire, a rarely cited influence on R.E.M. In fact, nearly a decade later, the influence of the band, and 'Strange' in particular, resurfaced on 'Departure' on *New Adventures In Hi-Fi*. "It's a great song," Buck said of 'Strange.' "Really, if we were going to write another song for this record, I couldn't have written one that better suited that side of the record." Indeed the lyric about something strange, something that's "not quite right" perfectly suited the chaos and disorder theme of *Document*.

Wire's slower, more robotic original, released on the 1977 album *Pink Flag*, was nearly four minutes of throbbing madness. R.E.M. opted for a

'Strange,' by British post-punks Wire, perfectly suited the mood of *Document*.

more compact two minutes and 32 seconds, making it sound more like a traditional garage rocker. Additionally, Stipe saw fit to customize the lyrics. He changed the original's "Joey's nervous and the lights are bright" to "Michael's nervous…" (In fact, the lead singer of Wire was Colin Newman, and none of the other members of the band were named Joey.)

It's The End Of The World As We Know It (And I Feel Fine)

After five fairly downbeat and intense songs, R.E.M. finally gives the listeners some comic relief, albeit black humor, with this rapid-fire Stipe rant that has become a fan favorite.

In the song, Stipe's frantic, speak-singing recalls 'Subterranean Homesick Blues' by Bob Dylan, whom Stipe once parodied in photographer Laura Levine's low-budget, rarely screened super-8 film *Just Like A Movie*. Buck acknowledged the Dylan influence, but also pointed out that

"Chuck Berry did it first with 'Too Much Money Business.' It probably has roots in the old medicine shows, where some guy would go through town singing about what's in bottles he's selling," he told Vic Garbarini in *Guitar World*.

Stipe has said part of 'It's The End Of The World…' came to him in a dream. "I was at Lester Bang's birthday party and I was the only person there whose initials weren't L.B.," Stipe told Timothy White on a Westwood One radio special. "So there was Lenny Bruce, Leonid Breshnev, Leonard Bernstein… So that ended up in the song along with a lot of stuff I'd seen when I was flipping TV channels. It's a collection of streams of consciousness."

The apocalyptic vision expressed in the song's lyrics is also a frequent theme of Stipe's dreams. "It's mostly

style in the studio. "When they showed me that song in the studio I just said, 'It's the end of the world as we know it and I feel fine,'" he told *Melody Maker*. "I wanted it to be the most bombastic vocal that I could possibly muster. Something that would completely overwhelm you and drip off your shoulders and stick in your hair like bubble gum."

Comedian Lenny Bruce, one of the L.B.s in Michael Stipe's inspiring dream.

When the band took to performing the song live, the members of R.E.M. were a bit taken aback by the reaction. Although the song shared the apocalyptic theme of Prince's '1999,' Stipe wasn't suggesting the party atmosphere that concert-goers responded with. "I think Bruce Springsteen experienced that with 'Born In the USA,' which was a scathing attack on America, but was taken to be a very patriotic kind of flag-waving song, especially live," he told White. "I think the same thing happened with '[It's the] End Of The World…,' but not to the same degree. But it does have a good beat."

Although 'It's The End Of The World…' was inspired, in part, by a dream, it is also based, in part, on reality. The members of R.E.M. did go to a birthday party attended by legendary rock critic Lester Bangs in 1980, just prior to his death, where they ate jelly beans and cheesecake.

"We'd never been to New York before and we decided to go and we went with this guy whose mom had a van and we slept in the van and got drunk every night," Buck told John Platt in *Bucketful Of Brains*. "We were with Pylon—this was before we were a band or maybe we'd just started rehearsing that week or something—and Pylon said, 'These guys haven't eaten in days, we're going to a party, maybe they could come and eat some food.' Lester was so drunk, he just stood in the hallway and everybody would walk by and he'd call them names… He called me a rotten cocksucker." Despite the verbal abuse, Buck still considers Bangs his favorite rock critic. "I think Michael wove that into his dream, and maybe his dream was woven into that," he added.

destroyed buildings and bombed out cars and shit," he told Chris Heath. "Everything is destroyed, but I have complete clarity of vision and complete focus from the absolute foreground to infinity, and I can see every crack in every wall and every leaf on every tree."

Fittingly, Stipe wrote the song in a stream-of-consciousness

Aside from its status as a frequent closer in R.E.M.'s live set, 'It's The End Of The World…' continued to live on long after *Document* had run its course. With the lyrics "that's great, it starts with an earthquake," the song has become an anthem of sorts to residents who live in regions that are prone to tremors. It was also included on a 1990 Greenpeace album distributed in the Soviet Union. "They chose the song, we didn't," Stipe told White. "I thought it was kind of an ironic choice, it does mention Breshnev in it. I had to submit the lyrics for the government to OK them, and they did."

The song, which Stipe has called "the ultimate ambivalent anthem," also turned up on a few soundtracks. First, the song was featured on the 1989 soundtrack to *Dream A Little Dream*, which starred Jason Robards, Corey Feldman, and Piper Laurie. In 1996, the song turned up in *Independence Day*, the box-office blockbuster about aliens attempting to take over the planet. "They told us it was this movie about aliens coming down with Will Smith and Jeff Goldblum," Buck told Gary Graff. "Our question was, 'Is this going to be a quality deal?' You have to trust the people around you, and they said it seemed OK. I hear that the song is in a scene that gets a lot of laughs. I'll have to see it sometime."

The One I Love

Opening with a couple of Berry drumbeats and a Neil Young-style guitar riff, it was quite clear that 'The One I Love' was R.E.M.'s most commercial and traditional rocker yet, and it would be the band's most successful. "It's so straightforward, it is kind of unlike us," Buck explained, "although it does have a lot of our trademark things on it." The guitarist once compared the song to an old Appalachian folk song, but instead of an acoustic guitar, he played a Les Paul through a Marshall amplifier "and cranked it up to 11," he told Garbarini.

Aside from the unforgettable instrumental attack, Stipe's vocals were clear and upfront and the song's love theme was easy for the masses to grab a hold of, as the song's chorus seemingly spelled it all out, "this one goes out to the one I love."

Despite a lyric that appeared to be clear and simple, Stipe once again had a trump card up his sleeve, and naturally many once again missed the point. Following the dedication in the song, Stipe dismisses the one he loves as "a simple prop" to occupy his time. "It's that old cynical voice roaring up again," he said.

Of the repeated unexplained yells of "fire," Stipe explained to Garbarini "We wrote it on the road. It was just a feeling of complete anger and frustration coming out. Originally, I wasn't saying any word at all. I was just… screaming. The whole chorus was me screaming, and then that developed into the word 'fire' when it became time to put it down on tape."

"It's a brutal kind of song, and I don't know if a lot of people pick up on that," he told Steve Pond in *Rolling Stone*.

"But I've always left myself pretty open to interpretation. It's probably better that they just think it's a love song at this point. I don't know. That song just came up from somewhere and I recognized it as being real violent and awful. But it wasn't directed at any one person. I would never, ever write a song like that. Even if there was one person in the world thinking this song is about me, I could never sing it or put it out."

The misinterpretation of the song, which was performed regularly on the 1986 *Pageantry* tour, stunned Stipe, who recalled performing the song in concert. "Last night I sang it and this couple two rows back looked at each other lovingly and held hands," he said to Bill Flanagan in *Musician*. "I thought, 'Oh my God.'"

Misunderstanding and all, the song went on to become R.E.M.'s highest-charting single to date, peaking at No. 9 on *Billboard*'s Hot 100 singles chart, which was quite a feat considering that the band's three previous chart singles failed to crack No. 75. The fact that 'The One I Love' garnered a record amount of airplay for the band on commercial radio was a bittersweet victory for R.E.M. "Especially at first, there was a lot of resistance to what we did and the way we sounded," Buck said. "I've had program directors say to my face, 'We'll never play your records on this station.' But they are now."

Still, at the time of the album's release, Buck wasn't feeling too confident about the song's fate. "I didn't even think that would be the first single," he said. "It will go higher than we ever had a single, but we never got above 90 anyway." Stipe predicted that the song would not "float" and would plummet down the charts.

"I.R.S. definitely wants it to happen," Buck added, "but we will sell a lot of records without it going top 40. Having it up there is one of those things that makes the difference between 700,000 or 300,000, but the sales themselves aren't that important. We wanted to make a good record. I'm real proud of this record and want people to buy it. If we have a hit, fine, if not, fine. The people at the record company take it a little more seriously probably than I do."

With 'The One I Love,' not only did R.E.M. have one of its strongest songs, but the band also delivered its most commercial video. Directed by New York artist Robert Longo, who designed the cover of the Replacements 1985 album *Tim*, the clip wasn't standard MTV fare, but still managed to break through. Stipe doesn't lip-sync, and the band is only shown performing briefly. Instead, various mysterious dramas seem to be unfolding in the artfully shot clip.

"It's the closest thing to a "real" MTV video the band has ever done," said Rick Krim, director of talent relations for MTV. "The band has turned on new fans without turning off its older fans, and that has a lot to do with the band's success."

Apart from the video, R.E.M. also opted to release an acoustic version from the Texas Records benefit at McCabe's Guitar Shop. The take, which was released on the B-side of the 'It's The End Of The World As We Know It (And I Feel Fine)' 12-inch, appeared under its original title, 'This One Goes Out,' and only featured Stipe. "We were going to do an acoustic set and I was upstairs getting nervous and stretching and Michael wanted to surprise me," Buck recalled on *Rockline*. "He had taught a friend of his how to play the song, which, by the way, he plays better than I do, which is kind of unfortunate. I said, 'Wait a minute, I recognize that song. What is this?' And it just so happens we got it on cassette, so we put it out as a B-side."

With the success, even the members of R.E.M. soured on the song a bit. "I don't really like the song that much frankly," Stipe said on *Rockline*. "I got really tired of it."

Fireplace

With its title alone, 'Fireplace' is another song on *Document* that lives up to the recommendation on the spine that we should "File under fire." The song, which is based on extracts from a speech by Mother Ann Lee, the leader of the American Shaker sect from the 18th century, features Steve Berlin from the band Los Lobos on saxophone—a friend from R.E.M."s early days.

"We opened for the Plugz in 1982 when Steve was with them," Buck recalled. "We liked them a lot and they liked us so we just kind of hung out and had some drinks together. We wanted a sax player for this song, so I said, 'I know Steve Berlin, let's call him up.'"

Berlin was up for the challenge. "He came in and he did a little solo and then I told him, 'Just think Coltrane on *Love Supreme*, and he did that kind of thing when he goes up a scale and down a scale in a real warbling way that was really neat. It really suited the song. It was supposed to be bizarre. When we did the original track, we were listening to it and we all said, "It doesn't swing at those places. It's a little too wooden. We need something to loosen it up there.' So I said, 'Let's get a sax, it's a real warm personal voice and get it to do something really fairly chaotic and it will add swing to that part,' and it did."

Initially, the band was considering the track for the "Page" side. "That could have fit on side one, except that it is a Chinese heavy metal jazz kind of a song."

Lightnin' Hopkins

Despite its title, this song isn't about the Legendary Texas bluesman who died in 1982. "I love Lightnin' Hopkins, but it's not about him," explained Buck. "I just happened to have a Lightnin' Hopkins album in my hand when we went into the rehearsal studio that day, and Michael wanted to call the song that, so I said OK fine. It's actually kind of like an evocation of the South. It's almost cinematic. There's that one cinematic verse. That pan-to-hand silhouette thing."

Buck later said that 'Lightnin' Hopkins' was nothing more than nonsense. "In fact, Michael told me to say that doesn't

The making of *Document*. From left, producer Scott Litt, Mills and Stipe work at the Sound Emporium.

mean anything," he told Roy Wilkinson. "It's utter bullshit. There's the weird verse about camera directions—it almost seems like it was a film of someone filming a black person. It's kind of vaguely about being black." Since the song was named for Hopkins, Buck attempted a tribute of sorts. "I put that shitty slide guitar on. I really am the world's worst slide guitar player," he added.

The song actually dated back to the *Pageantry* tour of 1986. "We started to write it, but we didn't finish it," Buck added. "We may have done it once on the tour, but Michael didn't have words to it."

With it's heavy percussion and almost disco-like drums, 'Lightnin' Hopkins' is reminiscent of Michael Stipe's work with the Golden Palominos, a band led by drummer Anton Fier, whose revolving line-up featured Stipe on its 1985 album *Visions Of Excess*. On the album, Stipe sang lead vocals on

three tracks—the original songs 'Boy (Go)' and 'Clustering Train,' as well as a cover of Moby Grape's 'Omaha.' "I'm sure that has rubbed off," Buck confirmed. "Also, that was a disco-ish type song. I'm not afraid to confront those things head on."

Still, rather than go with a drum machine, the band opted to use Berry's live drum track. "We were talking about the effect we wanted on the drum sound and the first time I heard it I went, 'Nah, no way.' But I don't see why we shouldn't be heir to this technology just like everyone else." Buck said. "I think we use it in a pretty organic manner. It's not like a rhythm machine or something, it's a real drum."

87

King Of Birds

'King Of Birds' is another song that had been kicking around in some state for a few years. "We had the track written for *Lifes Rich Pageant* and we actually recorded a version that was about eight minutes long with no vocals," Buck explained. "It was real psychedelic and it had this wandering guitar freak-out section in the middle. We listened to it and we went, 'Nah forget it.' But Michael happened to like that one. On the next record, he said, 'I've got stuff for that, I just don't like that four minute jazz in the middle.' So we kind of cut a folky version." To flesh the song out, Buck "immediately bought a dulcimer and overdubbed all the dulcimer stuff on it."

Although some have speculated that the song was inspired by William Wharton's book *Birdy*, Buck can't confirm this. "'Standing on the shoulders of giants' is the only part of the song I remember, which Enrico Fermi or one of those people said. Whoever it was that won the Nobel Prize was quoted as saying, 'If I look tall, it is only because I am standing on the shoulders of giants.' Then some really ungracious guy years later won the Nobel Prize, and said, 'If I look tall, it's only because I'm surrounded by midgets.'"

Although Buck's story is amusing, it was actually Sir Isaac Newton who said, "If I have seen further, it is by standing upon the shoulders of giants." The philosopher and mathematician would later be mentioned in 'Man On The Moon' on *Automatic For The People*. Newton is known for formulating the laws of gravity, which itself were part of the theme of 'Fall On Me' from *Lifes Rich Pageant*.

With its tribal drumming and psychedelic guitar riffs, 'King Of Birds' is one of the R.E.M. songs that most recalls the band's prime influence, the Velvet Underground, in its feel. "That's just kind of a meditation," Buck said. "It doesn't go to some big chorus, it repeats, but repeats in weird places. That's kind of a fairy tale march song."

Oddfellows Local 151

Like 'The One I Love,' R.E.M. frequently performed *Document*'s closing track, 'Oddfellows Local 151,' on the *Pageantry* tour. "Those two kind of bookend all the new songs in between," Stipe explained.

When the band performed it at that time, it was known as 'Firehouse,' a word that is repeated throughout the song. Unusually, in live performances of the moody, angular rocker, Stipe has even been known to strap on a guitar and thrash away.

'Oddfellows Local 151' provided a suitably atmospheric ending to the album. "There used to be Oddfellow's Lodges all over the town just like the Mooses or the Shriners," Buck explained to Roy Wilkinson. "The song actually is about these winos who used to live down the street from us. They used to live in cars—we called them the Motor Club. These old guys would sleep in the cars and drink all the time. I think there was a guy called Pee Wee as well. Michael knew them because he lived right next door to them. Every once in a while you'd give them five bucks or drop off a bottle."

On another occasion, however, Buck was feeling less lighthearted about the plight of the homeless, which he described as a sign of the chaos the band was attempting to document on the album. "I read this essay in the *New Yorker* or *Atlantic* or one of those things that my mom subscribes to," Buck recalled. "It said that we, as a society, have to be very caring for street people and for the winos and all of that, because the sign of a society falling apart is when it's OK for certain segments of society not to be comfortable. When a neighborhood starts having people pass out on the ground and people living in parks, it means that the society in that neighborhood is already on the downswing, not because these people are bad, but because it represents the fact that people aren't taking care of their duties to take care of them."

With its ominous sound and feel, 'Oddfellows...' served as an appropriate closer to *Document*, R.E.M.'s grimmest, yet most hard-hitting album to date.

The *Document*-makers outside of Sound Emporium in Nashville. From left, Berry, Stipe, Mills, and Buck.

When the word got out that R.E.M. had left I.R.S. Records, their home for six years, for the greener pastures of Warner Bros., some accused the band of selling out. True, R.E.M. had signed a five-record deal worth $10 million—a sweet pact no doubt, but not out of line with their peers. By this point, R.E.M. had become a platinum-selling act, with a top 10 single to their credit. *Rolling Stone* magazine had proclaimed the band "America's Best Rock & Roll Band."

Yet with any amount of success, there's usually some sort of a backlash. Some also made an issue of R.E.M.'s move from an independent label to a major, when in fact R.E.M. hadn't been associated with an indie since its days on Hib-Tone. Although I.R.S. was independently owned, the label's releases had always gone through the major label pipeline, first through A&M, and later MCA. However, R.E.M. were not pleased with I.R.S.'s distribution in Europe, a factor that made the move to a bigger label that much more critical, since the band had their eyes on the global marketplace.

difficult to sign the contract with Warner Bros. because it was basically making the agreement with myself, that I want to make five more albums with R.E.M.," Stipe told Jon Storey and Stuart Batsford in *Bucketful Of Brains*.

With Stipe making that commitment, and the new deal complete, R.E.M. was once again starting over. In fact, one of the implications of the album title, *Green*—which was tentatively titled *Think Tank Decoy*—is "a new beginning." Another interpretation of the title perhaps mocks the band's big-label signing. "There's all the different aspects of the word green, all the different ways it can be taken," Stipe told Steve Sutherland. "One of them is definitely the political party, but there's all the other meanings… one being money, one being a sense of innocence or naiveté." The title also strongly linked Stipe to the environmental movement. "With *Green*, I came to be known as the recycle singer," he told David Fricke. "People think of me as this mastermind or toxic-waste incinerator." In typical R.E.M. fashion, the album cover was not green, but a bright shade of orange.

R.E.M., however, did continue to play off the green theme

GREEN

"We never entered this for a career, but now that we're here we want to give as many people as we can the opportunity to hear us," Buck once said. Although Stipe once joked that the reason R.E.M. opted for Warner Bros. was "Bugs Bunny," there were actually some other important factors. Warner Bros. had long proven itself as a haven where artists were allowed to create, free from executive interference. Not only that, in chairman Mo Ostin and president Lenny Waronker, a former record producer, the label was home to two of the most widely admired men in the business. "Mo represents something in the music industry that brought R.E.M. to Warner Bros.," Stipe said.

Still, the deal was difficult to make for some members of the band, and not for the obvious reasons. "It was very

It's great to be *Green*. Stipe, Mills, Buck, and Berry make their major-label debut.

by inviting environmental organization Greenpeace to set up booths in the lobbies of the arenas where the band performed during the *Green* Tour. It was on the *Green* Tour that the band successfully made the leap from theaters to arenas, which seated three times as many fans. "It's one of those rock-and-a-hard-place situations," Mills said of the move to arenas. "If there are that many people who want to see you, you have to let them in, because if you don't, you'll have a real serious scalping situation, and we don't like that. We'll have better sound, better light, and a backdrop," Mills promised, "but musically we won't change it that much."

Another aspect of the album's title had some fans scratching their heads and searching for a hidden meaning. On the cover there is the number "4," which is only visible when held in the right light, superimposed over the letter "r" in the title. Stipe revealed that the number had no significant meaning, it was just an accident that stuck. "Instead of hitting the "r" in *Green*, I hit a "4," which is right above the "r" on the typewriter." In addition, 'Stand' is listed as track "R," rather than "4."

It was *Green*'s sense of innocence that reminded Stipe of the band's first album. "For me, *Green* had so many connections to *Murmur*," he told Anthony DeCurtis. "It was very much in the back of my head the whole time we were working on it. From the album cover to the topics of the songs and the way the songs were carried out, to me, there's a great connection there. Signing to another label was a new

start for us. It did offer us an opportunity to sit back, scratch our temples and wonder, 'Where are we and where do we want to go?'"

Initially, at least, Stipe wanted to go in the acoustic direction the band would explore to greater lengths on *Out Of Time* and *Automatic For The People*. "I wanted it to be completely acoustic, but those guys dragged me out of the river and shook me off and said, 'C'mon.' So, we had a pretty good combination of what all four of us really wanted,

which was a lot of loud and a lot of quiet," he told *Melody Maker*. Early plans to have an acoustic side and an electric side also didn't pan out, but *Green* did offer an array of different sounds. In fact, Stipe told the band not to write any more R.E.M.-like songs, a notion Buck agreed with. "We threw out all the mid-tempo, minor-key guitar-riff songs that we can write in our sleep," he told Edna Gundersen in *USA Today*. "You have to be real critical of your own stuff. You see so many of these big happy rock groups that put out a piece

Stipe gave a thumbs-up to Democratic presidential candidate Michael Dukakis.

of trash and think, 'Everything we do is great.'"

For the first time, R.E.M. spent four months writing new material in Athens, Georgia. They also opted to work with co-producer Scott Litt for the second time, venturing to Ardent Studios in Memphis, Tennessee—the same studio where '70s pop legends Big Star, among others, recorded. "Ardent has a real nice feel, the people there are really nice, and it's got a great place that serves great margaritas right next door," Buck told Timothy White. "And, if you figure if ZZ Top can make records there, and the Replacements, and Al Green, then it has to be a decent studio."

Instead of working at their usual breakneck speed, the band spent three months recording the album. "We found out that three months is too much time," Stipe later admitted. Still, the band undoubtedly used the time effectively. "In the past one or the other of us would present a tune pretty much worked through," Mills said. "This time we all just made noise until we found a song. There were hard stretches, but there always are when you try new things."

However, there was no pressure from Warner Bros. during the making of the album, as the label lived up to its promise to give the band complete artistic control. "The pressure we feel is what we put on ourselves to make the best record we can," Mills explained. "I am a lazy person in a lot of ways," he continued. "When you go in the studio you want to make a record that you can be proud of. People are going to second guess-you, but you want to be proud and say that you did the best job you can."

That additional time in the studio may have resulted in the album being overproduced. "Overall, I think the record is a little too slick for me, but that's cool, because we were just in an evolution trying to figure out where to go," Buck said in retrospect. Stipe had similar feelings. "I think Green, if anything, wasn't quite loose enough," he said on the syndicated radio program Rockline. "I think Green is a really great record, although it seemed a little stiff to me."

Nonetheless, the album did seem to appropriately capture the direction that R.E.M. was moving in. "It was just a natural culmination of our career up to that point," Buck said. "For five or six records we had gone from this weird art folk band, then we were a rock band. We were playing in front of 20,000 people and it's kind of a big rock record. It reminds me of one of those Led Zeppelin records."

Like some Led Zeppelin records, Green also has some quiet acoustic numbers. "The diverseness is what saves it," Buck added. "Some of the rockers are fun, then you get the other stuff like 'Hairshirt,' 'You Are The Everything,' that last untitled song, or 'I Remember California,' which are actually fairly weird songs. In a way I really like the record, but it has a little too much of a sheen on it for my tastes."

The move to more slick production made sense, as the band was toying with pop conventions while continuing to move into the mainstream on its own terms. It was also experimenting with the conventions of its very being, as the band frequently switched instruments during the sessions. "Bill is supposed to be the drummer, and he doesn't play drums on four songs on this record," Buck told Julie Panebianco.

Also, R.E.M. were reacting against the vitriolic nature of Document. As Mills noted, "The last one was a little more alarmist and a little more dire." Stipe took a different approach on Green. "I felt that Green was a very uplifting album," Stipe told Jack Barron in New Musical Express. "I set out to write an uplifting album… I just feel people need a very positive music, a very positive voice right now. There is ugliness, there is cynicism, there is sadness in Green. Clearly you can't have one side of an emotion without continuing the entire spectrum–well you can, but I think it's very false."

The need for optimism wasn't lost on liberal Americans. The Reagan era was coming to a close but Reagan's Vice President, George Bush, was primed to be his successor. R.E.M. championed Democratic candidate Michael Dukakis,

with Stipe personally taking out advertisements in college newspapers. (The advertisements read: "Stipe says don't get Bushwhacked. Get out and vote. Vote smart. Dukakis.") It was also more than a coincidence that Green was released on election day. "We were hoping to get ads in some of the magazines—something like, 'There are two things to do on Election Day' with a picture of our record and a picture of Dukakis, the Democratic candidate, but it wasn't possible." (The ads appeared, but without a picture of Dukakis.)

Dukakis, of course, lost the election, leaving America to four more years of Republican rule. For R.E.M., however, Green proved to be a winning move, showing that the band could jump to a larger label with its integrity intact and continue to change its musical direction while watching its audience grow. The mystery behind R.E.M.'s success was no secret. "It's pretty easy to pin down," Mills explained. "The chemistry is what makes a band… not four or five guys playing together."

Still, Buck wasn't as easily impressed by the band's latest effort. "Melody Maker called Green the best record of the last 10 years, and I laughed," he told Edna Gundersen in USA Today. "I'm sorry, it just isn't." Maybe so, but it was another

Green grows R.E.M. at the Hammersmith Odeon, London, 1989.

Pop Song 89

Like such album-openers as 'Finest Worksong' and 'Begin The Begin,' 'Pop Song 89' is immediately appealing, thanks to Buck's catchy guitar riffs, Mills's fuzz bass, and Berry's slamming percussion. But the track is considerably lighter than the anthem-like songs that opened R.E.M.'s previous two albums.

For openers, it is easy to understand Stipe's lyrics and they are not particularly deep or mysterious, but rather a twist of the Doors' 'Hello, I Love You' without the hormones. Instead of the beautiful girl that Jim Morrison is coming on to on the Venice Beach boardwalk, Stipe could be making small talk with anyone about the weather and the government. It's also evident that Stipe has moved beyond his dislike of using the word "I" in lyrics, as he uses it repeatedly in the song. In

fact, every song on *Green*, with the exception of 'Stand,' is written in the first person.

In keeping with an R.E.M. tradition, the vinyl version of *Green* has an 'Air' and 'Metal' side. With its lightweight feel and mundane subject matter, 'Pop Song 89' was a logical first cut for the 'Air' side. It can also be taken as a parody of a pop song, which Stipe confirmed.

"It's a complete piss-take," he told Steve Sutherland. "I guess it's the prototype of, and hopefully the end of, the pop song. It would be the last pop song ever. And, maybe in making the video, I'll be able to make the last video ever to the last pop song ever. I think the song really describes a lot of where music sits now."

Stipe also claimed that the song's lyrics weren't just

'Pop Song 89' was a twist on The Doors' 'Hello, I Love You.' In the song, instead of trying to come on to a girl as Jim Morrison, above, had, Stipe, right, could have been making small talk with anyone.

nonsense. "I'd say I'm interested in both conversational devices and the weather and they do tend to cross over," he told Jack Barron in *New Musical Express*. "I'd say that before this century people were much more concerned with the weather. We have a lot of luxuries nowadays that mean we don't have to think about it so much."

On the Work Tour in support of *Document*, Stipe got quite a kick performing an early version of the song. "We didn't have the words then. But when we were doing it on the road it was so exhilarating—you know, ripping my shirt off, doing this early '70s metal kind of bump-and-grind routine," he told *Sassy*. "It was incredibly funny and we would all just crack up throughout the whole song. It's so liberating to be really stupid like that."

That aspect of the song was also highlighted in the video, which was directed by Stipe. The black-and-white clip featured a bare-chested Stipe shaking and shimmering with three bare-breasted female dancers, all wearing matching diamond-patterned trousers. "It's meant to provoke," Stipe told *Rolling Stone* of the uncensored clip, which was included on the 1990 video compilation *Pop Screen*. "It's in response to videos which objectify and berate women, which equate nudity with vulgarity." However, in order for the clip to be broadcast in America, Stipe had to prepare a censored version. He opted to superimpose black bars over the chests of the three dancers—and his own. "We took the view that a nipple was a nipple, so we got rid of them all," he explained.

Get Up

The upbeat mood of *Green* continues as Stipe and company go from casual conversation to an animated take on sleep and dreams. For R.E.M., named after the dream state of sleep, a song like 'Get Up' is a natural. Lyrically, the song can be taken as a precursor to *Monster*'s 'I Don't Sleep, I Dream,' but there are also hints of the anti-suicide message of *Automatic For The People*'s 'Everybody Hurts' tucked into 'Get Up,' as Stipe offers such comforting observations as, "You've got all your life" and "I know life is hard." 'Get Up' also compliments 'Stand' as a call to arms, a message to "get up" and take action.

At one point, the song sends a contradictory message. Stipe sings that dreams "complicate" his life, while the backing vocals offer dreams "compliment" life. Once again, Stipe has said that the lyrics aren't necessarily autobiographical.

"When I sleep it's pretty much a clearing house for everything that's come on me," Stipe told *Melody Maker*. "I feel very bombarded by the 20th century in general and I accept it and revel in it, but I also often feel like a victim of it. I think that's a very common thing, whether people recognize it or not or choose to discuss it or not."

Musically, Stipe has described the song as "great bubble gum," but even with its insistently catchy riff, the band had a hard time deciding what to put into the song's mid-section. Appropriately enough, the answer came to Berry in his sleep. "I had a dream that we should put 12, not 13, not 11, but 12 music boxes, and get them all going at once," Berry told Julie

Panebianco. "We had all the people that work in the studio call up their grandmothers in Memphis to get all of them we could. We got 12 of them and there were some pretty strange looking ones, too. We just wound them all up and turned them on and that's what you hear. It worked out pretty well too, which is really funny because that was before I heard the lyrics to it. I didn't know what the song was about, which is really weird because the song is about sleeping of course."

The fact that the music boxes and other studio effects were used led the band to assume that 'Get Up' wouldn't work well in a live setting. "It's a very studio song," Stipe told White. "It's got me singing at least 15 different voices on it at the end. I thought, 'Man, this is really going to be hard to do live,' but it really works."

The single of 'Get Up' included a cover of Iggy Pop's 'Funtime,' recorded and mixed in four minutes, on the flipside. The 7-inch and the singles of 'Pop Song 89,' 'Stand,' and 'Orange Crush' were issued collectively in the limited edition box set titled *Singleactiongreen*, which contained a color poster of workers attempting to clean up an oil spill in Alaska. The words "R.E.M., GREEN, FALL," printed in orange type, and "GET UP," in red, were superimposed over the photo. The poster also featured the names, addresses, and phone numbers for the Environmental Defense Fund, The Alaska Center For The Environment, Greenpeace, and the Natural Resources Defense Council, as well as headshots of the band members. The packaging was made of recycled paper.

You Are The Everything

After the upbeat opening two numbers on *Green*, R.E.M. effectively turned it down a few notches with this bittersweet number. As its title suggests, 'You Are The Everything' is a love song, even if it doesn't include the word "love" in the lyrics. Exactly who is the object of Stipe's affection is something of a mystery, but judging by some of the lyrics, it seems to be an elderly woman, perhaps the grandmother he has been known to dedicate the track 'Try Not To Breathe' to in concert.

The lyrics hint that Stipe is singing about an elderly woman since her memory has been eviscerated, perhaps as a result of Alzheimer's disease.

In the song, Stipe also paints the picture of falling asleep in the back seat of a car on a long trip. This has a universal appeal and brings back memories of childhood. He also admits to his fear, "I'm very scared for this world/I'm very scared for me."

The song, one of the first written for the album, came together spontaneously in the studio. "Pete came in with the mandolin line for that," Berry told Panebianco. "I picked up a bass and Mike picked up accordion. Literally, we weren't even thinking. We just walked in the room and Pete said he had this thing. In about 20 minutes it was a song."

'You Are The Everything' also benefits from the usual atmosphere created by the sound of crickets chirping, a throwback to 'Wolves, Lower' from *Chronic Town*. "I don't know why we put crickets on there," Buck admitted, "but at that point there was a lot of stuff we just threw on, sounds as opposed to music."

· "There's no shortage of crickets in Bearsville," Berry added to Panebianco. "The studio is just surrounded by mountains and woods and it is… deafening at night. We also had a very cooperative cricket. He was underneath a board outside in the parking lot, and he was just going to town. He's featured on this record. We had a special microphone just for him. He was great. I think he knew we were recording. So we put two mikes out, one right out in the field and right on that sucker. So listen to him."

Stand

After the somber and reflective 'You Are The Everything,' R.E.M. effectively shoots *Green* into orbit with 'Stand.' It is their most straightforward, simple, irresistibly catchy or—depending on your mood and temperament—annoying song to date.

Beginning with Mills playing what sounds like a circus organ, and a goofy Buck guitar riff, the song has more bounce per ounce than any previous R.E.M. track. "It's a good dumb song, but it's not something I will want people to play at my funeral," Buck admitted.

It was Buck who initiated the song. "'Stand' originated when I came up with this dumb riff," he told Vic Garbarini in *Guitar World*. "Then Mike said, 'Man, I've got this kind of Beck, Bogart, and Appice bass line that can go in there!' It was getting silly, so we played it through and modulated up. Then we did it again, and we did one more modulation up, a full step, and we were just howling with laughter."

Stipe had a similar reaction. "The guys had the music in the works and I just thought, 'God, this is the stupidest music I've ever heard,'" he told Steve Sutherland. "It takes a great deal of courage to write a really stupid song, but these guys did it and I really admire 'em for it. I really think it was great and I wanted to match that with a lyric or a voice that was equally as stupid, but… really kind of great." Mills opined that 'Stand' was "a good pop song" but "pretty inconsequential, but you can't have a *magnum opus* every time you do something."

As if the song wasn't dumb enough, Buck took it a step further by employing one of the most annoying guitar effects known to man during a rare solo. "I thought as long as I had to have a real kind of rock guitar solo, I might as well use the wah wah pedal, which is one of the most over-used and despicable effects possible," he told Panebianco. "It's not a bad solo, but you should also get kind of a smile out of it."

Still, with all the lightheartedness contained in 'Stand,' the song does have a simple, but important, message: you should take a stand and become involved in the decision-making process "in the place that you live" and work.

**Comedian Chris Eliot, left, got a life with 'Stand,'
R.E.M.'s "stupidest music."**

"It is very stupid, but underneath all the stupidity there is something there," Stipe said on *Rockline*. "'Stand' is about as broad as we get, but at least it's not another dumb radio love song that leaves you cold," he added in *Musician*. "I'm glad that four-year-olds enjoy it."

In a possible attempt at capturing that innocence, R.E.M. opted to put a photo of a shirtless young Buck on the back of the single sleeve. The Warner Bros. logo is superimposed over his belt buckle. The caption simply reads: "P.B. at an earlier age." The single was issued in different territories with different B-sides. The American single contained the instrumental 'Memphis Train Blues,' while the European issue had the acoustic version of 'Pop Song 89' and a cover of the Ohio Players's funky 1974 hit 'Skin Tight.'

As if 'Stand' wasn't silly enough, the song became even more ridiculous on the television screen, first in the Katherine Dieckmann-directed video, and later as the theme song to *Get A Life*, a sitcom starring comedian Chris Elliot.

The video features dancers, cavorting on a compass pattern on the floor, intercut with everyday people involved in acts of environmentalism, such as recycling newspapers. The band isn't shown performing. Instead, they are featured in a Monkees-like sequence, jumping over a ditch in a field. As the clip winds down, the camera focuses on each member of the band. When it's Stipe's turn, he breaks up laughing, and ultimately hides his face from the camera. "Katherine Dieckmann had the idea that my public image was a little too staid," Stipe told David Fricke. "She wanted to crack that veneer, and she did."

That myth was further splintered by the use of 'Stand' as the theme to *Get A Life*. "They came to us before the show was ever real and they asked us if they could use 'Stand,'" Stipe explained on *Rockline*. 'Get a life,' the phrase, was so great, that we decided to give it to them without ever seeing the show."

World Leader Pretend

After the sugary sweet experience of 'Stand,' R.E.M. once again opted to dramatically change the mood of *Green* by contrasting the lightweight song with the album's most serious track. 'World Leader Pretend' is a song that Stipe has called "probably" his "greatest triumph" as a singer and lyricist. "It's probably the most political song I've ever written," he told Panebianco, "and perhaps at the same time the most personal."

To drive home the song's importance, Stipe chose, in a first for R.E.M., to include the complete lyrics of the song in the liner notes. Prior to *Green*, Stipe was not comfortable about showcasing a complete lyric on paper. "The idea of separating the words from the rest of the song seemed really alien to me," Stipe told Timothy White. "Since the words were written for the song, just to kind of hack them off and put them on paper didn't seem right."

Stipe's feelings changed, however, after he penned 'World Leader Pretend.' "It's a very cathartic song and it has been since its inception," he added. "The reason we chose to print the lyrics is that that song, more than any other for me, really stated what *Green* was about. If there has to be a synopsis of the title, why we chose to call the record *Green*, that song does it. Kind of the statement and intent of that song is that you pretty much have to straighten out what is going on with yourself before doing anything else outside of yourself."

In concert, Stipe further drove home the importance of taking responsibility for one's self by prefacing 'World Leader Pretend' with a few lines from Gang Of Four's 'We Live As We Dream, Alone,' performed *a cappella* as he banged a stick on the back of a metal chair *a la* Gang Of Four's Jon King.

In the song's lyrics, Stipe put new emphasis on the word "I." "In some of the early stuff I refused to use the word 'I' or the word 'you,'" he told Panebianco. "I did that for a long time. I did that until I broke it, then I broke the rule and I started doing it a lot. I think the first 14 lines of 'World Leader Pretend' start with the word 'I.'" Actually, a number of lines do begin with the word "I," but not the first 14. The first begins with "I," but the song's second line begins with "it," followed by 10 lines that begin with the word "I" or "I've."

The emphasis on the first person pronoun naturally led some to assume that Stipe was singing about himself, a notion that would recur with the popularity of 'Losing My Religion.' "A lot of people who wrote about 'World Leader Pretend' seemed to think that it was about myself and stardom and it had nothing to do with that at all," Stipe told Andy Gill. "When I say, 'I am World Leader Pretend,' I was, of course, using myself as everyman."

Instrumentally, the band opted to capture the ominous mood of the track with a few twists. Mills played the mellotron at Ardent Studios that was used on the legendary Big Star's third album, while Jane Scarpantoni's cello and Bucky Baxter's pedal steel guitar were employed for added effect. In all, 'World Leader Pretend' is a chilling song, showcasing the fact that R.E.M. could be as effective by being direct as it had been in the past by being enigmatic.

The Wrong Child

The mood of *Green* continues to slide down a notch with this heartfelt song about a child that doesn't quite fit in. "I think the original title was 'Beethoven,' because Michael thought it sounded like some Beethoven or Bach thing," Buck recalled. "The lyrics were inspired by this Irish writer, Christopher Nolan, who is handicapped. He wrote this book called *Under The Eye Of The Clock*, which I read several years ago. He can't really communicate and he's physically challenged in a very severe way. It's a very moving book. Michael read it and didn't steal from the book so much, but he captured some of the feeling lyrically. Musically, I haven't played it since we did it. It kind of flows from here to there." Stipe has also stated that the song was inspired by an incident from his own youth.

"I know a lot of people who are physically handicapped," Stipe told Gavin Martin in *New Musical Express*. "It just sort of came to me. I think everybody at one point or another feels like they are left out of something and I think that song pretty much captures that through the eyes of a child. When you're in that emotional state, I think you probably see yourself as a child, or as an adult who is being treated like a child."

Musically, 'The Wrong Child' has an eerie feel thanks to a combination of minor key mandolin and mellotron riffs, and Stipe's discomforting, at times slightly off-key, vocals. On a few occasions, however, the song is lifted from the depths by a stunningly beautiful piano line. At other times the song is reminiscent of one of Led Zeppelin's acoustic numbers.

The musical approach effectively captures the song's subject matter, which is sort of a sad flipside to the joys of childhood expressed on *Murmur*. It's hard not to be moved when Stipe sings of a child who asks children to play with him and tell him what it is like to go outside, because he's never been. Later, the protagonist is laughed at by other children. When the track winds down with Stipe crooning, "I'm not supposed to be like this, but it's OK... OK?," the effect is riveting.

Christopher Nolan, whose *Under The Eye Of The Clock* inspired 'The Wrong Child.'

Orange Crush

With its urgent feel, Buck's ringing guitar, and Berry's drill-sergeant drumming, 'Orange Crush' made sense not only as *Green*'s first single, but also as the opening cut on the 'Metal' side of the album.

The fact that the song borrowed its name from a popular citrus flavored soft drink may have lead some to assume that it would be another sugary sweet number in the vein of 'Stand,' but make no mistake, 'Orange Crush' is not lightweight pop. The name 'Orange Crush' is in fact a reference to the defoliant Agent Orange, which was used by the American forces in Vietnam. Years after the war, US military personnel exposed to the agent developed cancer and fathered children who were born with defects.

"It's a strong song and I intended it that way," Stipe told Keith Cameron. "It's certainly no direct reference to any personal experience of mine, but that I grew up in the Vietnam

era. I remember eating French fries and getting ketchup all over my lap, because I was watching *The Flintstones*, and they would interrupt the show to show these soldiers running through North Vietnam. Pretty wild, for an eight-year-old."

Although Stipe had no military experience himself, he was a military brat, who frequently moved as his father took on different jobs in the armed services. His father, in the helicopter corps, also served in Vietnam. 'Orange Crush' wasn't the first R.E.M. song to deal with Vietnam. An early number called 'Body Count,' which was in the band's early live sets but never commercially released, also dealt with the war.

'Orange Crush' wasn't only about Agent Orange, or Vietnam for that matter. "It's largely about that and it's also just about the bad side of being drafted and having to go fight a war that you certainly may not believe in and don't want to fight for," Mills told White. "Once you turn 18, it's something you live with. I missed the draft fortunately, but it's something that is very scary if you are very close to that age."

As Buck added, "You don't just learn a career in the army." To drive the point home, Stipe frequently prefaced the song in concert by singing the US Army's own advertising jingle, "Be all that you can be, in the Army," before launching into the aural assault that is 'Orange Crush.'

Despite its heavy topic, 'Orange Crush,' at least musically, emerged accidentally. "Sometimes it's literally noise from chaos," Mills told Ira Robbins. "We all play without listening to the other and then all of a sudden some of it starts to go together. One of the first to come out of the chaos method was 'Orange Crush.' That was literally everybody just making noise in the studio and then it just fell into place."

Aside from a stunning, discordant guitar solo, which is the closest Buck has ever come to sounding like U2's The Edge, R.E.M. employed a number of sound effects on the song. Stipe is heard imitating a drill sergeant with a nonsensical monologue as a group of troopers fall in line over the sounds of a helicopter. "There are a couple of big cracky things we found on a sound effects record," Buck explained. "In our own modest way, we were getting away from worrying about overdubbing music, and getting sounds on things. So there are a lot of little things on those tracks that aren't really musical and aren't even musical instruments."

For a further examination of those sounds, fans were treated to an instrumental version of 'Orange Crush,' as a bonus track on the 'Find The River' CD single.

A stark black-and-white video for the song, directed by Matt Mahurin, alternates footage of a soldier preparing for battle and a young boy at play. At one point, a glass bottle is shown that looks suspiciously like an Orange Crush bottle, although the soda-pop's logo is not visible in the clip.

The band also opted to use a military image for the sleeve of the single. The cover art was a US Navy photo of a makeshift Christmas tree assembled by military personnel. The three-inch CD single also included cover versions of Suicide's 'Ghost Rider,' and Syd Barrett's 'Dark Globe.'

With 'Orange Crush,' R.E.M. evoked the horrific images of the Vietnam War.

Turn You Inside-Out

With 'Turn You Inside-Out,' the "Metal" side of *Green* continues to live up to its title, as this often overlooked throbbing psychedelic workout is one of R.E.M.'s most effective rockers. It also inspired the title of this book. The song features Buck, Berry, Mills, and guest percussionist Keith LeBlanc locked into a potent funk groove, which gives Stipe ample room to lay down an impassioned vocal.

Initially, the band had a hard time making the song work in its live performances. "I thought '…Inside-Out' would work really great as a live song and it falls on its face, it just doesn't work," Stipe told White. However, 'Turn You Inside-Out' improved with age and occasionally surfaced in the band's set on the 1995 *Monster* tour.

"That was the very last song written for the record," Buck explained. "We had four days off and rehearsed and we came up with that and this other song. It came together really quickly, the lyrics and everything, so it's one we never got tired of, because it was so spontaneous. You can tell it was written in about 10 minutes because the arrangement is really weird. It goes from here to there and back. That was the one that, when we toured, the two extra guys had a really hard time with, because things don't just repeat in any rational order. Parts have eight repetitions here, 10 the next time, six the next time, which is kind of cool. It was this type

of thing that Michael said, 'I got lyrics that are this long here, so go that long,' which I kind of like. I like the fact that people might not notice that the songs are really kind of lop-sided and strange."

In concert, and in the James Herbert-directed in-studio performance clip, Stipe used a megaphone. In the studio, the band also experimented with his vocal. "Part of it was done live," Buck said. "We might have put the vocal through an amp and we might have used one of those silver bullet mikes used for harmonicas."

As is often the case, Stipe's lyrics were once again misinterpreted. "You can't take that as a literal one-on-one situation," Stipe warned Adrian Deevoy. He later further explained his intent. "I understand that all high school boys think it's about fucking," Stipe told Anthony DeCurtis. "That's the report I've gotten back from the grade schools. It's about manipulation and power. To me, it had a great deal to do, emotionally, with what a performer can do to an audience. A performer could be myself, it could be Martin Luther King, it could be Jackson, it could be Reagan, it could be Hitler—any preacher that is able to manipulate a large group of people."

Hairshirt

After the back-to-back explosions of 'Orange Crush' and 'Turn You Inside-Out,' R.E.M. once again opted to throw things for a loop, with a slow, plaintive number named for a garment worn for self-punishment by penitents.

It's also another song on *Green* that features the mandolin, an instrument R.E.M. would use to a greater extent on *Out Of Time*. "I had just bought that mandolin and I wrote a couple of songs with it, but I was out of the studio one day and Bill picked up the mandolin and came up with the chord changes for that and the melody," Buck explained. "So that's Bill playing mandolin, I'm playing bass, and Mike is playing organ. We just cut the track totally live. Michael hadn't come up with lyrics yet. He just said, come up with five

or six minutes. It can be long. We said, 'It was just two parts over and over.' We just did it until we felt like we were going to die."

Stipe had a different memory of what went down in the studio. "They were really pushing their boundaries on a lot of these songs," he told Panebianco. "It was very interesting to watch them write 'Hairshirt,' where Bill had a tambourine on his foot and was playing bass, and Peter was playing this mandolin, and Mike was playing an accordion, and it worked. It was a very strange thing."

I Remember California

With its ominous guitar, tribal drumming, and haunting title and vocal, 'I Remember California' is one of the more menacing songs on *Green*. "It's a love song," Buck revealed to Panebianco. "It's not a love song about California, nor is it about a stretch of earth. It's about someone and times in California."

In the song's lyrics, Stipe takes snipes at some of the California stereotypes, singing of "motor boys and girls with tans, nearly was and almost rans." He also effectively captures the contrast of California's natural beauty and the fact that it is the home to much of America's defense industry by dropping lyrics about "redwood trees," "Trident submarines," and "lemons, limes, and tangerines."

"I have this theory that people in California, they're the people that just went and went until they couldn't go any further unless they fell into the ocean," he told Keith Cameron. "So they set up a lemming camp and it became Los Angeles. And there you are."

Nonetheless, California has played an important part in the R.E.M. story. For one, Peter Buck was born in Oakland on December 6, 1956, and spent his early years in San Francisco. In 1996, Mills rented a home in the Hollywood hills, becoming a part-time California resident. The headquarters of I.R.S. and Warner Bros. are both located in California, and R.E.M. has often recorded and mixed its albums in Los Angeles and shot a good number of its videos in the city and surrounding areas.

Stipe, captured on the *Green* tour, used a megaphone to perform 'Turn You Inside-Out.'

(Untitled)

Long before it became an alternative rock cliché to put a hidden bonus track on CDs, R.E.M. released a song with no title. There is no mention of track 11 on the back of the *Green* CD jewel case. The actual disc does, however, list track 11 and a running time for the song, but there is no title.

Exactly why the song doesn't have a title is a mystery, and an unfortunate one at that. The song is a rarely noted gem that might have gained more notice had it been properly titled. Lyrically, the song soars with a chorus about a person asking a friend or family member to look after his loved ones.

Again, R.E.M. opted to switch instruments on the track, with Buck settling down behind the drum kit. "Bill can't play that drum beat to 'Untitled' the way Peter can," Mills told White. "I don't think anyone could, but it really adds to the charm of the song. We tried to see if Bill could play it on the record, but it just did not sound the same."

"He's a great drummer," Berry said of Buck. "He's got good rhythm, he's right on it. We discovered a whole new songwriting technique. Just grab an instrument you don't know how to play and fool around until it sounds right."

Buck wasn't as impressed with his talents behind the drum kit. "I don't think you can listen to the record without realizing which song it is that I play drums on," he told Panebianco. "Bill is still amazed. He says it's impossible to play that drum part, not that it's hard, it's just so bad, no one can play it perfectly all the way through. It's one thing to make a mistake like that, but it's another thing to do it on purpose."

Mike Mills not only remembered California, he became a part-time resident of the state in 1996.

following the success of *Green*, R.E.M. celebrated its new worldwide fame with its biggest tour to date. It was a tour that found the band playing more than 130 dates in 17 countries, while attempting to adapt its music to suit large arenas built for hockey games rather than concerts. During the trek, documented on the 1990 home video release *Tourfilm*, the band mocked traditional arena-rock behavior by using projected greetings on the stage backdrop, rather than lowering itself by dishing out the usual arena-rock clichés.

By all accounts the *Green* world tour, which ended in late November 1989, was a success. However, the grueling experience left the band's members searching for a new direction once they returned to the rehearsal studio.

plans to support the new album with a tour, and that fact influenced the sound of the record. "If your surroundings change, your songwriting does change a bit, which is why we stopped touring in '89," Buck explained. "The idea was that we don't want to be influenced by these basketball arenas and the 20,000 people that are screaming."

To other bands, such a move away from their trademark sound could be disastrous, but confident Buck said that going with less electric guitar would not affect the quality of R.E.M.'s music. "We're songwriters and we can make a great record with no guitar whatsoever," he told Chris Willman of the *Los Angeles Times*. "[*Out Of Time*] was kind of a chance to get away from being a guitar band. It was written mostly with mandolin and bass and keyboards, no guitar at all."

OUT OF TIME

"First we were going to take four or five months off," recalled Buck. "But we were younger then and didn't have families or anything, so we took Christmas off and we started rehearsing again on January 2." When the band's members plugged into their amplifiers, they realized that the months on the road had taken their toll. "We set up the amps and I heard the buzz and I was like, 'This just zaps my energy completely,'" Buck said. "Michael didn't even come in for about a month or a month and a half, so we just kind of sat in a circle with acoustic guitars and mandolin. Bill would play bass or guitar, I would play mandolin or bass, and Mike would play organ, bass, or guitar."

When Stipe turned up to begin putting words to the band's new material, he realized that a dramatic change had taken place. Buck was no longer playing guitar. "He just wanted to explore more acoustic things and get away from loud guitar," Stipe said. In addition, the band had retained the services of former dB's member Peter Holsapple, who served as the band's "fifth member" on the *Green* tour.

Despite the success of the *Green* tour, the band had no

Time-keepers. The grueling *Green* world tour took its toll on the members of R.E.M.

Although electric guitar was virtually absent from the songwriting sessions, it's a mistake to assume that R.E.M. didn't plug in for *Out Of Time*. Buck does play electric guitar on several songs on the album, but the album does have a more acoustic feel in general. The move to more acoustic-based sounds was certainly a risky one. In 1988, Tracy Chapman's self-titled debut album turned out to be a surprise hit in the US, but aside from that, acoustic-based music was largely absent from the upper regions of the charts, which were dominated by hard rock and upbeat danceable pop. With the support from their new label, Warner Bros., R.E.M. had seemingly only begun to tap into their potential as a rock act with global appeal. Certainly the success of *Green* and the single 'Stand' showed the band's potential. Other bands might have attempted to continue to follow the same path, but R.E.M. saw it differently.

After months of rehearsals in Athens, the recording of what would become known as *Out Of Time* began in the summer of 1990 with producer Scott Litt, who had worked with the band on *Green* and *Document*, once again manning the mixing board. The band also returned to Bearsville Studios in Woodstock, New York, to cut the basic tracks, followed by an overdubbing session at John Keane's studio in Athens, Georgia. There was also a string session, featuring members of the Atlanta Symphony, at Soundscape Studios in Atlanta, Georgia.

Mark Bingham and Jay Weigel, whom Stipe had befriended while working on a cover version of 'Little April Showers' for the 1988 album *Stay Awake: Various Interpretations of Music from Vintage Disney Films*, were tapped to handle the string and horn arrangements on *Out Of Time*. The move would help make the album R.E.M.'s most baroque-flavored effort to date.

Holsapple, Bingham, Weigel, and the Atlanta Symphony weren't the only outsiders to lend support. Other guests included legendary New Orleans-based saxophonist Kidd Jordan, Boogie Down Productions's rapper KRS-One, B-52's vocalist and fellow Athenian Kate Pierson, and Henry Mancini's flugelhorn player, Cecil Welch.

In recording the album, R.E.M. and Litt opted to use both new and old technology. "We did kind of a peculiar thing… which was to record most of the… instruments analog and record the vocals digital," Stipe said on the syndicated radio show *Rockline*. "Everyone does it the exact opposite, Michael Jackson included. My voice has got so much warmth to it that recording digitally doesn't take away from that. It gives me a degree of precision that I always wanted to hear."

R.E.M. also opted to go with a spontaneous approach, playing most of the tracks live in the studio. "I put down the vocals without doing a whole lot of overdubbing," Stipe added.

Another change with *Out Of Time* was the subject matter of Stipe's songs. While the band's music had become increasingly political from *Lifes Rich Pageant* through *Document* and on to *Green*, on *Out Of Time* the singer opted to focus on personal politics and love. Stipe even said that the album contained his first love songs, a claim that those familiar with the band's earlier material could clearly dispute.

Despite the clear change in musical direction, or possibly because of it, the members of R.E.M. had a difficult time coming up with a title that would effectively sum up the album. "*Catbutt* was a favorite of mine, but thematically, it didn't seem to work somehow," Stipe quipped. Other possibilities included *Imitation Crabmeat*, *Last Train to Disneyworld*, *Love And Squalor*, and *The Return Of Mumbles*. The latter title was deemed appropriate because Stipe's vocals are once again buried in the mix on some of the album's tracks.

"I wanted to call the album *Fiction*," Stipe told Andy Gill of *Q*. "I thought that was descriptive—all the songs are basically fictions, they're all love songs. At one point we thought about calling it *Love Songs*, but that seemed a little too stupid. *Out Of Time* seemed appropriate. Thematically, the record deals with time and memory and love and *Out Of Memory* or *Out Of Love* didn't make much sense… One of the reasons for writing an album of love songs is that I didn't want to be known as just the political activist-singer of a band."

Another possibility, *Time And Love*, suggested by a Paisley Park staffer while the band was mixing the album at Prince's Minneapolis studio, was thrown out because it sounded too much like a title by the Fifth Dimension. Ultimately, with a deadline approaching, the band opted for the appropriate *Out Of Time*. "We were literally out of time. We had to pick a title." Stipe said. Later, the singer seemed surprised to learn that it was also the title of an early Rolling Stones hit. "Well, fuck 'em," he told *Spin*. "But, I think there are a lot of meanings to it. Now that we're aging dinosaurs."

In a continuing R.E.M. tradition, the vinyl version of *Out Of Time* had a Time side and a Memory side, rather than the traditional side one and side two. "That's what the record is about," Buck explained on *Rockline*, "but now there aren't records any more. In the old days there used to be albums— side one and side two. We kind of preferred to let the listener pick which side that they want to listen to first."

The band also picked a release date that was of some historic significance. Just as *Green* was released on election day in the US, *Out Of Time* was released on March 12, which would have been the 69th birthday of Jack Kerouac, the acclaimed beat writer whose landmark book *On The Road* fueled the band's early desires to travel across the US.

Although the band kept to its promise not to return to the arena circuit in support of *Out Of Time*, it did play some intimate acoustic showcases for TV and radio shows in Europe and in the US. These settings perfectly fitted the band's new baroque-style material, proving to any potential naysayers that R.E.M. had effectively retooled itself from an arena rock act into an intriguing acoustic ensemble. Above all, what mattered most was the music. On *Out Of Time*, R.E.M. showed the world that it had more up its collective sleeve than jangly electric guitar riffs and an incomprehensible vocalist.

Radio Song

R.E.M. fans were likely thrown for a loop on their first listen to *Out Of Time*. The first sounds on the album weren't a Berry drum beat, a Buck guitar riff, Mills's melodic bass, or even Stipe's vocals, but the voice of rapper KRS-One from the hip-hop act Boogie Down Productions. "Hey, I can't find nothing on the radio," complains KRS-One. "Yo, turn to that station." Only after the spoken-word gambit did some familiar R.E.M. trademarks kick in—Buck's guitar begins to ring, Mills bass pulses, and Stipe sings. After Stipe's opening lines

KRS-One wasn't the only guest who appeared on 'Radio Song.' With Mills splitting time between organ and bass, Peter Holsapple played some additional bass parts, Kidd Jordan added tenor, alto, and baritone saxophone, and producer Scott Litt added some echo and tape loop effects. The track also offered the first taste of the Mark Bingham-conducted strings.

However, it's not only the guest performances that make the song. Mills's Hammond organ sounds as if it would be at

---

KRS-One also complained about the radio, making him a suitable guest on 'Radio Song.'

---

about the world "collapsing around our ears," R.E.M. takes another unexpected turn. The band launches into a full-funk workout for the first time since *Fables Of The Reconstruction*'s 'Cant Get There From Here.'

This time, however, the funk riffs sound more relaxed and convincing, rather than a tongue-in-cheek exercise. Part of the added legitimacy can be attributed to the participation of KRS-One. "It was really exciting to involve him in the project," Stipe said. "He was really into it and it made sense since we both had similar gripes about radio and formatting. He fit right into the track."

Stipe was a fan of Boogie Down Productions, thanks to KRS-One's social consciousness and his employment of "edutainment"—using entertainment as a means to educate listeners. Stipe counted Boogie Down Productions' 1989 album *Ghetto Music: The Blueprint of Hip Hop* as one of his favorites of the '80s.

The singer wasn't the only one impressed by KRS-One. In fact, Berry said that the rapper, whose real name is Kris Parker, helped salvage the track. "The song kind of sucked before we put that stuff on it," Berry told Harold DeMuir in *Pulse*. "It had a good groove to it, but it just wasn't that exciting. When Michael sent the tape to KRS-One, all he asked him to do were the 'hey hey hey' parts, but he came up with this whole rap that was exactly what the song was about."

home on a Stax record, Buck opts for funky-but-chic guitar riffs, and Berry's syncopated drumming swings. On top of it all, Stipe's vocals are alternately heartfelt and humorous.

Lyrically, the song attacks radio programmers for playing the same old insipid love songs over and over again. While Stipe wasn't going as far as the Smiths did with their 1986 song 'Panic'—which included the chorus, "Hang the DJ,"—'Radio Song' did boldly lash out at some of the powerbrokers that could affect R.E.M.'s career. Berry made it quite clear that R.E.M. weren't biting the hand that feeds. Commercial radio had left the band hungry early in its career. "We don't owe radio shit," Berry told DeMuir. "Commercial radio never wanted to play us, but we sneaked through the cracks just because we had a fan base that couldn't be denied."

While Berry apparently took the subject quite seriously, Stipe later said that 'Radio Song' should be taken with a grain of salt. "I hope people have enough of a sense of humor to realize I'm kind of taking a piss at everyone, myself included," Stipe told *Vox*. "Hopefully, they'll get the humorous intent of the song, with my opening plea about the world collapsing and KRS-One's closing rap, which I find really funny and thought-provoking."

In addition to the album version, an alternate take of 'Radio Song,' subtitled 'Tower Of Luv Bug Mix,' with additional production and a remix by Salt-N-Pepa collaborator Herby "Luvbug" Azor, was issued on a promotional CD single. On the disc, Azor is listed incorrectly as "Hurby" Luv Bug. The rare track includes the radio parody spoken-word intro, "More music, less talk—WREM," female backing vocals, and additional jazzy keyboards and percussion. The promotional single also contains the band's cover of The Troggs' 'Love Is All Around,' recorded live for the *Rockline* radio program, and a live version of 'Belong,' recorded during the *Green* tour in November 1989 in Greensboro, North Carolina.

'Radio Song' wasn't the only collaboration between Stipe and KRS-One. The rapper appeared in a public service announcement for Stipe's C-Hundred film production company, and the two, along with Harmony, performed the title track on the consciousness-raising 1991 Elektra Records album *Civilization Vs. Technology*.

A rarely shown video for the song, directed by Peter Care, shows Stipe working in a darkroom and features KRS-One.

Losing My Religion

With its universal appeal, unique instrumentation, and intriguing but perplexing title and lyrics, 'Losing My Religion' is a landmark R.E.M. song. While the band had previously scored top 10 hits in America with 'The One I Love' and 'Stand,' it was 'Losing My Religion' that elevated the band into the ranks of superstardom in the US and around the world.

"I guess I really hit the nail on the head with that one," said Stipe. "My idea with that song was to try to rewrite 'Every Breath You Take' [by The Police] and I did a pretty good job of it, I guess."

Initially, the song took shape when Buck fiddled with a mandolin while drinking beer and watching a baseball game. Buck took that material, recorded on a boom box, to rehearsals. "Bill played bass on it at first," he recalled, "then we switched it, so it was drums and bass and mandolin and made it more of a band arrangement, but originally all the songs were written sort of sitting in a circle." In the studio, Buck played mandolin and electric octave guitar, Mills played bass and keyboard strings, Berry played drums and percussion, and Holsapple played acoustic guitar. When the band previewed the song weeks before the release of *Out Of Time* at the 40 Watt Club in Athens, Georgia, it was in an all-acoustic set without Berry.

When R.E.M. initially met with Warner Bros. to discuss the marketing of *Out Of Time*, executives at the label didn't think 'Losing My Religion' was the appropriate choice for a first single. "At the time, the record company said, 'There are other songs that are hits on this record,'" Buck recalled. However, the band's choice prevailed. "We just put that out like we do a lot of times. We put something that is unlikely as the first single, but it just kept on going." The fact that the song became a hit was a total surprise. "Nobody expected that at all," Mills said. "It was nice to see that a mandolin-based quasi-folk song could be a big hit in America."

The song's appeal wasn't limited to America, as Mills explained to the crowd at a benefit show for Greenpeace at the 40 Watt Club in Athens, Georgia on November 19, 1992: "Peter and I just spent a week in Israel... We were there talking to our friend Karen Rose... she DJs sometimes and she wondered why nobody ever requested 'Losing My Religion.' She asked a friend of hers and the guy said, 'They do, but they don't know the English. They don't know what to call it, so they just call it, 'Oh Life.'"

That phrase also struck a nerve in Spain, where Berry said he first realized that R.E.M. had become global superstars while performing 'Losing My Religion' on the *Monster* tour. "You know when it hit me?" Berry asked David Browne in

Entertainment Weekly, "When we played 'Losing My Religion' in Madrid and they sang the first two words, 'Oh life,' it was louder than the band. That was the difference between what we were in 1989 and being like Bruce Springsteen or Michael Jackson. But it was a great feeling, I must say."

As if the song wasn't enough, 'Losing My Religion' also benefited from a unforgettable video that was directed by a visual artist from India known simply as Tarsem. "We had the idea of strictly a performance video, which would just have had the band in it," Stipe said on the syndicated radio program *Rockline*, "And he,

Berry, Mills, Stipe, and Tarsem celebrate at the 1991 MTV Music Video Awards.

being a fan of the band, expected the band not even to appear in the video, much less lip-sync. He had come up with this whole idea, and what we did when we talked was kind of grafting the two together and that's what you see now."

The clip begins with Stipe seated with his back to the camera in a strangely lit room. Mills stands around impatiently while Buck and Berry run in and out of the picture frame, apparently chasing something. Once the music kicks in, a pitcher of milk falls off a window sill and smashes to the ground, coinciding with the song's first drum beat. In other moments, Stipe, wearing the wings of an angel, lip-syncs and dances like the midget from *Twin Peaks*. Buck, shown briefly on the mandolin, is the only instrumentalist in the band shown performing in the clip, which is also intercut with several actors in quasi-religious and historical settings, including the depiction of a shirtless, heavily made-up young man tied to a tree, and a blonde-haired African-American man with angelic wings. MTV lauded the clip with several awards, including the best video of the year, best group video, breakthrough video, best direction in a video (to director Tarsem), best art direction (Jose Montana), and best editing (Robert Duffy).

Some read a little too much into the striking images featured in the video. In Ireland the clip was banned from broadcast television. "They mistook some of the mythological stuff that Tarsem put into the video to be religious and thought it might be offensive to some of the Irish Catholics," Stipe explained.

Despite its title, the song had little to do with religion. "The term 'losing my religion' is slang in the South," Stipe explained on *Rockline*. "It means 'fed up' or 'at the end of your rope.' A lot of people have misinterpreted it to be about religion and it's really not. It's really a secular song, a classic obsession song if you will."

Initially, even Buck was suspicious of the origins of the phrase "losing my religion." "When Michael came up with the lyrics to 'Losing My Religion,' I thought that was a pretty evocative title," he told Vic Garbarini in *Musician*. "But when he claimed it was an old Southern saying that meant 'at wit's end' or 'at the end of your rope,' I had my doubts. I figured it was just another Michael-ism." A few months later, on a visit to New Orleans, a friend introduced Buck to his 80-year-old grandmother as a member of the band that recorded 'Losing My Religion.' The elderly woman told Buck that she hadn't heard someone say that phrase since she was a little girl back in the '20s and '30s. "Score one for Michael," Buck added. "I was sure he made that up himself."

Another misconception was that the song was in some way autobiographical, an easy conclusion to draw based on the lyric "that's me in the spotlight." Even Buck once said he thought Stipe was singing about himself in the song. Stipe, however, maintained that this was not the case. "I wish I'd said, 'That's me in the kitchen' or 'That's me in the driveway,'" he told Jeff Giles in *Rolling Stone*. In *Vox*, Stipe went on to add that 'Losing Me Religion' "could be a comment on the state of the world very easily. In fact, it's an extension of 'World Leader Pretend.'"

Whatever the case, 'Losing My Religion,' which reached No. 4 in the US, and No. 19 in the UK—R.E.M.'s highest charting single—helped drive *Out Of Time* to the top of the charts in the US and UK, giving R.E.M. their first No. 1 album. It also garnered the band several honors from the readers of *Rolling Stone* magazine, including best single, best band, Stipe as best singer, and R.E.M. as artists of the year. Not

everyone was pleased, however. *Out Of Time* also placed sixth as worst album of the year. (A live version of 'Losing My Religion,' recorded on November 19, 1992, in Athens, Georgia at the benefit for Greenpeace, was included as a bonus track on the 'Bang And Blame' CD single.)

An angelic Michael Stipe in Tarsem's video clip for 'Losing My Religion.'

Low

"This is a difficult song to listen to," Stipe once said as an introduction to 'Low,' one of the darker songs on *Out Of Time*. With Mills's funeral parlor-organ serving as the musical backbone of the song, 'Low' effectively brings *Out Of Time* down a few notches after the one-two punch of 'Radio Song' and 'Losing My Religion.'

Frequent R.E.M. video collaborator James Herbert, right.

'Low,' which was often played on the *Green* tour, was one of the first songs completed for *Out Of Time*. The band also submitted the song to Wim Wenders for use in *Until The End Of The World*. The director, however, opted instead to use 'Fretless' on the film's soundtrack.

As in 'Radio Song,' Stipe used 'Low' to reflect on love songs with the lyric, "I skipped the part about love/It seemed so silly/It seemed so shallow." "That's how I always felt about love songs," he told Roy Wilkinson in *Sounds*. "It was like, get them out of my face, they're all horrible and manipulative." Nonetheless, for the first time since 'The One I Love,' Stipe chose to use the word "love" in his lyrics.

Apart from Mills on organ, the instrumentation is rounded out by Berry on congas, Buck on guitar, Holsapple on bass, another Bingham string arrangement, and Kidd Jordan on bass clarinet.

For Buck, 'Low' brings to mind a unique mental picture. "Whenever I hear it," he told Jim Macnie in *Musician*, "I picture people 10,000 years ago sitting around a campfire wearing fur rugs with the fog drifting by."

In the song, Stipe uses the lyrics to dramatic effect. "I would think that not being dramatic in pop music would mean being mediocre," he said. "To me a prime example of that is 'Low.' The whole song hinges on the word 'time.' In the last verse I say, 'You and me, we know about time.'"

Despite the somber mood of the song, Stipe has said it shouldn't be taken too seriously. "It's just a song," he told Gavin Martin in *New Musical Express*. It was written on the road and I put together a bunch of nonsense phrases. I never meditated on it… I wrote it in a feverish moment somewhere touring around the world. I think it's funny actually."

A rarely broadcast video for the track, directed by longtime R.E.M. video collaborator James Herbert, features an interesting mix of live action and art, as several paintings from the Georgia Museum of Art at the University of Georgia in Athens seemingly come to life.

Near Wild Heaven

R.E.M. didn't let the mood of 'Low' weigh down *Out Of Time*. Just when things seemed to be headed south, this Beach Boys-influenced pop delight brings *Out Of Time* up with its optimism. The song's title brings to mind an early critical rave. "When I get to heaven, the angels will be playing not harps, but Rickenbackers. And they will be playing songs by R.E.M.," read a review of *Reckoning* in *New Musical Express*. The joyous 'Near Wild Heaven' is one of two tracks on the album that featured Mills as the primary vocalist.

"It's kind of a duet with Michael," Buck explained, "and

they wrote the lyrics together." Buck admitted that the Beach Boys were definitely an influence on the song. "When we were making that record Capitol came out with those Beach

Boy two-fer records where they have about five outtakes," he said. "I was listening to the one with *Smiley Smile* and *Wild Honey* a whole lot." Buck isn't the only member of R.E.M. who is into the Beach Boys. "Mike and Bill used to drive around Maçon 20 years ago and sing along with Beach Boys

on the radio. ['Near Wild Heaven'] certainly had a Beach Boys influence. I think I even suggested the high harmony part, just so it would sound kind of like the Beach Boys."

'Near Wild Heaven' was influenced by the sound of the Beach Boys.

While Buck—who has called the Beach Boys landmark *Pet Sounds* one of his all-time favorite albums—was happy to tip his hat to the group, Stipe has claimed that he is not a fan of the quintessential California band. "I heard *Pet Sounds* twice. I stand on record as having listened to it tied to an armchair with Mike and Peter raving at me about how great a record it was," he told Jon Storey and Stuart Batsford in *Bucketful Of Brains*. "I don't get it... I think Brian Wilson was amazing... but I never dug the Beach Boys." This statement is quite puzzling, since Wilson was the driving force behind *Pet Sounds* and the rest of the Beach Boys' best music.

Although it wasn't included on the album, the band employed a similar vocal approach with Stipe backing Mills on the band's cover of the Troggs' 'Love Is All Around,' which R.E.M. frequently included in its acoustic showcase gigs in support of *Out Of Time*.

Endgame

While 'Near Wild Heaven' recalled the Beach Boys with its vocal harmonies, 'Endgame' sounds like some lost Brian Wilson orchestral piece. Although the song doesn't have any words, Stipe does add some "la la las" to the majestic instrumental track.

As the title suggests, the song was conceived as an end theme for a film that doesn't exist. "I wanted to call it 'End Title Sequence,'" Buck told Tina Clark in *Music Express*. "It sounds like the movie's over and that's the last theme."

The evocative piece of music gave Stipe a different mental image. "The picture that I see when I hear 'Endgame' is Peter sitting on this giant stage surrounded by classically trained musicians, him playing this little guitar and them rolling around him like the ocean," he told Harold DeMuir in

Pulse!. "It was my first real attempt at composing with live musicians. What I basically did was take my vocal line and replace it, except for the first verse, with instruments that I thought sounded like my voice."

Although Stipe is the band's lyricist, he didn't want to attempt to write words for 'Endgame.' "I often feel that imposing a lyric on to a song limits it and moves it away from something that can be taken in any possible way," he told Clarke. "Music of course has its shifts and ebb and flow, but the minute you put a word on it, you've truncated it, tunnel-visioned it into something and run it through someone's mind, the singer's—and you've lost something. That's why 'Endgame' has no lyrics. I just couldn't stand the idea of writing words to go into that song."

An added thrill for Stipe was working with Cecil Welch, a flugelhorn player known for his work with Henry Mancini. "I grew up listening to Mancini," Stipe told Clarke. "I adore his work. I was so thrilled to be able to work with him. The part that I wrote and he performed sound so much like a Mancini part that it's astonishing."

While many rock acts have attempted to work with strings in the past, only a handful have been successful. "I think I read George Melly talking about that one," Buck told Roy Wilkinson of *Sounds*. "He was saying that most rock musicians don't have any idea what classical music is—they're all upwardly mobile lower middle class kids who think that if they rip off a little bit of the '1812 Overture' everyone'll think they're really high brow. I kind of prefer the small string quartet kind of thing. 'Endgame' certainly doesn't have the bombast that my generation tends to associate with classical music."

'Endgame,' however, isn't just a piece based on the work of hired hands. Berry played percussion on the track, Buck played acoustic and electric guitars, Mills contributed bass and backing vocals, and Stipe sang, played bass melodica, composed the horn arrangement, and handled the string arrangement with Bingham. Jordan is also featured on the track, playing bass clarinet and tenor saxophone.

Shiny Happy People

If 'Stand' was "just a dumb pop song," 'Shiny Happy People' may be R.E.M.'s dumbest. But the song does have a certain historical significance, marking as it did the first collaboration with Athens homegirl Kate Pierson of the B-52's. Nonetheless, Stipe has referred to the song as an "abortion."

Buck has a different take. "It is what it is," he said. "We wrote this kind of silly song in three-quarter time and Michael gave us this sort of silly lyric, but it wasn't like we spent hours and days doing it. We recorded it in one take. Michael sang it and Kate came in and sang it. If our career was predicated on us having hits that sound like that it would be embarrassing. I'm not afraid to do foolish things. That's a silly, stupid little song. I don't have any interest in playing it live, but I like it."

It was the participation of Pierson that made the song special for Mills and Stipe. "It was fun working with Kate," Mills said. "That was a highlight. We just sort of knew her, we've seen the B's play a lot, but I don't think we've actually worked together before." Added Stipe, "She's probably my favorite female singer."

Although Buck has said 'Shiny Happy People' was "tongue-in-cheek," on at least one occasion, Stipe claimed that the song was sincere, bragging that it was "the happiest song" he has ever written. "You can't sing the words without smiling, because there's so many E sounds," he told Brantley Bardin in *Details*. "I'm an extraordinarily happy person."

Even when the band was compiling material for *Out Of Time*, Stipe already had a strong initial reaction to what would become 'Shiny Happy People.' "The other guys just gave me this song for the next record that is so beyond 'Stand.' It makes 'Stand' sound like a dirge," he told David Fricke.

While 'Stand' was fairly straightforward, 'Shiny Happy People' likely surprised more than a few people with its strange time signature in the middle section. Mills, however, wasn't so sure such a move was to his liking. "I personally think that 'Psychotic Reaction' is the only good song that changes time in the middle," he told *Musician*. "But what the hell. Toying around with these things is our *forte*." Berry enjoyed the experimentation. "We've found that the best way to keep our records interesting is to just keep throwing wacky new ideas in. Like the waltz-time section in the introduction and the middle of 'Shiny…'—it's almost sure to keep the song out of the top 10," he told Harold DeMuir in *Pulse!*.

Berry's prediction proved to be a little off the mark. Even with the unusual mid-section, 'Shiny Happy People' did become a hit, reaching No. 10 on *Billboard*'s Hot 100 and No. 6 in the UK. Still, as Buck once said, the song "is so relentlessly upbeat you want to throw up."

As was the case with 'Stand,' R.E.M. used a similarly upbeat approach for the video for 'Shiny Happy People.' Katherine Dieckmann, who directed the 'Stand' clip, was also the eye behind 'Shiny Happy People,' which featured the band and Pierson cavorting with dancers and schoolchildren. (The backdrop for the clip was a mural painted by Ms. April Chapman's 5th grade class from Oglethorpe Ave. Elementary in Athens, Georgia.) Stipe, dressed in a gold suit and sporting a backward baseball cap, is positively over the top, not only lip-syncing, but smiling. "I fainted the first time I had to do it," he told Jim DeRogatis. "I feel like we pushed

video as far as it could be pushed without lip-syncing. I'd taken such a strong stand against it, I think I finally had to prove to myself that I could do it."

The band is featured with instruments in the clip. Berry bangs a drum, while Mills plays upright bass. Buck, looking a bit uncomfortable, strums a mandolin, although he actually played on electric guitar on the track. Holsapple, who contributed acoustic guitar to the track, is absent.

In all, the song and its accompanying video clip may be R.E.M.'s goofiest moment. But along with 'Stand,' 'Shiny Happy People' may be the most immediately appealing R.E.M. song. Just try playing it for a three-year-old.

Such over-the-top cheeriness didn't go unnoticed. British band Fatima Mansions, annoyed that R.E.M. had the nerve to display such optimism, recorded a brutal punk version of

Athens homegirl Kate Pierson of the B52's guested on 'Shiny Happy People.'

the song. Early R.E.M. producer Mitch Easter recorded a more faithful version for the tribute album *Surprise Your Pig*. Even R.E.M. couldn't leave well enough alone. A promotional single featured three different versions of the song— 'Music Mix,' 'Pop Mix,' and 'Hip Mix.' The 'Music Mix' is of particular note, as it features a funkafied fuzz bass that sounds as if it was lifted from the Gap Band's 'You Dropped A Bomb On Me.'

Belong

Although its mood is slightly darker, 'Belong' owes more than a little to the obscure 'Voice Of Harold,' Stipe's alternate take of '7 Chinese Bros.' in which he substituted that song's lyrics with the liner notes from a gospel album. On 'Belong,' R.E.M. opts for Stipe's spoken-word vocals, which were employed on a good portion of 'Voice Of Harold' and would later resurface on *New Adventures In Hi-Fi*'s 'E-Bow The Letter.' Yet whereas 'Voice Of Harold,' included on the *Dead Letter Office*

compilation, was a goof, 'Belong' is quite serious. The song, which was performed frequently during the *Green* tour, is also much more reliant on Mills's and Berry's background vocals.

In the song's lyrics, Stipe mentions that a woman takes her child and opens a window. What happens next is unclear. "I think it's significant to state that it's not a song about defenestration," he told DeMuir. "I took great pains to clarify that in the vocal and worked on a few lines to make sure that there was no violent act contained within the song. There's an event that's occurred somewhere far away that has to come to the attention of the woman who's the protagonist of the song, and she realizes how significant that thing is to her child and herself, and she goes to the window to take a breath. I think that when I first wrote the song, it did seem like the woman hurled her child and herself out of the window, but that's not what occurs."

Even with Stipe's explanation, 'Belong' is still somewhat of an enigma. The evil forces in the song that give the heroine cause for concern are vaguely described in the lyrics as "creatures" that have "jumped the barricades and have headed for the sea."

"To me, it's very uplifting," Stipe once said. And for reasons that he is probably alone in understanding, it is "probably the most political song on the record."

In concert, Stipe has been known to provide a bit of background as to the intent of the song. "This is another song about war, but another type of war. A more intimate type," he once said before performing the song. A bit more

insight may also be found on the Jem Cohen-directed video clip for the song, which was included on the 1991 compilation *This Is On Film*. Before the song kicks in—a live recording rather than the *Out Of Time* version—a radio is heard picking up various news broadcasts. There are mentions of a number of "pro-democracy demonstrations," which suggests that the "creatures" that "jumped the barricades" may well be fascists launching an invasion into a democratic country.

Although Stipe speaks throughout the song, his vocals aren't exactly easy to decipher since they were recorded on a Walkman in a garage, rather than in the recording studio. "I wasn't happy with the way the vocals sounded in the studio. It was too clear, it was too studio, so I borrowed Scott Litt's Walkman and I took it to the rental home that we were using," he said on *Rockline*. "It was a three-car garage and it had a giant tank sitting in the corner of some type of noxious gas, which I ignored. I was just hoping it wouldn't explode. I did the main part of the vocal in that garage. I really liked the acoustics and that kind of reverb sound I got and it was perfect for the track."

Half A World Away

The bittersweet tone *Out Of Time* continues with 'Half A World Away.' Over the mournful hum of organ, acoustic guitar, and mandolin, Stipe opens the track by singing, "This could be the saddest dusk I've ever seen." In concert, he has introduced the song by saying, "This may well be the saddest song ever written."

Musically, the melancholy song about longing for a loved one was inspired by Buck's experiences while moonlighting with other musicians. "At the time we were making that record I was hanging out with a bunch of folk musician guys and playing on front porches," he said. "For me, that was different. I come from the rock'n'roll *milieu* where if you jam, you are playing loud guitar and someone is soloing, but I would play these traditional songs with these guys and I was the only guy who didn't know these songs or had never played them. I think some of that stuff leaked through a little bit."

'Half A World Away,' or any other R.E.M. tune, shouldn't be confused with traditional folk music. As Buck explained, R.E.M.'s songs are "more complex and use more chords and

time signatures than traditional folk music... I like folk music, but we're not folk musicians, so we would always screw it up somehow."

On 'Half A World Away,' apart from R.E.M.'s traditional instrumentation and the aforementioned organ and mandolin, Mike Mills also plays the harpsichord. This gives the track a nice baroque touch. A Bingham string arrangement is also utilized.

Despite the seemingly heartfelt story, Stipe said that 'Half A World Away' "doesn't make sense to anybody but me. And even to me, it's a totally fabricated experience. It's drawn from things that I know or saw on TV or that people I know told me," he told David Fricke. "It's a complete fabrication. But there's something there."

A black-and-white video, directed by Jim McKay, and featuring desert scenery, effectively captures the mood of the song, but adds no additional meaning. Nonetheless, 'Half A World Away' is a truly beautiful song and points to the more somber direction R.E.M. would explore on *Automatic For The People*.

Texarkana

Like 'Near Wild Heaven,' 'Texarkana' has Stipe assuming the role of background singer, while Mills moves into the spotlight as the lead vocalist. "It's a lot of fun to do, but I wouldn't want to have to do it all the time," Mills said. "It's nice that there are three different voices in this band. We are very fortunate that we have that. It makes it add so much texture and depth to any band that has more than one person that can sing."

Although the song is named for the city on the border of Texas and Arkansas, which has a separate municipal government in each state, it has nothing to do with the city, and Texarkana is never mentioned in the song's lyrics.

"Michael wrote the lyrics to a song and Texarkana was mentioned in the title, and he couldn't finish it, so Mike finished it and sang it," Buck explained on *Rockline*. To Stipe's chagrin, Mills finished and sang the song within a half-hour. "But we couldn't decide what to name it, so we decided to keep the old name," Buck added. "The new lyrics have

---
Former dB's member Peter Holsapple was a guest on *Out Of Time*.

---

absolutely nothing to do with the title, but I like Texarkana."

Stipe and Berry have also expressed an affection for the city. "I love the idea of a city that is named after three different states," Stipe said on *Rockline*. "It's a beautiful place, but you wouldn't go there for enlightenment," Berry told Roy Wilkinson. "There's a Grand Funk Railroad song about this infamous Arkansas groupie called 'Little Rock Annie,' and in some ways, that sets the tone for the place."

With its galloping bass line, combination of real and synthesized strings, and sweet and light melody, 'Texarkana' recalls the Moody Blues. R.E.M. studio chum John Keane adds some particularly tasty pedal steel guitar to the track, which also features Peter Holsapple.

Country Feedback

Like *New Adventures In Hi-Fi*'s 'E-Bow The Letter,' 'Country Feedback' effectively lives up to its title. It's a country song with feedback. The song was actually cut as a demo before the band began working in earnest on *Out Of Time*.

"We didn't have a song. I walked in, I had four chords and put them down with Bill playing bass," Buck told Jim Fanning and Russell Miller in *Discoveries*. "I put the feedback on it, Michael walked in and said, 'Oh, I've got words for that.' The total recording time, not including the mix, was 35 minutes."

Aside from Berry on bass and percussion, Buck plays acoustic guitar and is listed in the album credits for "loud guitar," Mills plays organ, Pierson contributes backing vocals but is nearly inaudible, and Keane once again contributes pedal steel guitar.

In writing the song's lyrics, Stipe used what he has called the "projectile vomiting" approach, scribbling down the song's lyrics in a stream-of-consciousness manner. Buck later revealed the song took a bit longer to compose than he initially let on, as a day passed between the time the band came up with the music and Stipe added the lyrics.

"Michael came in the next day and scatted the words," Buck told Jeff Giles in *Rolling Stone*. "Usually, he has pretty concise words. We get to look them over. We'll say, 'Repeat this. Pull this out. Maybe change this line.' With 'Country Feedback,' he just had two little drawings on a piece of paper, an Indian head and an arrow, I think, and he just kind of shouted."

In a particularly bitter and angry vocal, Stipe at one point appears to sing "Fuck off," but he's actually saying, "Fuck all." "It's a very desperate song," Stipe told Roy Wilkinson.

"It's a love song, but it's certainly from the uglier side. It's pretty much about having given up on a relationship." Whether that relationship was real or imagined, Buck found Stipe's lyric particularly compelling. "It was exactly what was on his mind that day," he said. "It was real."

Perhaps to reflect the ugliness in the song, Stipe has been known to perform the song with his back to the audience. He has also introduced the song as a favorite of his and Berry. (A live version of the song was included as a bonus track on the 'Bang And Blame' CD single.)

Me In Honey

With its genesis in a one-chord riff, 'Me In Honey' is perhaps the simplest song on *Out Of Time*. "That was literally a riff Mike played once," Buck told David Fricke in *Melody Maker*. "I put this guitar line over it and Bill added a drum beat. It was maybe 30 seconds long and it was on the end of a cassette tape of five songs and Michael fixated on that. Just 30 seconds, one chord. He went, 'That beat, that key, D flat. I've got a song for it.' So I said, 'What about another chord for the chorus?' He said, 'Perfect.' We broke up the riff in sections so that each verse was a different length. Then he worked it out on paper, scribbling out lines. And I thought, 'Weird. How did he get all of this out of one chord?' "

Thematically, 'Me In Honey' was inspired by a song written by Stipe's friend Natalie Merchant. "Specifically, the song to me is an answer to 10,000 Maniacs's 'Eat For Two.' It's a male perspective on pregnancy, which I don't think has really been dealt with," he told Parke Puterbaugh in *Vox*. "There's a real push me/pull me issue saying, 'I had nothing to do with it,' yet on the other hand saying, 'Wait, I have feelings about this.'"

Somehow it seems fitting that the band returned to their traditional instruments for 'Me In Honey,' which closes the album, augmented only by guest vocalist Pierson. Yet strangely enough, as on *Out Of Time*'s opening track 'Radio Song,' it is the voice of the guest vocalist that is heard opening and closing the track, rather than the familiar voice of Michael Stipe.

With 'Me In Honey,' Stipe provided an answer to 'Eat For Two,' written by friend Natalie Merchant, right.

the international breakthrough success of *Out Of Time* and 'Losing My Religion' may have made R.E.M. richer financially, yet coming off the best-selling album of their career the band members were anything but shiny, happy people. That fact was reflected in *Automatic For The People*, the darkest, but most cohesive album in the R.E.M. catalog.

R.E.M. had reached new heights in popularity with *Out Of Time*, despite the fact that, for the first time in its career, the band failed to promote the album with a tour. *Out Of Time*

'Losing My Religion.' But the band, as usual, downplayed its accomplishments and the awards show glitter. Buck showed up to the ceremony in pajamas and insisted the only reason he was there at all was because his mother and wife wanted to attend. Once again, Stipe used the moment in the spotlight to raise awareness. He wore a black baseball hat that read: "White House Stop AIDS."

Even before the Grammys, the band triumphed at the *MTV Music Video Awards*, held in September 1991, taking home awards for best video of the year for 'Losing My

AUTOMATIC FOR THE PEOPLE

reached the top of the *Billboard* album chart in its eighth week, only to be dethroned by Michael Bolton's *Time, Love And Tenderness* a week later, when *Billboard* began utilizing a new point-of-sale technology called SoundScan to tabulate the chart. The following week, however, *Out Of Time* returned to the top of the chart. The album also went to No. 1 in Great Britain, Germany, and Israel, with combined sales that more than quadrupled those of any other previous R.E.M. album.

In addition, there were numerous awards and accolades. The band was nominated for seven Grammy Awards, taking home three trophies in February 1992, including the honors for best alternative album for *Out Of Time* and best video for

Automatic R.E.M.: Michael Stipe, Bill Berry, Peter Buck, and Mike Mills.

Religion,' best group video, breakthrough video, best direction in a video (to director Tarsem), best art direction (Jose Montana), and best editing (Robert Duffy). Rather than making the usual self-congratulatory rock star speech, Stipe used the triumph as a platform to express his political views. Each time he visited the stage to collect an award, he revealed a different T-shirt with slogans that ranged from "Rainforest," "Choice," and "Love Knows No Color," to "Alternative Energy Now," "Handgun Control," "The Right To Vote," and "Wear A Condom."

Despite all of the awards and accomplishments, things were not well in the R.E.M. camp. This was reflected in the somber mood of the new material the band had begun writing for what would become *Automatic For The People*. "We're all influenced by where we are as people and what we are going through," explained Buck. "That year was just a

119

weird, chaotic, kind of sad year. The good thing about that record is that we managed to capture all that. We didn't really write a lot of rock songs for that album."

During the period of *Out Of Time* and *Automatic For The People*, Buck had sunk into a deep depression, drinking large quantities of wine and rarely leaving his house. In photographs and television appearances, he appeared to be bloated and out of shape. His first marriage also unraveled, which prompted him, in part, to leave Athens for New York for a brief period before heading, ultimately, to Seattle.

As a result, rather than the pretty acoustic numbers that populated *Out Of Time*, many of the songs on *Automatic For The People* appeared to be lullabies only to be twisted by weird bits of feedback. Following on the heels of the grunge explosion that sent Nirvana and Pearl Jam into the upper regions of the charts, R.E.M. once again found themselves out of step with the times. When the rest of the world was turning up their amps to "11" and screaming, the members of R.E.M. were still toying with acoustic instruments, and Stipe was singing some of the songs in a whisper.

"I still think *Automatic* is a punk rock record, but it's just a very quiet one," Stipe explained. "It flew in the face of everything else that was going on musically at the time. We had the audacity to do an incredibly quiet, introspective record not using electric guitars and that was exactly not what everybody else was doing at the time." Indeed, with *Automatic For The People*, R.E.M. once again chose to forgo touring—much like the Beatles had done during their most creative period. Instead they concentrated on honing their craft in the studio. The result would be some of the finest material of R.E.M.'s career.

The subject matter—death, mortality, and passage—indeed called for a somber instrumental approach. However, these themes also began to lead some to speculate. Stipe, still thin and now balding, had no plans to do interviews. His reluctance to talk, coupled with his appearance—which some called sickly—led certain members of the press to conclude that the singer was suffering from AIDS. Interpretations of the lyrics to such death-themed songs as 'Try Not To Breathe' and the longing for the carefree times of yesteryear in 'Nightswimming' only added fuel to the fire. Rather than speak up to quell the rumors, he chose to remain tight-lipped on the subject.

The songs that would make up *Automatic For The People* evolved out of jam sessions that the band held in their home base in Athens. "We just used to go into the studio every day and mess around for a couple of hours," Buck recalled. "We had this body of work that was really slow. Musically, a lot of the songs are kind of like old folk or blues songs." Peter Holsapple—the former member of the dB's who introduced the band to Mitch Easter, served as an auxiliary player on the *Green* tour, and played on *Out Of Time* and the subsequent rare acoustic promotional performances—was no longer affiliated to the band.

"After we did all the demos we went to New Orleans," Buck added. "I think it was a the last day of Mardi Gras so you could imagine how nuts it was when we got there. It was going to be more demos, but we started doing more recording and we ended up keeping things."

Among the songs recorded at Daniel Lanois's Kingsway Studio in New Orleans, Louisiana, were 'Drive' and 'New Orleans Instrumental No. 1.' The studio, owned by Lanois, who is known for his work with U2, is located in the French Quarter and is said to be haunted.

The *Automatic For The People* sessions turned into a travelog of sorts, as the band chose to record it in severall different studios following the initial stint in the Crescent City. R.E.M. also stopped in at Bearsville Studio in Woodstock, New York, where it had worked on *Out Of Time* and *Green*. Following Bearsville, the next stop was Criteria Recording Studios in Miami, Florida, a studio with a rich history. In the fall of 1970, Derek and the Dominos cut the landmark 'Layla' there, and four years later Clapton returned to record *461 Ocean Boulevard*, his first No. 1 solo album in America. It was in Miami that R.E.M. chose to shoot much of the artwork that appeared in the CD booklet, including shots of the band posing on the beach and Stipe swimming in the Atlantic Ocean.

At Bobby Brown's Boss Studios in Atlanta, closer to R.E.M.'s home base of Athens, string arrangements–featuring some of the same musicians from the Atlanta Symphony who played on *Out Of Time*–were added to 'Drive,' 'Everybody Hurts,' 'The Sidewinder Sleeps Tonite,' and 'Nightswimming.' For the task of arranging the strings, the band called on John Paul Jones, best known as Led Zeppelin's bass and keyboard player. A partnership between R.E.M. and Jones may have seemed like an unlikely alliance to some, but there were some similarities between R.E.M. and Led Zeppelin that ran deeper than Mitch Easter's off-handed comparison of *Reckoning* and *Led Zeppelin II*. For one, *Green*'s combination of rockers and slower, moody acoustic tracks recalled *Led Zeppelin III*.

Another involved Jones himself. While Zeppelin singer Robert Plant and guitarist Jimmy Page were in the spotlight, some felt that Jones was the band's true musical driving force. A similar situation exists with R.E.M. Stipe and Buck are the most visible and charismatic members of the band, but Mills is considered by many the musical backbone of the group.

Besides his work within the confines of Led Zeppelin, Jones had also made a name for himself arranging strings for other artists. "He arranged strings for all those '60s British bands—the Stones, the Yardbirds, Herman's Hermits, and

Billboard's Melinda Newman. "[The listener] shouldn't walk away with down feelings, but they probably won't walk away with a bounce in their step either."

Despite the melancholy mood of its content, the album's title had an upbeat ring to it. The name is actually the service mark and motto of Weaver D's Delicious Fine Foods in Clarke County, Georgia. (It wasn't the first time the band had given a nod to one of its favorite eating spots—'Walters Theme' on the *Dead Letter Office* compilation *was* a tribute to Walters Bar-B-Que.)

Donovan," Buck told Kerry Doole in *Music Express*. "His stuff was remarkably nonsweet; I really hate those big sugary washes." Also lending a hand was cellist Knox Chandler, known for his work with the Psychedelic Furs, who played on 'Monty Got A Raw Deal' and 'Nightswimming.'

The band eventually opted to mix *Automatic For The People* at the Heart-owned Bad Animals Studio in Seattle, so completing R.E.M.'s whirlwind album-making excursion that touched down in four different cities across America.

While much of the album was downbeat, there were some bright, optimistic spots. "It's a little melancholy, but all the songs about dark things have a hopeful message," Mills told

Weaver D serves it up "automatic for the people" of Clarke County, Georgia.

At Weaver D's, when customers order food, the waiters at the soul food restaurant respond with the word "automatic." As Berry once explained, "Anything you ask for, whether it be catering 5,000 or just another refill for your sweet tea, his answer is always, 'Automatic!'" To acknowledge the debt, R.E.M. felt it was suitable to mention the restaurant in the album's liner notes: "A gracious thanks to Weaver D and his great establishment—'Automatic.' "

Drive

With the ominous and somber opening strains of 'Drive,' R.E.M. made it quite clear from the onset that the band was moving in a new direction with *Automatic For The People*. From 'Radio Free Europe' to 'Radio Song,' the opening songs had typically been rather upbeat tracks. Even the moody 'Feeling Gravity's Pull' from *Fables Of The Reconstruction* had a kick to it. 'Drive,' on the other hand, was a relatively low-key affair with Stipe's dry, echo-laden vocal plus sparse, mostly acoustic instrumental support from the band. Still, the song was subtley powerful.

The central lyrical phrase "Hey kids, rock'n'roll" earned the song comparisons to 'Rock On,' the 1973 hit by British singer David Essex. It's a song that Stipe had liked as a teenager growing up in St. Louis. Some also cited Pylon's 'Stop It,'—an influence closer to home. R.E.M. had covered the Athens band's 'Crazy' for a B-side that subsequently turned up on *Dead Letter Office*. 'Stop It,' from the 1980 album *Gyrate*, released the same year that R.E.M. formed, is a much more upbeat track, but contains repeated phrases "rock'n'roll" and "hey kids," much like 'Drive.' The Pylon song also appeared on the soundtrack to the 1987 documentary *Athens, Ga—Inside/Out*, which also featured R.E.M.

"I could see both of those comparisons," Buck said. "But the chords, before we started playing them, literally could be any old Appalachian ballad in the world... There's that song 'A Cuckoo Is A Free Bird,' it's like 1,000 years old. Townes Van Zant has recorded it, but I've heard 100 people play it. It kind of has the same chords. That D minor to G thing with an F and A minor. It is just kind of this weird Appalachian haunting kind of chord progression. When the band started playing it, it just got kind of weirder and weirder."

'Drive' was cut live with acoustic guitar, vocals, bass, and drums at Kingsway Studios in New Orleans. "We did it about 15 times in a row," Buck recalled. "The vocal is live, all the effects were on it. It was really a locked-in type of thing. It does have a little 'Rock On' groove and has a little of that Pylon feel too, although both of the songs aren't similar [musically] at all. When I wrote it originally, I thought we would have a banjo, and a harmonium and it would be an old Appalachian ballad-type thing."

However, the folk strains of the song are broken up by a striking mid-song electric guitar solo by Buck that cuts through the largely acoustic track like a hot knife through butter. In order to achieve the right effect, Buck played the solo with a nickel rather than a guitar pick, a trick he borrowed from Queen's Brian May, and he overdubbed the track six times.

Another element that separates 'Drive' from 'Rock On,' 'Stop It,' and its folk predecessors is the political bent that Stipe added to his lyrics. The opening three words, "Smack, crack, bushwhacked" can be taken as either just a nonsense rhyme or a scathing indictment directed at the United States government. Stipe had used the word "Bushwhacked" before to express his dislike for George Bush, the 41st President of the United States of America. In October 1988, Stipe had personally taken out ads in the classified sections of college newspapers in support of Democratic presidential nominee Michael Dukakis, which read: "Stipe says: Don't Get Bushwhacked. Get out and vote. Vote Dukakis." Of course, Bush won that election and continued to govern the country using the blueprint laid down by Ronald Reagan. While the Reagan administration was in power, the Iran-Contra scandal surfaced, in which the White House was accused of illegally selling arms to Iran in order to fund the Contra rebels in Nicaragua. There had also been allegations that the U.S. government was selling drugs, such as crack cocaine, in order to fund the war in Nicaragua.

Many believed that one of the chief conspirators in the Iranian-Contra scandal was Lt. Col. Oliver North, who was convicted of crimes connected with the scandal, but later had his conviction overturned. Stipe may be alluding to North in the phrase "Ollie, Ollie, Ollie in come free, baby," as North managed to emerge from the scandal with what was seen as a little more than a slap on the wrist. Then again, Stipe could just be referring to the children's game Hide-And-Seek, which uses the phrase "ollie, ollie, ollie" to alert players that the game is over and they can come out of their hiding place without getting caught.

With or without any deep political meanings, 'Drive,' the first single from *Automatic For The People* was certainly a different turn for R.E.M. "We record this stuff and sometimes we think it is really weird and it turns out to be really normal, and sometimes we do normal things and people think it's weird," Buck explained. "When we put 'Drive' out as a single, everyone was going, 'That's really weird. Your first single doesn't have a chorus.' We thought about it and we said, 'You know, you're right.'"

Prior to the release of *Automatic For The People*, 'Drive' had been known by another title. When participants in the Peter Care-directed video were handed lyric sheets, the song was known as 'Tried,' another word that features prominently in the lyrics. The video, filmed in black-and-white, shows Stipe crowd-surfing over fans in slow motion. Buck, Mills, and Berry appear briefly as a part of the crowd only to be blasted away by what appears to be a firehose. With its use of slow-motion and stark black-and-white photography, the video is extremely effective in fitting the mood of the song.

Although the only live performances R.E.M. were doing at that point were one-off benefits and occasional television appearances, the band soon learnt that the sparse arrangement of 'Drive' didn't work well in a live setting. "To be completely honest, we couldn't play that thing very well live," Buck admitted. "It never really worked." As an alternative, the band worked out a funk-rock version that once again showed the influence of Gang Of Four. "We played it in the rehearsal studio and it came out like that and we thought that was pretty cool," Buck said. "I think we did it on TV a week or two after the record came out. I

"Smack, crack, and bushwhacked?" George Bush was a target on 'Drive.'"

scorching funk rendition of 'Drive', which caused more than a few jaws to drop.

That alternate version of 'Drive' appeared the following year on *Alternative NRG*, a multi-act benefit album for Greenpeace that was recorded and mixed using solar power.

like the fact we did a really different version on TV to promote the record." Indeed, R.E.M. may have caught some viewers off-guard when they appeared on the MTV Video Music Awards on September 2, 1993 performing 'Everybody Hurts.' As the soul-comforting ballad faded out, they launched into a

Dave Wakeling, formerly of The Beat, and with whom R.E.M. had shared several early bills, was one of the album's producers. R.E.M.'s contribution, which also appeared as a bonus track on the 'Strange Currencies' single, was recorded at the 40 Watt Club in Athens on November 19, 1992.

Try Not To Breathe

Even in the initial album copy for *Automatic For The People*, this song sported the titled 'Passion (Try Not To Breathe).' However, before the album actually went to press, 'Passion' was completely dropped and the parenthetical phrase became the title.

"What usually happens is that we have a whole body of work, sometimes before Michael ever hears them, we'll have 15 things kind of demo-ed. Michael said, 'I will call this one 'Passion,' because I've got a page of lyrics called 'Passion,' but he never used them for the song."

The song's title was inspired by something that Buck said while making a solo recording of the original demo for the song. "I started playing it and John Keane, who was taping it, said, 'Peter, the mic is really close to your guitar and I can hear you breathe.' And I just said, 'O.K. I'll try not to breathe,

take two.'" When Stipe heard the demo, he took the phrase and added it to the lyrics, which are about an 87-year-old woman who has "lived a full life" but is considering suicide, so that her loved ones will remember her in good health, rather than withering away. In concert, Stipe has dedicated the song to his "nana."

The song continues the somber mood of 'Drive,' but is more upbeat, thanks to a waltz-like rhythm and a call-and-response section that recalls the Beatles' 'Yellow Submarine,' which sounds as if it is coming from a megaphone.

"There's all kinds of stuff going on there," Buck explained. "There's electric dulcimer, nylon-string guitar, feedback, and all kinds of weird things." The weird musical touches that were thrown in, Buck added, kept the song from becoming overly sentimental.

The Sidewinder Sleeps Tonite

'The Sidewinder Sleeps Tonite' is one of two celebratory songs on *Automatic For The People* that ensures the album isn't a complete downer. In fact, at one point, Stipe can be heard laughing. The singer apparently had a hard time pronouncing the name of Dr. Seuss, the author of such famed children's books as *The Cat In The Hat*. "I kept trying to get Michael to say 'Seuss,' not 'Zeus,' anyway, and that made him laugh," Mills told Ira Robbins in *Pulse*.

Invoking the name of Dr. Seuss in the song wasn't the only nod to nostalgia. 'The Sidewinder Sleeps Tonite' bears such a strong resemblance to 'The Lion Sleeps Tonight,' a 1961 No. 1 U.S. hit by the Tokens, that R.E.M. felt the need to note that the use of the title and musical material in the song was done with permission from Abilene Music Inc.—the publisher of 'The Lion Sleeps Tonight.'

"We knew that if we changed our title we could maybe have done it, and nobody would have known," Mills told *Billboard*. "But the nod was obvious, and as far as Michael was concerned, it was the best title. We figured, rather than change our artistic direction, it would be easier to go ahead and see what [Weiss, Creatore, and Peretti—the writers of 'The Lion Sleeps Tonight'] would want to let us have it. So, we called these guys and asked what would be equitable for

them. They said, 'Well, we'd like it if you'd cover ['The Lion Sleeps Tonight'],' and we said, 'O.K., what about a B-side?' And they thought that was fine."

R.E.M.'s version, recorded in Athens in November 1992, turned up appropriately enough on the B-side of 'The Sidewinder Sleeps Tonite.' Just as they had done with the Everly Brothers' 'All I Have To Do Is Dream,' R.E.M. produced a stunning version of 'The Lion Sleeps Tonight,' proving that they were as adapt at tackling certified classic pop hits as well as more obscure cover choices by the likes of the Velvet Underground and Syd Barrett.

"We would never have agreed to cover the song if we didn't like it," Mills added. "It's something we've all enjoyed over the years growing up. But we weren't doing it to get radio play; we were just doing it to provide a B-side and fulfill the terms of our deal. I hear the writers are pretty happy about the way it came out."

While 'The Sidewinder Sleeps Tonite' borrowed heavily from the Tokens' hit, it also contained some of R.E.M.'s more

---

The Cat In The Hat **by Dr Seuss was one of the pop culture references in 'The Sidewinder Sleeps Tonite.'"**

unconventional trademarks. The song has three verses and choruses before the bridge. Most songs have just two. Also the chorus is one of the most indecipherable in the post-Green era. What sounds like, "coney jah waker," is actually said to be "call me when you try to wake her up," but only the sidewinder knows for sure.

Everybody Hurts

'Everybody Hurts' is perhaps the most stunning, heartfelt, and moving song that R.E.M. have ever written and recorded. In a perfect world, it would have been a chart-topper around the globe.

It was Berry who brought in 'Everybody Hurts,' but oddly enough he wasn't on the basic track. Instead, a $20 Univox drum machine provided the rhythm, while Buck played guitar and Mills played keyboards. The combination gave the song a unique blend of robotic and human elements.

When Stipe first heard the instrumental track, he stood in the corner of the studio and cupped his hands over his mouth and left ear, perhaps attempting to find a voice in which to sing the moving ballad. He would eventually arrive at a sound that he would subsequently refer to as his "soul voice"— a style which effectively matched the feel of the song.

With 'Everybody Hurts,' Michael Stipe attempted to reach out to the despondent.

"That was written for teenagers basically, saying don't kill yourself," Stipe told Robert Hilburn in the *Los Angeles Times*. "My sister is a teacher and someone she knows, who is 15, tried to kill himself, and it led to this song. The idea was to write something that would appeal to someone who is having trouble… so that if they hear the song, they might be able to say, 'God, that's me,' and feel some sense of hope or that someone might care about them."

With its swirling string arrangement provided by John Paul Jones, and dramatic lead vocal by Stipe, 'Everybody Hurts' is, in some ways, reminiscent of Simon & Garfunkel's 'Bridge Over Troubled Water'—a 1970 No. 1 hit in America that also attempted to reach out to the despondent. However, rather than muddying the waters with metaphors, Stipe went to the heart of the matter with his most direct set of lyrics.

"He wanted that particular song to reach teenagers and not be misunderstood," Buck told Jim Irvin in *Mojo*. "You don't want something that needs a Math degree to go through when you're trying to reach a 17-year-old and say, 'It's OK, things are tough but they get better.' There's not a line out of place."

Stipe added that the song was a bold move for R.E.M.

"'Everybody Hurts' was a very fucking ballsy song," he told Jim DeRogatis of *Request*. "It could be and can still be heard as one of the most sappy, maudlin, sentimental, cry-in-your-coffee songs. But it succeeded. For some reason, the majority of people think that song speaks to them in some way. That really worked, but we could have just as easily taken a step that didn't work."

In concert, the song was a favorite, performed with an urgency only suggested by the studio take. During the song's climax, Mills has been known to knock over his keyboard stool for dramatic effect.

The video clip for the song, directed by Jake Scott, the son of acclaimed *Blade Runner* director Ridley Scott, is also among the band's most stunning. In the clip, shot on Interstate 10 in San Antonio, Texas, the band, riding in a car driven by Stipe, runs into a traffic jam. To drive the song's lyrics home, initially they appear as subtitles, but as the camera shifts to the occupants of the other cars, various other subtitles appear, representing the thoughts of the parade of individuals who appear on the screen. The thoughts, some sad, others darkly humorous, range from "There's nothing I can do" to "No tenemos mas tiempo," which means "We don't have any more time" in Spanish. By mid-song, the members of R.E.M. have exited their car with Buck, at one point, lying in a crucifix-like pose on the roof of a car, while Stipe lip-syncs with the fervor of a Southern preacher. As the song reaches its climax, the occupants of all the cars lining the freeway evacuate their cars and join the members of R.E.M. in a march into the unknown. The clip closes after the song has finished with a static-filled aerial shot of the abandoned cars on the freeway. The frantic voice of a female television news reporter is heard over the whirl of a helicopter. "We have no official explanation… Police estimate some 300 or 400 people… They just got out and walked… God, we've gotten confirmation… We cannot find anyone. I've never seen anything like this …"

Indeed, R.E.M. fans had never quite heard anything like 'Everybody Hurts' from the band. It was simple, direct, and incredibly effective.

Two different versions of the song have been released. One was recorded on November 19, 1992 in Athens. The other on September 2, 1993 at the MTV Awards.

New Orleans Instrumental No. 1

This track has the distinction of being the first full, purely instrumental piece to appear on a regular R.E.M. album. In the past, R.E.M. had included brief untitled instrumental snippets on various albums, but never a full instrumental with a title. (Although *Out Of Time*'s 'Endgame' doesn't have any lyrics, it does have some vocals. 'White Tornado' is included on *Dead Letter Office*, but that's not a proper album, but rather a collection of B-sides and out-takes.)

Named for the city in which it was recorded, 'New Orleans Instrumental No. 1' was cut approximately four days into the band's demo sessions at Kingsway Studios during a spontaneous intoxicated late jam. "We went to a restaurant where I knew the guy and he kept bringing us bottles of wine and everybody got a little tipsy," Buck recalled. "We got back to the studio and Scott [Litt] suggested that we should make some stuff up on the spur of the moment. On that one, it was about 2 a.m. and everybody was pretty much blotto. It's probably the only instance when we've recorded stuff when we were drunk. I think that is Bill playing piano and I was playing one of Daniel's guitars that has a Universal sustain that sustains forever. It occurred and it sounded great. The original is about four-and-half minutes long." Mills played stand-up bass.

On *Automatic For The People*, the song, edited down to a brief two-minutes-and-12-seconds, provided a nice tuneful and atmospheric gap between 'Everybody Hurts' and 'Sweetness Follows.' What is billed as 'New Orleans Instrumental No. 1 (Long Version)' was included on the CD single of 'Everybody Hurts.' That version, which runs three-minutes-and-28-seconds, ends in a howl of feedback.

Sweetness Follows

'Sweetness Follows' is another melancholy song that deals with death. In this particular song, Stipe's character appears to be singing to his siblings after the passing of his parents. The song touches on themes of loss, regret, and ultimately joy when reflecting back on happier times and realizing one must enjoy life while one can. To make sure that his own parents weren't offended, Stipe reportedly called to clarify that the song, which contains such bitter lines as "distanced from one, deaf to the other," was not about them.

The song, which begins in a quiet and somber way with session player Knox Chandler's churning cello and Mills's funeral parlor-like organ, takes a turn about halfway into the track with shards of squealing feedback contrasting with the sweet sounds of acoustic guitar. The effect is reminiscent of an approach used by Big Star on the song 'Kangaroo' from the album *Big Star's 3rd: Sister Lovers*.

"'Sweetness Follows,' particularly, is just an old blues song with some weird jazz chords thrown in," Buck explained. "We recorded it in the '90s and we wanted to add all these elements that would turn it into something else."

Monty Got A Raw Deal

Although his following isn't as large as James Dean's, the legendary 1950s screen idol Montgomery Clift, star of such films as *The Misfits*, *From Here To Eternity*, and *A Place In The Sun*, continues to live on in pop music. 'The Right Profile' is the seventh track on *London Calling*, the landmark 1979 album by British punk legends the Clash. In the song, Clash frontman Joe Strummer detailed Clift's decline into alcohol and drug abuse after a car crash left him disfigured and required filmmakers to shoot him only from the right side.

'Monty Got A Raw Deal,' which happens to be the seventh track on *Automatic For The People,* also uses Clift as its subject, but his surname and the names of the films he starred in are absent from the lyrics, which were inspired by Stipe's meeting with a man who took photographs of the

In the world according to Michael Stipe, 1950s screen idol Montgomery Clift, right, got a raw deal.

actor during the filming of *The Misfits*. "The Clash song is real specific and ours isn't," Buck told Ira Robbins in *Pulse*. "It's more of a mediation on the movies and reality."

The music for the song came from Buck, who composed the tune on bouzouki, a Greek stringed instrument, in a New Orleans hotel room while a couple in the next room were apparently enjoying a particularly lively love-making session. Oddly enough, Buck's pre-chorus bouzouki riff has an Oriental feel to it. On the studio recording, Chandler's cello is once again employed for added effect.

Ignoreland

Automatic For The People's one all-out rocker, which recalls the work of the Who and Neil Young, changed the tone of the entire album, but it almost didn't make it to the final record. "'Ignoreland' was one of the last things we wrote. If we hadn't come up with that, the other song that was going to make the record was 'The Devil Rides Backwards On A Horse Named Maybe,' and that was slower than anything on the record," Buck explained. "That was about three-quarters finished. If we didn't come up with 'Ignoreland,' the record would have been even slower, which I think would have been good."

Lyrically, the vitriolic 'Ignoreland' puts R.E.M.'s politics in plain view, as Stipe rails against the "heartless" Reagan and Bush administrations that "stole their power from the victims of the 'us versus them' years," and focused on funding the military, while the media was afraid to report on anything that wasn't fed to them on "a presidential spoon."

In retrospect, no members of the band are really happy with the track, which features co-producer Scott Litt on harmonica and clarinet. "It's an awful mix," said Buck. "The day we wrote it was like on a Friday and that was the last day of rehearsals and then we went down to record at John Keane's studio and we didn't even have an ending for it, but it sounded great. It sped up and slowed down and all that. We did all these overdubs and it sounded great, but you could really tell it was a fucked-up take. The ending just kind of died. Rather than just being brave and keeping that take, because it was really kind of a weird scary take, we re-recorded it and it got cleaner and we got fussier and it took all the heart out of it...What we should have done was put the vocals on the original take and not worry about the tempo."

Nonetheless, with its powerful guitars and distorted vocals, 'Ignoreland' offered the biggest clue as to where R.E.M. would venture musically on its next album.

Star Me Kitten

This is a seductive and twisted love song that, as the lyrics suggest, was originally known as 'Fuck Me Kitten.' However, the band opted to change the title, in part due to a suggestion by actress Meg Ryan, then working in the film *Sleepless In Seattle*. Ryan, who visited the band while they were mixing the album at Bad Animals Studio, said it would have been difficult to buy an album with the word "fuck" on it in the town were she grew up. But there were also other considerations. R.E.M. didn't want the album slapped with a parental advisory sticker, which would prohibit such major department stores as Wal-Mart from carrying the album and make it more difficult for the band's fans to buy. The decision to substitute "fuck" with the word "star" wasn't unheard of in the rock world. Although there are no similarities musically with 'Star Me Kitten,' the final track on the Rolling Stones' 1973 album *Goats Head Soup* contains the chorus, "star, fuck a star, fuck a star," but the song is titled simply 'Star Star.'

While R.E.M. may have looked to the Stones for an alternate title, the musical inspiration came from other sources. "Mike started playing these oddball chords, and I said, 'That sounds like it needs tremolo guitar and some lovely little

Twin Peaks lead," Buck told Ira Robbins in *Pulse*. "Me and Bill and Mike did it in like ten minutes, put it on cassette and walked out. We said, 'Michael is never going to put words to that.' And that was the first one he got a melody and words to."

Aside from Angelo Badalamenti's *Twin Peaks* theme music, the band also turned to 'I'm Not In Love,' a 1975 hit for the British pop act 10cc. "Our treatment on the record was sort of inspired by 10cc and vocal tape loops," Litt said in the documentary *R.E.M. Rough Cut*, which aired on public television in the U.S. "I sang about eight different notes and we sampled them and we loaded them on to a track—each note on to one track of an eight-track machine, so when I raise the fader that note comes up," Mills added. "I'm actually playing the mixing board to get the notes. It's that 10cc effect that they did on 'I'm Not In Love.'"

It was somehow fitting that the song borrowed from 'I'm Not In Love,' because the relationship Stipe sings of in 'Star Me Kitten' seems to be based not on love, but on lust and submissiveness.

A demo version, slightly shorter than the album cut, turned up as a bonus track on 'The Sidewinder Sleeps

Beat legend William S. Burroughs evoked the ghost of Marlene Dietrich on his version of 'Star Me Kitten.'

Tonite.' In the demo, an organ fills the space where Mills's 10cc-style vocals were dropped in.

Another version popped up on the 1996 album *Songs In The Key Of X*, which features music from and inspired by the sci-fi TV series *The X-Files*. This unique collaborative version features legendary author William S. Burroughs reciting the lyrics in his cigarette-soaked gruff voice. Before the *Automatic For The People* track begins, Burroughs offers a humorous monologue. "Here's something I picked up," he says. "A knack of going along with someone else's song, putting myself into it. It evolves from 'Lili Marlene,' Marlene Deitrich. Not one of my favorite people, but that's where it came from."

Man On The Moon

'Man On The Moon' was a crowd favorite on the *Monster* tour of the magnitude of 'It's The End Of The World As We Know It (And I Feel Fine).' The song, with its numerous references to 1970s pop culture and undeniably catchy chorus, was the result of a happy accident involving Berry. "We were sitting around in our rehearsal studio and I hit that C chord on the guitar and then turned around to grab my beer, and my hand and the chord slid up to the third fret… and everybody went, 'Oh, that sounds great! Let's use that for the verse bit.'"

Stipe's lyrical contribution was equally as astonishing: "I just fell off the chair when I heard that," Buck said. "We were in Seattle and he finished the song quickly, in a day. We were all just dumbfounded. It was, uh… mind boggling."

In the song—rounded out by a samba beat, a dozen overdubbed guitars, and some tasty slide guitar work by Buck—Stipe name-drops Mott The Hoople, the glam-rock band fronted by Ian Hunter. When producer Mitch Easter first met R.E.M. for the 'Radio Free Europe' sessions back in 1981, Easter thought Stipe, then sporting long, curly hair and sunglasses, was a Hunter lookalike. Also mentioned in 'Man On The Moon' are popular 1970s games *Life*, *Twister*, *Risk*, and such evergreen favorites as *Monopoly*, twenty-one, checkers, and chess, as well as a diverse list of characters and historical figures including wrestler Fred Blassie, Elvis, Moses, Sir Isaac Newton, and Charles Darwin. However, it is the late comedian Andy Kaufman, rather than some obscure hidden subject, who is the primary inspiration of the song.

"When Michael sings about Andy Kaufman and Elvis, he's singing about Andy Kaufman and Elvis," Buck told Ira Robbins in *Pulse*. "It's not about wheat prices in Russia." Andy Kaufman, the comedian who was famous for his role as Latka in the sitcom *Taxi*, had a huge impact on the singer, comparable to his love of Patti Smith. Stipe recalled one of Kaufman's appearances on *Saturday Night Live*. "He came out with a child's turntable and put it on a stool and put on the song from *Mighty Mouse*, which was my favorite cartoon

as a kid, and he mimed the choruses," he said in an interview with the internet magazine *iGuide*. Although just a teen at the time, Stipe realized that Kaufman was "doing one of the most profound things I've ever seen in my life," he said. "It was so shockingly wild and hysterically funny. It really blew me away." Stipe added that Kaufman's Elvis imitation was "better than most impersonators." It should be noted that when Stipe breaks into an Elvis impersonation in 'Man On The Moon,' singing, "Hey, baby are we losing touch?," he's not just doing Elvis, but imitating Kaufman doing Elvis. (Stipe's Elvis-vocals are preceded by his singing question, "Hey, Andy are you goofing on Elvis?") In the Peter Care-directed black-and-white video clip for the song, another one of the band's finest, Stipe assumes the persona of *Giant*-era James Dean, rather than Kaufman. As he walks through the desert, sporting a cowboy hat and jeans, images

The antics of the late comedian Andy Kaufman had a profound effect on Stipe.

of Kaufman wrestling and imitating Elvis are superimposed on the screen. In mid-clip, Stipe hitches a ride on a big rig piloted by Berry, which deposits him at a truck stop where Buck is tending the bar, Mills is a cowboy-hat wearing pool player, and footage of Kaufman imitating Elvis appears on the TV. At the truck stop, the various other customers at the bar mime selected lines from the song, giving the standard practice of lip-syncing in videos a new twist.

Nightswimming

'Nightswimming' is the first of two moving songs, with the central theme of water, that close *Automatic For The People*. Both were composed primarily by Mills and feature him prominently on piano. On 'Nightswimming,' in a nod to rock history, Mills played the piano at Criteria Studios that was used on Derek And The Dominos' rock classic 'Layla.'

The lyrics of 'Nightswimming,' about the carefree days in Athens when the band members and friends went skinny-dipping in a local swimming hole, were actually penned by Stipe prior to the recording of *Out Of Time*. The band, it seems, had trouble coming up with an instrumental track to fit the words until Mills, months later, eventually found the right approach. The hard work was worth the effort, as Mills feels that the song effectively captured the experience. He's said that 'Nightswimming' is one of his favorite R.E.M. songs of all time. "Michael did such a beautiful job with it," he said during a radio interview. "It's the most evocative song, because it is mostly a true story. It is definitely about times we had around Athens. To play that and listen to that is really meaningful to me."

Strings, arranged by Jones, fill out the song. "When you use strings, you don't have to rely so much on that rock'n'roll combo aspect," Buck explained to Kerry Doole in *Music Express*. "'Nightswimming' for instance, was either going to be just piano and vocal or with strings."

Jem Cohen's artfully directed clip for the song, which shows desolate scenes of Athens at night, effectively captures the mood of the song. In the clip, people are shown disrobing and swimming naked, as the song's lyrics suggest. For the home-video release of the *Parallel* collection, two versions of the 'Nightswimming' clip had to be prepared. The original, with nudity, led to a parental advisory warning that it "may be unsuitable for viewing by minors." A second version, which was not as explicit, was also assembled so a version of *Parallel* without the parent warning could also be put on the market.

Apart from the two versions, the 'Nightswimming' video clip offers another interesting twist. About halfway through, the song fades out giving way to various natural night time sounds, such as crickets, for approximately a minute-and-a-half before the song resumes.

Find The River

'Find The River' is another song composed by Mills, primarily on the piano. "It was done completely before we even went into the studio," Buck explained. "Mike put like almost every instrument on it and after that we just added vocals."

The black-and-white clip, directed by Jodi Wille, is the only video of the *Automatic* era that shows the band in performance together. (The clip for 'The Sidewinder Sleeps Tonite' shows band members playing their instruments separately in different rooms.) The in-studio band performance, featuring Stipe on vocals, Buck on acoustic guitar, Mills on keyboards, and Berry on bass, is intercut with an elderly man

hiking in the wilderness with an Alaskan Husky. The clip ends with the man sleeping and the dog on the beach of an ocean, rather than a river. As the lyrics say, "the ocean is a river's goal."

With the back-to-back combination of 'Nightswimming' and 'Find The River,' *Automatic For The People* effectively fades out with a wistful and bittersweet ending. "I wanted the record to end with 'Man On The Moon,'" Buck admitted to Ira Robbins in *Pulse*. "Now it ends with two slow songs, ending songs. 'Find the River' is kind of—dare I say it?—elegiac. It's a natural end to the record."

f or *Monster*, R.E.M. packed the acoustic instruments away and plugged in to record the hardest rocking album of their career. As a result, the band, which managed to increase in popularity despite a hiatus from touring, hit the road for the first time in five years with the mammoth *Monster* world tour.

"We never like to react to our own work," said Stipe, "but to go on the road with three albums of slow, quiet material would be kind of a snore, so we made a loud record."

The electrified roar of *Monster* caught some listeners off-guard. It was following the release of the relatively tame,

mostly acoustic-based *Out Of Time* and *Automatic For The People* albums that R.E.M. had reached the status of international superstardom, so it would have been fairly easy for those unfamiliar with the band's entire catalog to have mistaken R.E.M. for a quaint folk-rock group. "If they're not familiar with our ways they will be surprised," Stipe said of *Monster*. "But if they have known our music for a while, it fits into place. We've always kind of done this." Berry, who once threatened to quit the band if it recorded another somber acoustic-based album, summed up the *Monster* album by calling it "bold and in your face."

The *Monster*-makers: Bill Berry, Michael Stipe, Peter Buck, and Mike Mills.

R.E.M. started writing material for *Monster* in September 1993. The album was recorded between March and July 1994 at Kingsway Studio in New Orleans, Criteria Recording Studios in Miami (both used on *Automatic*), Crossover Soundstage in Atlanta, Ocean Way Recording in Los Angeles, "and a couple of parking lots," Stipe said. The bulk of the harder-rocking songs were recorded in a pseudo-concert setting at the Crossover Soundstage, which would pave the way for the live approach the band would favor on its next album, *New Adventures In Hi-Fi*. "We were originally scheduled to rehearse about a week," Mills recalled, "but what we were coming up with felt so good, we ended up staying for three weeks." In order to capture those quasi-live recordings, the group had a P.A. system and a 24-track mixing board moved on to the soundstage.

Despite the drastic change in sound, R.E.M. opted to stick with producer Scott Litt for their fifth consecutive effort. Stipe said that changing producers to alter the band's sound would have been a cop-out. "That's the easy way to go about bringing in a new sound or whatever it is that people might be searching for," he said. "The four band members aren't the

Both Stipe and bassist/keyboardist Mills said that *Monster* was one of their most difficult albums to record. "It took about one-eighth of my life," joked Stipe. "It was pretty rough. Like five months. There were a lot of life things happening around us—births and deaths, stuff like that. It was a very intense record." Stipe amused himself during recording downtime by signing on America Online as "Stipey" and fielding questions from fans. "The studio is more of a hurry up and wait than touring. It takes a long time to get all the machines to do what you want them to do. There's ten seconds of inspiration and actually something going on tape that is going to make it on record, and ten hours of tweaking the machines and making the lights blink. So after five months I was looking for a diversion and that was an available one."

Years later, Stipe revealed that the band actually called it quits while making *Monster*. "We broke up," he told Chris Heath in a 1996 interview in *Rolling Stone*. "We reached the point where none of us could speak to each other, and we were in a small room, and we just said, 'Fuck off,' and that was it. We were crazy, making that record. Our eyes were like kaleidoscope whirly things. All of us were nuts."

During the recording process, Buck became the father of twin girls, Zoe and Zelda, and Stipe's sister Lynda gave birth to a child. Mills compared the making of *Monster* to such an experience. "The creative process is also like giving birth, but

MONSTER

easiest people to get along with and Scott is one person who can tolerate all four of us, and us him, without wanting to strangle each other over a number of months. It's a good working relationship," Stipe added. "We can kind of beat each other up and emerge friends. He's an extraordinary producer. We're lucky to have hooked up with him."

The album's title came from Buck. "It is kind of a creepy group of songs," he said. "Also, it's a Steppenwolf album title, which I found out a couple of months after we had the record, so there you go. I think it's our Steppenwolf influence coming to the fore," he quipped.

I can't really presume to know exactly what that's like, but in a way it's like creating this thing out of nowhere," he said. "You never really know what's going to happen until you get into it."

While R.E.M. were recording *Monster*, Stipe also lost two close friends. The first, actor River Phoenix—to whom the album is dedicated—died of a drugs overdose on Halloween night, 1993, at the Viper Room in West Hollywood, California. The second, Nirvana front man Kurt Cobain, took his own life with a shotgun blast to the head in his Seattle home in April 1994 after years of battling with heroin, the pressures of stardom, and personal demons. Stipe has said that he felt a

deep connection with both of the young artists. They reminded him of himself when he was in his early 20s and beginning to grapple with the pains that often accompany stardom.

Still, taken in its entirety, *Monster* isn't a downer, but generally rather upbeat, loud, and raucous. "There were a lot of external factors that sort of put obstacles in the road to making this record," Mills explained, "but even with all that I think it is a very positive record."

"We set out to do that with *Automatic For The People*," Stipe added. "It was going to be a really loud punk rock record, but then it went the other way." Mills said that the loud rock approach utilized on *Monster* was "definitely by design." "I think Peter has put his acoustic instruments away for at least a while," Stipe added. "On this whole record, I think there might be one acoustic guitar on one song." After three albums of playing musical chairs, the band returned to its original instruments, for the most part, on *Monster*.

Nonetheless, the songs on *Monster* generally each have a sound all of their own. "The thing that surprises me is that

---

Monster **was dedicated to Stipe's friend, actor River Phoenix, who died on Halloween night, 1993.**

---

each song is sort of its own little world," said Mills. "When you go from song to song, you go from world to world. We felt like we had really good material to work with, so we wanted to do really strange things with it. We didn't want this [to be] just another R.E.M. record, or to sound in any way similar to things we've done before. With the good tracks we had, we felt like we could take the liberty to do strange things with them." At one point, Buck picked up a Sparklett's bottle, drilled some holes in it, and proceeded to use it as a percussion instrument.

In another example of toying with sound, Stipe's vocals were altered beyond recognition on a number of the *Monster* songs and, once again, his lyrics are close to indecipherable on a few of the tracks. "He's singing more distinctly than he did on the first record or two," Mills confirmed, "but the vocals are mixed in more with the track. That was on purpose. It just seemed natural. It wasn't really like we had to think about it, but as it happened it seemed to fit really well." Mills added that some of the vocals were "recorded through a Walkman, some through a harmonica microphone, and some are just really distorted. We really wanted to mess with

the vocal sounds a lot on this one and make it not so clear, clean, and pristine."

That was just fine with Stipe, who said he has always been most comfortable using his voice as an instrument, rather than communicating in a literal fashion. "I feel the human voice is a really welcome element in music and to the universality that music can have in terms of it being a really emotional kind of cathartic experience. It's something that is more than just a wallpaper to our lives. Unfortunately, when you include language in the human voice, it takes it out of the more universal and puts it into the specific. And I was never very comfortable with that."

To appreciate the full beauty and brutality of *Monster*, Mills had a suggestion for R.E.M. fans. "Play it loud, turn it up and check the headphones too," he said. "It's cool with headphones."

While it may make for an interesting headset listening experience, in retrospect, Buck isn't certain the band hit the mark on *Monster*. "Somewhere in there was the record we had to do," he explained. "It's the only record that we ever made that we actually sat down and thought it out and did what we said we were going to do, and I think it suffers for it a little bit. We wrote more songs, a wider, more diverse group of songs than we ever had for a record. We had 40 or 45 things written that were really good, but we just kind of kept throwing away stuff that didn't fit the rock perspective. I think by limiting ourselves, that's what kind of hurt the record. I really like the record still, but we could have made a record that would have been a little broader based and it would have made a bit more sense."

Monster, R.E.M.'s ninth full album (not including the compilations *Dead Letter Office* and *Eponymous*) came as the band's 15th anniversary approached. Throughout the years, R.E.M. found success, while retaining its artistic integrity and original line-up. "The secret to R.E.M.'s longevity would have to be our extreme love of money and power," Stipe joked. On a more serious note, he added, "We have a great deal of respect and love for each other and we like working together. There has yet to be a real turd in the punch bowl in terms of records we've put out, so it seems whatever we are doing, we're doing it right."

With *Monster,* R.E.M. managed to effectively reinvent itself as an aggressive, hard-rocking unit in preparation for touring. Coming on the heels of two relatively low-key albums, it was a bold and dramatic turnabout that roared.

What's The Frequency, Kenneth?

As *Monster*'s opening track and first single, 'What's The Frequency, Kenneth?' was a clarion call that R.E.M. was indeed ready to rock again. Opening with a Buck guitar riff that sounds anything but jangly, the track's straightforward-ness is miles away from the tempered melodies of the band's previous two album openers—*Automatic For The People*'s 'Drive' and *Out Of Time*'s 'Radio Song.' With 'What's The Frequency, Kenneth?,' *Monster* kicks off with an urgency that is similar to *Document*'s 'Finest Work Song' and *Life's Rich Pageant*'s 'Begin The Begin.'

The video for 'What's The Frequency, Kenneth?,' directed by Peter Care ('Drive' and 'Man On The Moon') also revealed

that R.E.M. had stripped down its approach. The clip—an artfully shot performance piece—marked a major departure from such elaborate *Automatic For The People*-era clips as 'Man On The Moon' and 'Everybody Hurts.' It also effectively debuted R.E.M.'s new look. Stipe, who had favored wearing hats to cover his balding head, had shaven his dome completely clean, while the once bookish-looking Mike Mills now appeared to be the biggest rock star of the bunch, sporting shoulder-length hair and a shimmering rhinestone cowboy suit.

Musically, unlike R.E.M.'s early recordings, Stipe's vocals are prominent in the mix, but at times his lyrics are difficult to

decipher. Perhaps in an effort to make things a bit more clear, the lyrics were included with the single—a rare move for R.E.M., whose albums have never included a full lyric sheet. Yet even with the printed words, they remained for the most part enigmatic. One line, "Richard said, 'Withdrawal in disgust is not the same as apathy,'" is a reference to the independent filmmaker Richard Linklater, acclaimed for the "Gen-X" film *Slacker*. There's also the recurring line, "You wore a shirt of violent green." Stipe wears an olive green star T-shirt in the video clip.

The title 'What's The Frequency, Kenneth?' was inspired by an incident involving Dan Rather, in which the CBS news anchor was accosted by a man on the streets of New York. The assailant, later identified as a convicted killer named William Tager, repeatedly screamed, "What's the frequency, Kenneth?" as he accosted Rather. "It's a little buzz phrase on

The subject of 'What's The Frequency, Kenneth' was "far beyond" CBS news man Dan Rather.

the street or something," Stipe said of the song's title. "It's a song lambasting the media, much like 'S.F.W.' or something like that. It would make sense that I would pick on Dan Rather, although I'm not just picking on him. It's so far beyond him really."

Rather apparently took no offense to the song and even appeared with the band in a comedy bit on CBS-TV's *Late Show With David Letterman*. (R.E.M. made their U.S. network television debut on NBC-TV's *Late Night With David Letterman* in 1983, performing a then-untitled track that would later be known as 'So. Central Rain'). Before going to a commercial break, Letterman announced to *Late Show* band leader Paul Shaffer that he had attended the first of the band's June 1995 Madison Square Garden concerts, where as Letterman put it, "something weird happened." Letterman announced that he had tape of the strange incident. The clip, actually shot on the Letterman set, featured Rather, wearing a suit and a black T-shirt, stiffly leading R.E.M. through 'What's The Frequency, Kenneth?' For Rather, a usually stonefaced talking-head, and R.E.M., sometimes criticized for taking themselves too seriously, the gag showed they both had a sense of humor. It was a win-win situation.

In a subsequent interview with Vic Garbarini in *Musician*, Stipe said, "'Kenneth' is such a joy to sing I don't care what the words are about. I know that they're very well written and they get an idea across to a lot of people." He later elaborated on the theme. "[It's] about people playing into the bullshit about the media drawing lines among young people in this country—that group is about cynicism and this group are idealists. And yes, it's also commenting on how we go about trying to research and analyze things we don't understand, like people younger than ourselves, rather than using your intuition and figuring it out from that end."

While R.E.M.'s medical emergencies made headlines during the *Monster* tour, the string of medical procedures began during the recording of 'What's The Frequency, Kenneth?' "You know how most punk songs speed up?," Buck asked Garbarini in an interview in *Guitar World*. "Well, 'Kenneth' slows down at the end. The truth is Mike slowed down the pace and we all followed, and then I noticed he looked strange. It turned out he had appendicitis and we had to rush him to the hospital. So we never wound up redoing it."

The CD single of the song included live versions of 'Monty Got A Raw Deal,' 'Everybody Hurts,' and 'Man On The Moon.' The three *Automatic For The People* tracks were recorded live on November 19, 1992, at a benefit concert for Greenpeace that was held in Athens, Georgia.

Crush With Eyeliner

If fans first listening to *Monster* thought R.E.M. would drop its hard-rocking swagger after 'What's The Frequency, Kenneth?,' the tremolo-drenched 'Crush With Eyeliner' likely hit them like a slap in the face that confirmed that R.E.M. indeed intended to rock on *Monster*.

Following the death of actor River Phoenix, Stipe said that he didn't write a song for five months. When he finally got over that depression-induced case of writer's block, 'Crush With Eyeliner' was among the first songs he wrote.

Thurston Moore, guitarist for New York noise-rockers Sonic Youth, is featured on backing vocals as a nod to his band's influence. "When I was writing the lyric, I thought I stole it from a Sonic Youth record, so I thought the best way to pay homage to them is to ask Thurston to be on the song," Stipe said. "We've known Sonic Youth for over ten years and it made perfect sense at the time. But in fact, I think I stole it from a Coke commercial."

That wasn't the only confusion about the song. Courtney Love, the singer of Hole and the widow of Nirvana frontman

Love, who has called Stipe the sexiest man in America, may have had a crush on Stipe, who has been known to wear eyeliner, but in subsequent interviews, the singer cleared up any misconceptions about the song. 'Crush With Eyeliner' is actually, in part, a tribute to the New York Dolls, with the inclusion of the title of their song 'Frankenstein,' and also an ode to people assuming different roles in their lives.

Courtney Love and Michael Stipe, left, at the MTV Awards in June 1994.

"I don't think the idea of slipping in and out of different personalities is unique to performers or people who are part of the pop-culture pageant," he told Charles Aaron in an interview for *Spin*. "Everybody does it every day, no matter what their job or life is like."

Perhaps to drive that point home, in the Spike Jonze-directed video for the song, a group of Asian youths are shown assuming rock star poses and mime along with the track while the members of R.E.M. are shown only briefly, looking on.

Buck suggested that the literal meaning behind some of the lyrics, which once again were included with the CD single, shouldn't be given deep thought. "All of Michael's songs are filled with a line or two that seems to be nonsense, just there to fill the space," he said in an interview with Vic Garbarini in *Musician*. "On 'Crush With Eyeliner'... He describes a person as 'kiss breath turpentine.' Well, that doesn't really mean

Sonic Youth's Thurston Moore, right, sang backing vocals on 'Crush With Eyeliner.'

Kurt Cobain, once claimed that the song was written about her. In one of Love's first public appearances following Cobain's suicide, she accompanied Stipe to the *MTV Movie Awards*, held in Los Angeles in June 1994. That night, Mills and Moore performed as members of the *Backbeat* band, the alternative rock supergroup assembled by producer Don Was to recreate the sound of the early Beatles.

anything literally. But the way it's sung, and the particular place in the song he sings it, makes total sense."

The CD single of 'Crush With Eyeliner' included live versions of 'Fall On Me,' 'Me In Honey,' and 'Finest Worksong,' also recorded live during the Greenpeace benefit show. A live version of 'Crush With Eyeliner' recorded in Detroit on June 6, 1995, was released as a promotional single.

King Of Comedy

Along with 'Tongue,' 'King Of Comedy' is perhaps the *Monster* song that sounds the least like any of R.E.M.'s prior work. "Those two just kind of appeared about within the last week of recording, even though we demoed them like a year before," said Buck. "They broadened the record out a little bit."

A robotic sounding vocal track leaves Stipe sounding virtually unrecognizable, while the electronic-like backing track sounds as if it was lifted from a Devo outtake. The sole human-sounding element in the song is a sweet backing vocal provided by Sally Dworski.

"The whole thing was recorded from a toaster—it's all machines," Stipe explained. "It was kind of fun. It only made sense that my vocal should sound like a machine, too. And that was the range I was comfortable in, so that's how we put it down."

Mills further explained how the song was recorded. "It's got some funky vocal treatment and it's the only one we used a computer on," he said. Although the song sounds as if it has a drum machine on it, Mills said that's not the case. "It's live drums," he said. "I play a synthesizer bass pedal run

through a computer, but it's all humanly played." He also credited Litt with playing a large role in assembling the song. Buck has admitted that it's the one song on *Monster* that he "never cared for."

"Content-wise the vocal kind of matches the lyric, which is extremely cynical and coming from kind of an ugly place," added Stipe, who also called the song his "Leonard Cohen rip-off." The barbed-filled music of the veteran poet and songwriter was certainly familiar to R.E.M. The band had recorded a brutal version of his 'First We Take Manhattan' for

> **Michael Stipe has called 'King Of Comedy' his "Leonard Cohen ripoff."**

the Cohen tribute album *I'm Your Fan*, which had been released in 1991.

Following the release of *Monster*, Stipe admitted that 'King Of Comedy' shouldn't be taken as deadly serious as it sounds. "That song is about as tongue in cheek as it could ever be," he told David Fricke in *Rolling Stone*. "I wrote it to be in the most cynical voice possible. I went to cynicism as a device to get the lyrics done. Because I had two days to finish the record."

Initially, the song was about an individual enrolled in an experimental drug research program who becomes obsessed with undeserving media celebrities. "Nice story but it made a shitty song," Stipe added. "I kept the title 'King Of Comedy' because I liked the movie and in the 11th hour, I went, 'Aha cynicism!' But, of course, I'm a commodity. I know that. And I'm fine with it. Really."

Working titles for 'King Of Comedy' included 'Disco Song' and 'Yes, I Am Fucking With You,' but not every lyric in the song is lighthearted. With the lyric "I'm straight, I'm queer, I'm bi," Stipe addressed his ambiguous sexuality in a manner similar to early Prince. "I do think little categories have crept in where it's a bit too easy to say this is straight and this is queer or even this is bisexual," he told Vic Garbarini in *Musician*. "Again, I think where those lines are drawn is way too constrictive."

I Don't Sleep, I Dream

'I Don't Sleep, I Dream' is another song that at least partially explores sexuality, but only a small part of it. As Stipe himself suggested in concert after performing the song. "Sometimes things aren't all they seem," he said. "If you just wanted to skim the surface of that song, you would think it's about a blow job, but actually there's a whole lot more going on there."

Those skimming the surface are most likely to have latched on to the lines "Do you give good head? Am I good in bed?," but the song, as its title suggests, is about dreams, some of which are sexual. "That song's nothing if it's not

---

Both R.E.M. and Gang Of Four borrowed from the work of novelist Joseph Conrad.

---

some sonic version of the dream state," Stipe told Jim Irvin in *Mojo*. In the song, Stipe's character is having his dreams analyzed by a person, either real or imagined.

In a subsequent interview, Stipe further revealed his feelings about attempting to manipulate his dreams. "I'm a little bit trepidatious myself about fucking around with my dream state," he told Vic Garbarini in *Musician*. "People have told me that you can train yourself to enter your dreams, stare at your hand, have a dream within a dream and all this stuff, and maybe that's fine for them. But I don't want to manipulate that."

Dreams are a familiar topic to R.E.M. The band's name, of course, is a abbreviation of rapid eye movement, the stage of sleep that is closely associated with dreaming, in which the eyeballs move jerkily under closed lids. 'Get Up' from *Green* was largely about dreaming and in concert on the *Green* tour Stipe usually prefaced the song 'World Leader Pretend' with an *a cappella* rendition of Gang Of Four's 'We Live As We Dream, Alone.' The band also recorded a cover of the Everly Brothers' 1958 hit 'All I Have To Do Is Dream,' wrongly titled '(All I've Got To Do Is) Dream' for the 1987 documentary *Athens, Ga—Inside/Out*.

Although musically the hypnotic R.E.M. track is quite different from the funky, percussive 1982 song recorded by the British post-punk act Gang Of Four, Stipe admitted that the songs share an inspiration: "I actually lifted it from a Joseph Conrad novel and that's where Gang Of Four got it from."

R.E.M.'s song, which is one of Mills' favorites, begins with a tribal flavored drumbeat—courtesy of Berry—which is embellished by a repetitive guitar figure and touches of piano and organ. Buck said that the song was spawned from a jam session take, with lyrics and melody added by Stipe. It was initially just "a drumbeat and one chord," Buck told Jim Irvin in *Mojo*. "I figured he'd come up with something very amorphous for it and I was really shocked that he had this concise, melodic thing over the top that totally changed the song. He doesn't come up with stuff that I dislike." Stipe

sings the song in a cool detached voice, but by the song's chorus, he's raised his voice to a falsetto, a style used even more blatantly in 'Tongue.'

Rather than finishing with a fade out, 'I Don't Sleep, I Dream' ends abruptly just as the band appears to be heading into a crescendo, a nod perhaps to the "interruption" Stipe is looking for in the song's lyrics. As Stipe told Jim Irvin in *Mojo*, "At the end of the song, it's like somebody dropped a huge book at the end of your bed while you're sleeping, BANG! and you're out of it."

Star 69

If the end of 'I Don't Sleep, I Dream' woke listeners from a sonic dream state, the guitar-frenzied 'Star 69' likely hit them like a bucket of ice water dumped on top of their heads. Again, to new fans, this was a totally different R.E.M., but to those who had collected every B-side and soundtrack cut, this song was completely in character with some of the band's harder rocking material, such as 'Windout' and 'Burning Hell,' which turned up on the odds-and-ends collection *Dead Letter Office*.

What is different from the R.E.M. of old is the song's subject matter. On *Monster*, more so than any of the previous R.E.M. albums, the band had moved into the future. Not only does 'King Of Comedy' sound truly futuristic, but 'Star 69' takes its very name from a then-new technology employed

R.E.M. '94: Michael Stipe, Peter Buck, Bill Berry, and Mike Mills.

by American phone companies that allows people to call back the previous caller by simply dialing "*69." This technology is particularly handy in dealing with prank callers and that's what Stipe has his mind on in the song, with the accusatory chorus, "I know you called."

Not only is the subject in the song a prank caller, but he is also apparently involved in "extortion and arson, petty larceny." Stipe later reveals that the whole episode reads like "some dork *Inside Edition/Hard Copy*," a reference to two sensationalist American tabloid TV shows.

The relatively short, sharp blast of a song, recorded in New Orleans, was initially quite different. Buck said, "We really overwrote it. I had two more pieces than it did on the record, so it was about six minutes long. It was really ungainly, but everyone really liked the chorus and the B-section, the thing right before the chorus. When we went to record it, we said, 'Let's chop everything out.' It had a bridge, we chopped the

bridge out. It had a different chorus, which we chopped out, and we made the B-section the chorus… It was kind of the most immediately direct song, because there was very little to it, it has one little chord sequence that repeats over and over with some kind of chaotic elements to it."

A rarely seen video clip for the track, which was included on the 1995 collection *Parallel*, featured the band performing a frantic version of the song live to the studio track. If the home video camera information that is included on the clip is correct, the footage was shot in Hong Kong on February 5, 1994. In the video, a particularly animated Stipe throws the microphone stand around and leaps around the stage, falling on top of a speaker cabinet one moment and shimmering on top of the monitors at the foot of the stage the next. The clip was directed by Jonathan Dayton and Valerie Faris, whose work with R.E.M. dates back to the band's very first video clip, the rarely seen 'Wolves, Lower.'

Strange Currencies

With a similar feel to 'Everybody Hurts,' and with Stipe singing in his newly discovered "soul voice," 'Strange Currencies' almost didn't make *Monster*.

"Originally we weren't going to put it on the record because it was a little too similar to 'Everybody Hurts,'" Buck said. "It wasn't really in consideration, but then Michael came up with some amazing melody, and it was like 'Gosh, we'll have to kind of follow that through.'" Because of the similarities in rhythm to 'Everybody Hurts,' Buck said the band had to "really mess it around and pull it somewhere different." As a result the chords, the key, and the melody are quite different than those on 'Everybody Hurts.'

The subject matter of the two songs also had very marked differences. While 'Everybody Hurts' was intended to provide comfort for suicidal teenagers, 'Strange Currencies' is an obsessive love song in the vein of the Police's 'Every Breath You Take,' the song that Stipe claimed to be the inspiration for 'Losing My Religion.'

"'Everybody Hurts' is a really direct, straightforward kind of song," Buck explained. "It is exactly what it is. 'Strange Currencies' sounds like a love song, but if you listen to it a couple of times and you think, 'Gosh, does that guy even know the person he's singing about. I think he's a stalker.' If

you see it as a love song, you think it's a cute love song, but if you actually hear the lyrics more than once or twice, it's like, 'Geez, I think he's going to maybe kill the person.' It is very threatening, which is why we kind of mutilated the song with all the feedback and the weird discordancies and the dropouts and stuff."

The haunting chorus of 'Strange Currencies' didn't die with *Monster*. A portion of the central phrase "You will be mine," was turned into a title for another twisted love song, 'Be Mine,' which appears on *New Adventures In Hi-Fi*.

Another development that would be further explored on *New Adventures In Hi-Fi* was Buck's use of the E-Bow, which would serve as part of the title and the musical heart of 'E-Bow The Letter.' Buck used the E-Bow on 'Strange Currencies,' which was recorded in Miami, to give the song that "thing that sounds like violins."

As was the case with all of the singles released from *Monster*, the lyrics of 'Strange Currencies' were provided on the CD packaging for the single.

An artfully shot black-and-white video clip for the song, directed by Mark Romanek, features a band performance intercut with scenes of various unsavory characters. It was included on the 1995 home video release *Parallel*.

Tongue

Along with 'King Of Comedy,' 'Tongue' is perhaps the song on *Monster* that sounds least like R.E.M., as Stipe, singing in a falsetto, is nearly unrecognizable. With its Hammond organ-laced backing track, the song is steeped in the soul tradition, a musical terrain that R.E.M. had rarely ventured into previously.

Again, like 'King Of Comedy,' 'Tongue' was a late addition to *Monster*. "It ended up on the record last minute," Buck said, "and no one really knew where it came from. It was kind of this demo that all of a sudden changed the record."

The move into soul music wasn't completely unexpected. Berry acknowledged that soul music had been an influence on the band, as he and Mills had played soul music in some of their pre-R.E.M. combos in high school. "Yeah, and we grew up in the South, soul was what was going on," Berry

told Jim Irvin in *Mojo*. Berry went on to explain how the song originated. "'Tongue' started out as a weird drum track that we recorded at a place in New Orleans where they have these wild drums, like Indian drums turned sideways. I started playing this beat and Scott rolled the tape...Mike put on this big baseball park organ and then Michael decided to sing falsetto on it. I don't think he wanted to sound like Al Green or Smokey, but it does have that feel."

Stipe, who counted 'Tongue' among his favorite tracks on the album, acknowledged that his voice was "pretty high,"

It was during a performance of 'Tongue' that Bill Berry first became seriously ill.

---

but initially he wouldn't give away what his intent was. "I was kind of going for something there and I hope that I achieved it. Time will tell, I guess. I'm not really willing to give that away yet."

Stipe was, however, quick to scoff at any comparisons with U2's Bono, who sang in a similar-sounding falsetto on 'Lemon,' a track from the 1992 album *Zooropa*. "Oh God," Stipe said, "falsetto's pretty common isn't it?"

In a later interview, Stipe came clean about his intentions. "I was trying to sing like a girl," he told Vic Garbarini in *Musician*. "If Michael Hutchence and Roland Gift from Fine Young Cannibals can sing like that, why can't I?"

On the *Monster* tour, Stipe further explained the song's intent while introducing the song. "This song goes out to all the women in the audience," he said. "This is ladies' choice. Gentlemen stick your fingers in your ears." The song was performed with a disco ball spinning above the stage, adding the feel of roller-rink nostalgia.

However, 'Tongue' took on a different meaning 27 dates into the *Monster* World Tour. During a performance of the song on March 1, 1995, Berry was forced to leave the stage due to a severe headache. The band completed its set with Joey Peters, from the opening act Grant Lee Buffalo, on drums. When Berry's condition worsened he was rushed to the hospital where he underwent brain surgery to repair two ruptured blood vessels. The tour resumed on May 15, 1995, at the Shoreline Amphitheater in Mountain View, California. On subsequent dates Berry admitted that it gave him an eerie feeling every time the band performed 'Tongue.'

Another footnote about Berry's life-threatening aneurysms: On the special edition of *Monster*, in a strange and perhaps prophetic coincidence, an illustration of a cartoon character called Migraine Boy was superimposed on a close-up of Berry's face.

Bang And Blame

As the title suggests, 'Bang And Blame' is another nasty relationship song. Stipe described it as a song "about domestic violence." One journalist took it a step further, theorizing that it may have been about the O.J. Simpson case. "It was written before that," Buck explained. "The character that would be singing that song isn't too dissimilar. I don't get the feeling he's a really nice guy. But people find O.J. everywhere. He's hiding in closets all over the world."

Despite its brutal subject, there are parts of the song, sung by Stipe with a certain amount of resignation in his voice, that are actually pretty and have a reggae-style feel. "It has a verse that could have fit on any R.E.M. record and it could have gone real pretty and drifty, but since the way we were going, we added the huge guitars and the noise and made it less of an R.E.M. song," Buck said. "I kind of like the way that halfway through, it doesn't change tempo or even the beat much, this layer of sound comes in and swamps it and it turns into something else."

The ugliness of the song's topic is driven home with the accusing chorus that is rocked by Buck's crunching guitar. Five background vocalists, including Stipe's sister, Lynda, who was formerly a member of the bands Oh-OK and Hetch Hetchy, add color to the song.

After the conclusion of 'Bang And Blame,' R.E.M. once again saw it fit to include one of its now trademark brief untitled instrumental interludes.

I Took Your Name

This tremolo-drenched rocker was the first song written for *Monster*, and it signaled the band's new direction. "Had I used the same voice that I used on 'Everybody Hurts' it would have sounded really dumb," Stipe told Jim Irvin in *Mojo*. Perhaps as a means to achieve the different vocal sound, Stipe's vocals on the track were recorded through a Walkman, while some of the backing vocals were recorded over the telephone.

The main riff for the song, which alternated with 'What's The Frequency, Kenneth?' as the opening song for performances on the *Monster* tour, was penned by Berry.

Although it sounds as if the guitars on this song and the other *Monster* rockers are compiled from several overdubbed tracks, Mills said that this was not the case. "Most are just one guitar," he explained. "There aren't that many walls of guitar. It is a wall of guitar noise, but it is usually only one guitar making all that noise."

Lyrically, Stipe assumes the role of some sort of psychotic character who has stolen someone's identity in a story that reads like the plot of a science fiction movie. At one point, he wryly sings, "I wanna be Iggy Pop," in a nod to the artist and his late-1960s combo, the Stooges. One of the group's best-known songs is 'I Wanna Be Your Dog.' R.E.M. also recorded a version of the 1979 Iggy Pop song 'Funtime,' which it learned from watching a video of Pop's appearance on *The Dinah Shore Show*. The studio version was released as the B-side to 'Get Up.' A live version appeared on the CD single of 'Strange Currencies.' As Stipe told Jim Irvin in *Mojo*, "a lot of [*Monster*] is referring back to Iggy and The Stooges and Patti Smith and Television, and stuff like that."

This track again has Stipe assuming the role of a psychotic character. "More than most of our records, Michael did tend to sing in character on *Monster*," Buck explained. "The characters are all kind of really confused people."

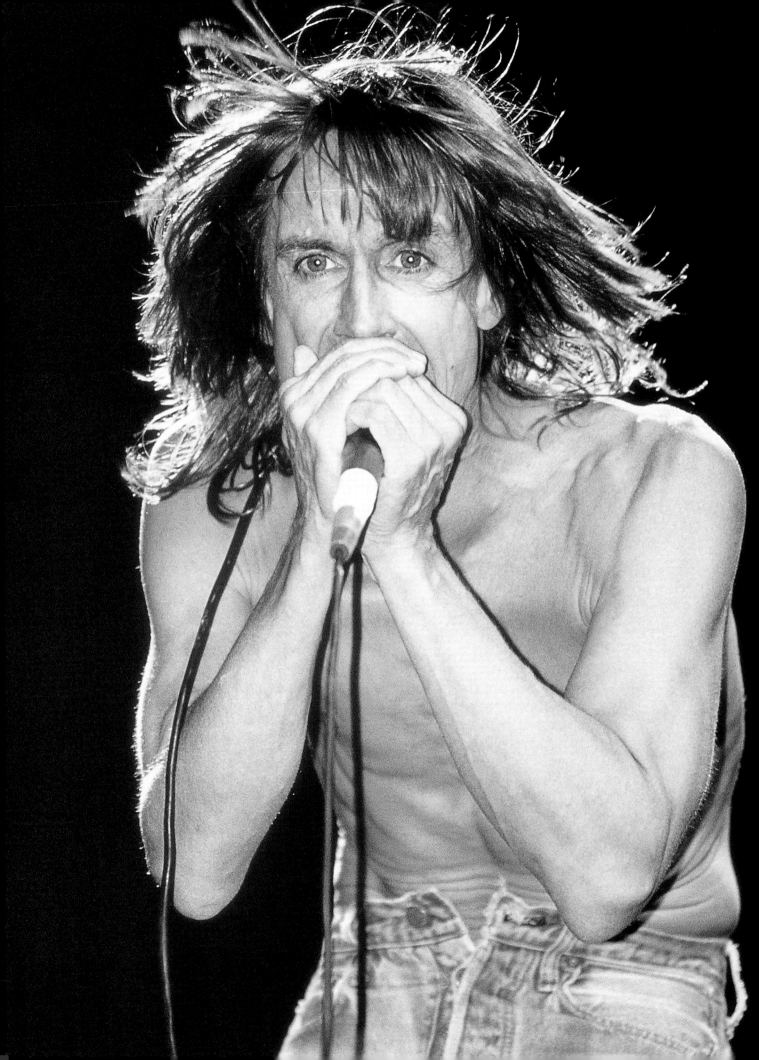

Let Me In

Following the suicide of Nirvana frontman Kurt Cobain in April 1994, Stipe released a statement saying the two had planned to collaborate on a project. "In the last few weeks I was talking to Kurt a lot," the statement said. "We had a musical project in the works, but nothing was recorded. He loved [his wife] Courtney and [daughter] Frances Bean, and he loved Krist [Novoselic] and Dave [Grohl] and Nirvana. He really loved those guys. His death is a profound loss and I just don't think I can say anything else right now."

Stipe wanted to be Iggy Pop, left, in the song 'I Took Your Name.'"

Kurt Cobain, right. 'Let Me In' was written "to Kurt, for Kurt, and about Kurt." Stipe said.

Cobain had professed his admiration of R.E.M. in a *Rolling Stone* interview. "God, they're the greatest. They've dealt with their success like saints, and they keep delivering great music."

More than a year later, on the eve of *Monster*'s release, Stipe elaborated on his relationship with Cobain. "The whole thing was via telephone," he said. "He was coming to Atlanta and I knew basically what was going on, so I was trying to offer a diversion to where he was at. He was recording stuff the whole time I was talking to him, about a week-and-a-half before he disappeared. He talked a great deal about what he wanted it to sound like. As far as I know there's tapes somewhere, but I don't know where they are. He was working in the basement on some stuff."

"I'm certain that if Nirvana had made their next record, it would have been a very quiet, very introspective, very beautiful acoustic record," Stipe added. "That's totally where his head was at."

Monster contains a printed dedication to actor River Phoenix, but 'Let Me In' was dedicated to Cobain. "I wrote that to Kurt, for Kurt, and about him," Stipe said. "I had just

written an entire record [*Automatic For The People*] about death, mortality, and passage and really didn't want to repeat myself on this record. I was really working against anything having to do with those topics. His death profoundly affected me. I couldn't really ignore it much longer." Although Cobain is not mentioned by name in the song, Stipe said, "I think people will be able to figure it out."

The haunting track pits Stipe's vocals against a wall of reverb guitar, organ, and tambourine, but no drums. "It's just

one guitar and it is mostly the reverb effect of the guitar that you are hearing," Mills explained. "The actual guitar is turned down and the reverb effect is turned way up. There's a little bit of keyboard and a little bit of tambourine, that's all there is." The combination gave the song a chilling effect.

Mike Mills, playing his customary bass, donned one of Kurt Cobain's guitars during performances of 'Let Me In.'

Cobain had readily praised R.E.M. in interviews, noting that the band had been able to achieve huge mainstream success without sacrificing their integrity. With the mutual respect and Buck's move to the same Seattle neighborhood as Cobain, R.E.M. and the Nirvana camp became close.

Buck attended Cobain's funeral and Stipe comforted his widow, Courtney Love, accompanying her to the *MTV Movie Awards*. In recognition of their support, Love presented the band with a lime green Fender guitar designed by Cobain.

R.E.M. put the guitar, which had to be restrung for a right-handed player, to good use during the *Monster* tour, appropriately on 'Let Me In.' For live performances of the song, the members of R.E.M. switched instruments—a practice they first experimented with during the *Green* tour.

Bassist Mills played Cobain's guitar, drummer Berry kept time on a tambourine, while guitarist Peter Buck played keyboards.

With the track's spotlight on Stipe's plea for Cobain "to let him in," and the ceremonious strumming of Cobain's guitar, it was one of the tour's more moving performances. 'Let Me In' is also one of the most heartfelt songs on the album, as Stipe eschews mystery in favor of focusing on the heart of the matter. Cobain undoubtedly would have approved.

Circus Envy

'Circus Envy' is another *Monster* rocker about emotional abuse with "messed-up" vocals. There is also plenty of distortion on the guitar and bass. "It's total fuzz bass all the way through," Mills explained.

The rave-up rocker was developed out of a jam session. "It's got two chords at the verse and another couple at the chorus, although the bridge is really complicated, surprisingly enough," Buck said. "Usually when you are just kind of making songs up the bridge is the simplest part. Mike had his fuzz bass on, so there is all that kind of distorted noise. We tried to capture it as rough as possible. We only played it a couple of times. There's not much on it, I think there's one extra guitar overdub and a vocal overdub."

Stipe commented on the track's rawness to Jim Irvin in *Mojo*. "The basic part of 'Circus Envy' is really fucked up, totally fucked up. Prior to this record that has happened, but it hasn't been profiled in the same way. Ultimately it's down to the mix, but with that stuff down you realized that it didn't need all the shit on top of it."

In its lyrics, the song repeatedly uses the word "*Monster*."

You

The album-closer, 'You,' was recorded early in the *Monster* sessions at Crossover Soundstage in Atlanta. "That was recorded while we were actually doing demos on an eight-track, so the drums are in mono, but no one noticed," Buck explained. "We had four or five mics on the drums, bounced to one channel. We had two bass lines, a guitar line, and a vocal line. We didn't even have a finished vocal, so we just kind of cut the track. We were going to re-record it, but the track was just really great, and a lot of the guitar lines I had never played before. We were just kind of playing and not knowing it was being recorded. We just decided, 'This is the take, we'll just slip it in and not worry so much about the aspect of the drums being on one channel.'"

The ominous-sounding song features a guitar riff that is reminiscent of the Doors' 'The End,' a comparison that Buck doesn't see as accurate. "I heard the Doors a lot in my life. I couldn't say they were a real influence," he said. "And Michael, I don't know. I don't think he ever listened to the Doors. I've read poetry in high school and after. When you read real poetry, you tend to realize that rock poetry isn't really poetry, so you tend to lose a lot of the interest in some of the things that people think is real poetic. But I really like the Doors' rock stuff a lot."

"If it is in there, it's way in the background," he added. "I hear all kinds of stuff in there. There's some Beatles-type harmonies and I know that kind of modal guitar line is some Richard Thompson-derived thing. It all gets shuffled together and comes out like some weird pop song."

The band acknowledged its debt to the former leader of Fairport Convention by recording 'Wall Of Death' for the 1994 Thompson tribute album *Beat The Retreat*.

On 'You,' some of the background vocals were recorded into a Walkman. The song is one of the more discomforting tracks on *Monster*, particularly the way in which Stipe sings the word "you" in a slightly off-key and shrill manner that recalls *Green*'s 'The Wrong Child.' However, after repeated listenings, the song does grow on you. As Mills explained, "If you give them more listens, they sort of suck you in."

At nearly five minutes in length, 'You' is one of the longest songs in the R.E.M. catalog and points in the direction of the lengthier compositions that the band would explore further on *New Adventures In Hi-Fi*.

With rumors about a band break-up beginning to circulate in the British press, R.E.M. quelled the gossip by signing a new five-album contract with Warner Bros. that was reported to have been worth $80 million. They also delivered what the band's members, label representatives, and insiders called the finest album of R.E.M.'s career.

New Adventures In Hi-Fi, the band's fifth album for Warner Bros., evolved out of the 1995 *Monster* tour. It was a tour that took its toll on the band's members, with only Buck surviving with his health unimpaired.

The $80-million-dollar men: Mike Mills, Bill Berry, Michael Stipe, and Peter Buck.

First, on March 1, 1995, Berry suffered a brain aneurysm in Lausanne, Switzerland. In July, after the tour had resumed, Mills became ill in Cologne, Germany, and had to be operated on for an adhesion in his abdominal tract—the result of a development of scar tissue from the appendectomy he underwent in 1994 during the recording of *Monster*. The scar tissue had caused part of his intestine to grow on to the lining of his stomach. After the tour had resumed once again, Stipe went under the knife for a hernia. The singer may have had a premonition of what was to come. In an interview prior to the release of *Monster*, he joked that touring was "a pain in the ass."

In between hospital visits, however, the band managed to complete the tour and record more than 110 concerts and more than 100 hours of material which had been road-tested during soundchecks. "Bill and I came up with this idea while doing interviews. We were going to write 12 new songs, record them on the road, and put it out a week later. It would be all-new live songs with applause," Buck said.

However, the band—supported on tour by auxiliary members Nathan December and Scott McCaughey—opted for another route. Virtually every show was recorded, but it was decided to go with live recordings from dates in Charleston, Boston, Detroit, and Phoenix, as well as material recorded during soundchecks in Atlanta, Memphis, Philadelphia, and Orlando. The band also checked into Bad

Animals Studio in Seattle to write additional material, add overdubs, and mix. "We ended up with about seven finished songs and 12 unfinished ones," Buck added. "By the end of the tour, we felt really creative and good about the work we had done, so the idea was, 'Let's go to the studio as soon as possible and let's capture the craziness, the dislocation, and weird scenes of the tour,' but without writing, 'We're an American band, come to party down in your hotel room,' because Grand Funk did that, and there will never be another song as good as 'We're An American Band' for what it was."

New Adventures In Hi-Fi isn't Grand Funk; rather, it's classic R.E.M. The album lives up to Mills' comparison with early albums, "a combination of *Monster* and *Automatic For The People*," capturing the hard-rocking swagger of the former, as well as some of the mellow and introspective qualities of the latter. It also adds some "new adventures" of its own.

There were also outside influences. Buck acknowledged similarities to such classic road albums as Jackson Browne's *Running On Empty* and Neil Young's *Time Fades Away*, but noted that the band had also turned to its contemporaries. "What was kind of an inspiration to us was to see Pearl Jam go out and do like a week of shows and then stay in the last town of the tour and record all the things they jammed on at soundcheck," he said. "We wanted to capture that spontaneity. We're a really good live band, but never really do capture that in the studio. The feeling was that if we can capture ourselves doing what we do live, it would be a great thing to work with."

There was also another factor. "It was partly motivated by laziness," admitted Mills. "If we could do as much as possible on the road, that's stuff we didn't have to do in the studio. That's one reason why this album was so easy to make." During a radio interview, Stipe added that he "really dug the idea of being able to somehow cross-graph the live stuff with the studio stuff and make it so you couldn't tell what was live and what wasn't."

Initially, even some members of the R.E.M. camp were skeptical that such a concept would work. "We brought up the idea that we were going to take an 8-track machine on the road and that was going to be the next record, and I don't

According to the *Los Angeles Times*, Holt was dismissed after allegedly sexually harassing an employee at the band's home office in Athens, Georgia. When asked about Holt, Downs, the band's longtime attorney, said, "We don't want to talk about it and, in fact, we have agreed in a settlement not to have any comment other than our official comment." The lawyer then proceeded to pull out a laminated card from his wallet and quickly read an official statement: "R.E.M. and Jefferson Holt have terminated their relationship by mutual agreement. The reasons for this decision are private and confidential, and no further discussions in these matters will be made by any of the parties."

NEW ADVENTURES IN HI-FI

think anyone was real positive about it," Buck said. "You should have seen their faces. Bertis [Downs] would kind of roll his eyes, but about halfway through the tour, he said, 'These are great songs.'"

Writing the new material on the road and gradually introducing it during the live set also proved to be a great morale booster throughout the tour. "The crew gets really tired of the same set every night… but we were putting in new songs and the crew started showing up at soundcheck and cheering us on," Buck explained. "Overall, it was a really great, positive experience."

The release of *New Adventures In Hi-Fi* came at a crossroads of sorts for R.E.M. The band had recently parted company with longtime manager Jefferson Holt, who along with Downs was often listed as a member of R.E.M. in the liner notes of the band's albums.

When Downs said that the band "has been through a lot of adversity," he may not have been talking only about the mishaps on the road. However, things were generally upbeat in the R.E.M. camp, despite a fatiguing week of work in Los Angeles in late July 1996, about two months before the album's release. During that one week, the band taped videos for the album's first two singles, posed for photo shoots, and conducted numerous interviews with the American and international music press.

Although Mills was fatigued from a night of partying, Buck was optimistic. Prior to the release of *New Adventures In Hi-Fi*, R.E.M.'s previous three albums had sold nearly 10 million units combined in the U.S. alone, making the band one of the hottest free agents on the market.

There had been much speculation about who R.E.M. would sign with. Candidates included DreamWorks, the new

label spearheaded by Warner Bros. veterans Mo Ostin and Lenny Waronker, who were instrumental in bringing the band to Warner Bros. in the late 1980s. Another possibility was Outpost, a new Geffen-distributed label, run by longtime R.E.M. producer Scott Litt, former Smashing Pumpkins manager Andy Gershon, and ex-Virgin A&R executive Mark Williams. Sony was also said to be interested, but it was Warner Bros. that won the prize.

In what was seen as a major coup for the label, R.E.M were signed for a second five-album worldwide deal, this time reportedly worth $80 million. The announcement was made August 24, 1996 at the WEA convention in Anaheim, California, to a roomful of cheering Warner Bros. employees.

"When we made the announcement, people—and a lot of them—actually broke down and cried," said Warner Bros. U.S. chairman Russ Thyret. "For the first two days that I was talking about it, I actually got choked up, because I was so happy."

Steven Baker, Warner Bros. U.S. president, called the signing a "pivotal" move for the label. "Making the deal and the thought of continuing to work with R.E.M. is the greatest thing in the world," he said. The news of the deal came just 17 days before the release of *New Adventures In Hi-Fi*, proving to the world that it was not the end of R.E.M. as we knew it.

Prior to the signing of the new deal, the band greeted reports of its demise as a minor annoyance. The talk stemmed from its split with Holt and the fact that in 1986, when Berry or Buck—no one can remember which one—was asked when the band would break up, one predicted it would dissolve on December 31, 1999.

R.E.M. and long-time manager Jefferson Holt, left, parted company amid scandalous allegations.

"The thought that the band would have planned that far ahead for anything is laughable, but now it's being reported as news," said Downs at the time. "We could start a pool about when that day would be, but at this point they are doing what some people consider their best work, and they are probably better friends than they ever have been as individuals." Explained Buck, "Either Bill or I said it, but the point is that breaking up is usually beyond your control. It was just a glib little answer."

Since the band wasn't touring, the label made use of the feature-length *Road Movie*, which was released on home video and laserdisc on October 1, 1996, as a marketing tool. Although the near-simultaneously released album and film share some song titles, this was by no means R.E.M.'s *Rattle And Hum*. The 90-minute film, directed by Peter Care, documented the three final nights of the *Monster* tour. In the film, the band performs 'The Wake-Up Bomb' and 'Undertow' from the new album, as well as other favorites.

Just prior to the album's release, Buck called *New Adventures In Hi-Fi* his favorite R.E.M. album. "I think prior to this, my favorite record was *Automatic*," he said. "They're pretty much equal. *Automatic* sustains a mood better, it is kind of a moody one-piece album, but the songs are a lot better on this one, and it covers a lot of ground. It was more successful than I thought it would be."

The album's title is "a little tongue-in-cheek," Buck admitted. "We all like those '50s hi-fi demonstration records. It was a camp thing in the late '70s. The B-52's and a lot of our friends collected them." It was also a bit ironic. Buck once jokingly said that the *New Adventures In Hi-Fi* was "a new phase R.E.M. album… Using only the latest eight-track technology." Yet there was also some truth to the album's title. While Buck said the album "is kind of a sampler of all the things we have accomplished in the past," it also included "a bunch of things we haven't really approached before." Potential titles for the album included *R.E.M.'s Own Thing*, *Revolution Of Our Minds*, *In Stereo*, *West*, and *Low Desert*.

As Buck commented in the liner notes of a limited-edition version of the album, "The songs sound substantially as they did at the soundcheck in Ames, Iowa. And if the soundcheck in Ames, Iowa, seems like a strange thing to emulate, I guess you just had to be there. With this record, you are."

The R.E.M. faithful flocked to record stores so they too could "be there," but in an upset on the U.S. charts, *New Adventures In Hi-Fi* only managed to debut and peak at No. 2 on the *Billboard* 200, unable to surpass the sales of the reunited New Edition's *Home Again*. In other parts of the world, however, R.E.M. came out on top. The album hit the No. 1 spot in 15 countries, including Australia, Austria, Belgium, Canada, Denmark, Finland, Holland, Greece, Ireland, New Zealand, Norway, Sweden, Switzerland, the U.K., and Germany. With *New Adventures In Hi-Fi*, R.E.M. took the show on the road and fans all over the world were delighted to go along for the ride.

How The West Was Won And Where It Got Us

From the opening slow-jam funk drum beats, groan of a synthesizer, and squawk of an "Ennio" whistle to its off-kilter piano lines, 'How The West Was Won And Where It Got Us' is the one track that best lives up to the *New Adventures In Hi-Fi* title, as it doesn't sound quite like anything R.E.M. had ever recorded before. Along with 'Drive' from *Automatic For The People*, it stands as one of the most subdued album-openers in the band's catalog.

The song was one of four on the album that were recorded at Bad Animals Studio in Seattle, following the completion of the *Monster* tour. The track originated from an in-studio jam and shows influences from the British trip-hop movement, a musical style that has never been associated with R.E.M.

"It was written while we were in the studio mixing the rest of the record," Buck explained. Mills recalls that the song came together quickly in the studio. "I was sitting down at the piano goofing off and Bill started playing that drum beat. I started playing those chords, and boom, there was a song."

For Three Men The Civil War Wasn't Hell. It Was Practice!

CLINT EASTWOOD in ""THE GOOD, THE BAD AND THE UGLY""

co-starring LEE VAN CLEEF also starring ELI WALLACH in the role of Tuco ALDO GIUFFRE and with MARIO BREGA SERGIO LEONE

Screenplay by AGE-SCARPELLI, LUCIANO VINCENZONI and SERGIO LEONE   Directed by SERGIO LEONE   Music by ENNIO MORRICONE
Produced by ALBERTO GRIMALDI FOR P.E.A.—Produzioni Europee Associate, Rome
Re-released thru   Copyright © 1980 United Artists Corporation. All rights reserved.   TECHNISCOPE® TECHNICOLOR®
United Artists   A Transamerica Company

"THE GOOD THE BAD AND THE UGLY" INT'L 1 SHEET

Ennio Morricone inspired the sound of 'How The West Was Won And Where It Got Us.'

That kind of spontaneous combustion showed that R.E.M., some 16 years into its career, hadn't lost the chemistry that created such earlier classics as 'Radio Free Europe' in part of an afternoon. "It's real exciting to me because it reminds us that even at this stage in our career we can sit down and have this really serendipitous thing just occur," Mills added during a radio interview. "Through no planning or real effort, all of a sudden we had one of our favorite songs on the record."

"It was the most spontaneous thing we have ever done," Buck added. "From the time we started playing the little riff, to the time we finished recording it, it was about five hours." In fact, the song was recorded the third time it was played in its entirety.

On the track, Buck plays bass, guitar, mandolin, and a Greek stringed instrument called a bouzouki. "I doubled it with the guitars," Buck said of the latter instrument. "It's supposed to sound Ennio Morricone-ish," referring to the Italian soundtrack composer known for his scores for Spaghetti Westerns. Morricone is also referred to in the credits. Besides playing his usual drums and percussion, Berry is also credited with the "Ennio" whistle. Mills and Stipe both play synthesizer. "Mike and I played the keyboard parts at the same time, on the same keyboard, in one take," Stipe revealed in a radio interview.

It was Mills' piano work that is perhaps the song's most striking element. "I was just trying to think Thelonious Monk—not that I have any idea how to play like Thelonious Monk," Mills told Bobbie Ann Mason. Others spotted another influence. "I listened to 'Aladdin Sane' about a month ago and that piano solo came on and I went, 'Oh my God.' I bet that was kind of in the back of my head too, that whole deconstruct-the-song-for-16-bars thing," Mills told Tom Doyle in Q magazine, referring to the title track of David Bowie's 1973 album.

Lyrically, the song plays on the title of the classic 1963 film that starred Gregory Peck, Henry Fonda, James Stewart, and Debbie Reynolds, and stands as a warning about the consequences of environmentally damaging technological progress. Stipe's protagonist notes that a canary trapped in a uranium mine has died, his tears run dry, and he watches "the decline from a hazy distance."

All that said, the song was tentatively titled 'Hail, Grant,' a possible reference to Grant Lee Buffalo or the band's singer-guitarist Grant Lee Phillips. The Los Angeles-based trio opened several concerts on the Monster World Tour. On one date, while thanking the band for its opening set, Stipe let the audience know how much he liked them. "I think they are the finest group of three men in the entire world," he said.

The Wake-Up Bomb

Anyone lulled into thinking that New Adventures In Hi-Fi would be another Automatic For The People-like somber-fest by the hypnotic 'How The West Was Won And Where It Got Us,' was likely blown away when 'The Wake-Up Bomb' exploded in their face. What Mills called "a big, loud, stupid rock song" certainly wouldn't have been out of place on Monster alongside such stomping rockers as 'What's The Frequency, Kenneth?' or 'Star 69.'

"I can see that," Buck agreed. "It fit well with this record, because it captures some things in the live performance aspect. That would have definitely bumped a few things off Monster if we would of had it written then." The song, which features a guitar break reminiscent of 'Orange Crush,' was written in May 1995, performed frequently during the Monster tour dates, and is included on the Road Movie home video.

Fans also got a preview of the song on television a year before the release of New Adventures In Hi-Fi when the band, going against the standard practice of playing a song off the current album to spur sales, performed 'The Wake-Up Bomb' on the 1995 MTV Music Video Awards, checking in with one of the evening's most inspired performances even though it was with a song that most of the world had never heard.

The version on New Adventures was recorded on November 12, 1995, in Charleston, South Carolina, and captures all the piss and vinegar of a live recording. Supplemental touring guitarist Nathan December is featured

on second guitar. Mills played bass in concert and subsequently overdubbed some organ parts on the track, but it's Stipe's swaggering, pissed-off vocal that makes 'The Wake-Up Bomb' detonate.

Thematically, "it was kind of about the glam-rock scene," Buck said. "Michael was kind of looking at the whole 'Dress like we do' [scene] when we were teenagers. It's kind of a joyous pop song, too." In what has become a new Stipe trademark, the song makes reference to such rock acts as T. Rex and Queen, just as 'I Took Your Name' from Monster mentioned Iggy Pop. At least one British journalist took the mention of the word "supersonic" as a dig at Britpop darlings Oasis. "The word 'supersonic' has been around a lot longer than either of us," Mills said to Des Burkinshaw in Mojo. "Sorry Liam, Noel, it's not about you—no offense."

In the lyrics, Stipe also teasingly toys with such clichés as writing the Great American novel and teaching "the world to sing by the age of 21." It doesn't really make sense to attempt to interpret Stipe's claims as autobiographical, especially since they are coupled with boasts about having to "knock a few buildings over" and having "the neutron bomb." Also, this is a songwriter who doesn't like to include lyrics sheets with albums, let alone publish his writing in a novel. Additionally, the singer was born John Michael Stipe in Decatur, Georgia, on January 4, 1960. He was 21 when the band made its recording debut with the 'Radio Free Europe'

In 'The Wake-Up Bomb,' R.E.M. evoked memories of T. Rex and getting drunk and listening to Queen.

Hib-Tone single and the world wasn't singing along—at least not yet. Then again, the line about teaching the world to sing could have seeped into Stipe's consciousness via the Coca-Cola commercial that featured 'I'd Like To Teach The World To Sing (In Perfect Harmony).' The song was a hit single in America by the New Seekers and the Hillside Singers in 1972.

In fact, the year 1973 is mentioned in 'The Wake-Up Bomb.' It wouldn't have been the first time that Stipe was influenced by a soda pop advert. He claimed that the "real thing" line in 'Crush With Eyeliner' was also inspired by a Coke commercial.

New Test Leper

With your head ringing from 'The Wake-Up Bomb,' *New Adventures* takes a turn with what sounds like a mellow, almost lullaby-type, folk tune—until you catch on to the lyrics of this song, which Stipe has called one of his favorites.

"It's about a person on a talk show," revealed Buck. Stipe was inspired to write the song after catching an exploitative TV talk show on the road. "It's kind of a heartfelt commentary on it," Buck added. In the song, a talkshow guest who openly questions his belief in Jesus, but admires some of his philosophies, is mocked by a studio audience, and cut off by the show's host and numerous commercial breaks before having a chance to tell his story.

To some, the opening lyric about the protagonist's lack of faith in Christ was controversial. "…Are people going to think Michael's talking about himself not liking Jesus?," Mills asked Tom Doyle of *Q* magazine. "I don't think that people just take us that seriously. It's not like we're tearing up a picture of the pope on TV."

Musically, "it's kind of a weird folk-rock thing with surf guitar," Buck explained. For the song, written during the *Monster* tour, the band returned to its core line-up, with Mills once again handling bass and organ. The version, cut at Bad Animals Studio in Seattle, with Buck playing electric guitar, was chosen for the album. "I love that song," Mills has said. "It has a guitar through a Leslie [rotary speaker], which is a real cool sound." An acoustic version, recorded for MTV with acoustic guitar and Hammond organ, turned up as a B-side on the 'Bittersweet Me' single.

Undertow

This song is another turn on the road of *New Adventures*, as the sweet folk-rock of 'New Test Leper' is replaced by a flood of tribal drumbeats and feedback. 'Undertow,' at least thematically, is a return to the "water" songs of *Reckoning*. "Whether it is literally or metaphorically, it's about someone drowning," Buck explained. "Maybe Michael said the guy is going down in the water for the last time. Being on tour seems like a drowning situation sometimes." And 'Undertow' was a tour staple, written in Athens while Berry was recuperating from his brain surgery and the band was preparing to return to the road. "We played that almost the whole year," Buck said. "We started playing it in May and played it through Christmas."

The urgent, throbbing take that R.E.M. chose to include on *New Adventures In Hi-Fi* was recorded live at a concert in Boston during a three-night stand in the middle of June 1995. The song was not only included in *Road Movie*, but also appeared as a B-side on the 'Bittersweet Me' single. Also heard on the recording is additional guitar firepower from Nathan December, and Scott McCaughey of the Seattle-band the Young Fresh Fellows playing an Arp Odyssey keyboard. Buck describes the antiquated synthesizer as a "white noise generator," and admitted that the distorted sound of the song was inspired by veteran New York noise-mongers Sonic Youth, who opened the May 1995 dates of the *Monster* tour.

E-Bow The Letter

As the title suggests, this song features Buck playing guitar with an E-Bow. The lyrics were inspired by a letter Stipe wrote in the middle of the night on the tour bus, but never sent. 'E-Bow The Letter' is of primary importance because it features the first recorded collaboration between R.E.M. and punk godmother Patti Smith, whose mid-'70s material was a tremendous inspiration to both Stipe and Buck.

"Patti Smith singing on something that I helped write was just amazing to me. She changed my life in a real, literal way in 1976 when I saw her play live," Buck said. "She changed my perception of what music was. It was just an amazing experience having her in a room singing a song I wrote."

Stipe first became aware of Smith after picking up the November 1975 issue of *Creem* magazine that someone had left under a chair in study hall. "I remember it had a picture of Patti Smith and she was terrifying looking," he told David Fricke of *Rolling Stone*. "She looked like Morticia Addams." Nonetheless, Stipe found her inspiring. "I read in that [magazine] an interview with Patti Smith, and I thought, 'If she can sing, I can sing.' No one's ever really tied in how much I've lifted from her as a performer."

In fact, when R.E.M. included 'So You Want To Be (A Rock'N'Roll Star' and 'Gloria' in their early live sets, it wasn't likely a nod to the original performers—the Byrds and Them, respectively—but to Smith, who recorded covers of both songs and often performed them live.

'E-Bow The Letter,' like *Out Of Time*'s 'Country Feedback,' is another one of Stipe's "vomit songs," meaning that he just spewed it out. "I think it's one of the best things I've ever written," Stipe told Chris Heath in *Rolling Stone*. "I think it plumbs something inside of me… I wanted this record to have heart. And that song maybe comes as close as anything on the record to being really real."

The lyrical phrase "aluminum tastes like fear" left some wondering if Stipe had just thrown in a nonsense lyric because he liked the way it sounded, but Buck told Heath that it made sense to him. "Fear is adrenaline, and adrenaline has several byproducts, one of which is adrenochrome. Does Michael know that? Probably not."

Stipe may not have known the science, but he does know the taste. "Have you ever been really afraid?," Stipe asked Heath. "You get a taste in your mouth—it tastes like chewing on aluminum foil. Adrenaline tastes like aluminum, and when you're really afraid, you taste it in your mouth."

The E-bow was a relatively unused part of Buck's arsenal. "I've never used it a lot," he said. "In the early '80s it was kind of typecast as an art-rock-type thing, so I was kind of like, 'I don't want to use anything like that.'" However, Buck reconsidered, and the device gives his guitar an atmospheric sound that sets the tone of the folk-rock dirge. "It's actually really evocative," Buck said of the E-Bow. "It gives you something that doesn't sound much like a guitar, but fills the space in a cello-ish way."

Also adding to the melancholy atmosphere of the song is the contrast of Stipe's spoken-sung vocals, Smith's plaintive singing, Buck's electric sitar licks, and Mills's work on organ, Moog synthesizer, and mellotron. "The mellotron is such a great instrument," Mills said. "It's got such distinctive sound, but you have to be careful not to use it too much. It brings a lot to the song, and helps give it that mournful and plaintive sound."

Michael Stipe and Patti Smith—the punk godmother changed the lives of Stipe and Peter Buck.

Working with Smith in the studio was a pleasant experience, Mills added. "We flew her in and she came in and made a close emotional connection to the song and just kind of wailed," he recalled. "It was great," Buck agreed.

Smith also contributed indirectly to another song on the album. "It was really inspiring for me. We were trying to get this other song and we just couldn't get it right," Stipe told *iGuide*, an internet magazine. "One of the days that Patti was in the studio with us, when we were working on this other song, I think her being there just made everybody want to do real well and we got the take that wound up on the record and it's real good. It's all of us playing at one time, so that worked out really well."

The video clip for the song, directed by Jem Cohen, included footage of the band that was shot in Los Angeles, while Smith was featured in Prague, where she was on tour. In between takes, and in a scene from the 'E-Bow The Letter' video, Berry was seen reading *How To Talk Dirty and*

Influence People, the 1963 autobiography by controversial comedian Lenny Bruce—one of the names dropped in 'It's The End Of The World As We Know It (And I Feel Fine).'

At the band's request, 'E-Bow The Letter' was the first single released from *New Adventures In Hi-Fi*. It didn't perform particularly well on the charts, but then again it is hardly a traditional single. The CD single includes 'Tricycle,' an alternate version of 'Departure,' and a cover of Richard Thompson's 'Wall Of Death'—originally included on the 1994 tribute album *Beat The Retreat*. The band recorded a demo instrumental version of 'E-Bow The Letter' before the *Monster* sessions, but it was put aside until a later date.

Leave

As Buck explained 'Leave' isn't "really much like anything we have done before." The seven-minute-plus song, the longest in the R.E.M. catalog to date, begins with a quiet baroque-style acoustic passage before exploding into an ominous rocker with a persistent siren-like sound created by McCaughey on an Arp Odyssey. "Scott's holding down a key and moving the octave switch back and forth through the whole song," explained Buck. "We could only play it once every other soundcheck, because Scott's wrist would be numb by the end of it." The song was influenced, in part, by hip-hop act Public Enemy, who frequently employed siren-like wails in their tracks.

This reoccurring sound—somewhat reminiscent of a car alarm—is Mills' favorite part of the song. "You don't hear it

---

R.E.M. support player Scott McCaughey, third from left, fronts his own band, the Young Fresh Fellows.

---

after a minute or two, it just sort of becomes part of the song, but at the very beginning, you're like, 'What the hell is that?'"

Recorded during a soundcheck during the final three dates of the *Monster* tour, the track features Mills on bass and keyboards, and Buck and December on guitars. Stipe provides some of the album's most passionate and soulful singing, and Berry can be heard playing overdubbed acoustic guitar and synthesizer.

As for the song's unusual length, Mills said it "was not a conscious thing. It just worked out that way." Running more than 65 minutes, *New Adventures In Hi-Fi* is the longest R.E.M. album to date and the songs in general are longer than those on any previous R.E.M. album. "Our idea has always been if there is something that is not necessary or if they are not consistent with the song, we take it out and leave out parts that don't improve the song." The band did cut the song down some from its original version, Mills added. "It was about eight minutes with everything on it, but we chopped it up a little."

The fact that R.E.M. chose to go with a take of 'Leave' recorded in Atlanta, near its home base of Athens, is ironic, because the song is essentially about hitting the road. In the song's lyrics, Stipe's protagonist sings that he better go "where the land touches the sea" and that leaving "it all behind" keeps him down. The song flows nicely into 'Departure,' a song that effectively realizes those visions of life on the road.

Departure

Following in the wake of the lengthy 'Leave,' 'Departure' is a relatively simple and compact blast. "It's literally a road song," explained Buck. "Michael wrote the lyrics on a flight from Singapore to San Sebastian, Spain. Trips sometimes kick off memories of other trips. I like the way that song particularly captures the feeling of being on tour. You're always looking out a window somewhere. For me, it always brings back other trips I've taken, from when I'm a little kid standing in the back of the car looking out the window, to the last tour, or when I went on the road with my own family. It kind of captures that doing one trip, thinking of another."

Stipe elaborated on the inspiration in an interview with Chris Heath published in *Rolling Stone*. Everyone else on the plane from Singapore to San Sebastian was asleep when the singer witnessed a storm over the sea and claimed it was one of the most beautiful things he had ever seen. He was so inspired that he wrote the lyrics on hotel stationery once he checked into his room in San Sebastian. As for the mention of William Greider, "It rhymes with hang-glider and spider," Stipe told Heath. "He's the *Rolling Stone* political writer, right? I don't know. It just came out. Tell him it's an honor."

'Departure' is a "typical soundcheck song," claimed Buck. "One chord for the verse, two chords for the chorus, it literally took 10 minutes to write and has that kind of a cool energy that we would maybe have not have gotten had we done it in the studio."

'Departure' was recorded live on October 22, 1995, in Ann Arbor, Michigan, with the band's standard line-up augmented by Mills on fuzz bass and overdubbed Farfisa organ, and December on guitar. It bears a resemblance to the band's cover of Wire's 'Strange,' which was included on *Document*. "Yeah, there is a riff of that," Buck acknowledged, "and there's also a riff like a Tom Verlaine song. It's all amped up and noisy."

An alternate version, recorded on February 22, 1995, in Rome, was included on the 'E-Bow The Letter' CD single. This version is rougher and features the Farfisa organ much more prominently in the mix. The song has also appeared on bootlegs mistitled as 'Baby Come,' after the original chorus. That chorus was subsequently replaced by "Here it comes" by the time the band came to recording the track for *New Adventures In Hi-Fi*.

Bittersweet Me

"For me, it's all snapshots," Buck recalled. "I remember coming up with the initial riff at the Shoreline Amphitheater in San Francisco. It was the first show when Bill came back from his aneurysm. We had a couple of days' rehearsal, the chorus just fell together. The chorus is kind of a weird series of chords— F, B-flat major 7th—it's kind of neat because it changes from a real normal key to a weird key and back into the chorus."

Although 'Bittersweet Me' originated on the road, and the bulk of it was recorded at a soundcheck in Memphis augmented by McCaughey on piano, it wasn't completed until the band checked into Bad Animals Studio in Seattle after the tour. Mills added organ and mellotron overdubs, Buck beefed up the guitars, and Stipe recorded the finished

Michael Stipe and Peter Buck used the *Monster* tour to record some *New Adventures*.

vocal. "We played it every day for the past eight months," Buck said. "But Michael finished it really late in the recording process, so I never heard the melody and the lyrics until right before we were mixing."

In the studio, Buck just "went kind of guitar mad and dubbed about 40 guitars" on to the track, he told Dave Schulps of MJI Broadcasting. Buck added that the song "changed the most from the soundcheck tape to the finished version… The soundcheck version's just organ, acoustic guitar, and really quiet electric guitar."

On the finished version, Buck said, "the verse has a pretty-ish feel and strums, the B-section and chorus are really huge and have that kind of Iggy Pop 'Passenger' guitar sound over the top with the kind of labyrinth chorus."

As the title suggests, Buck says 'Bittersweet Me' is "kind of a disappointed love song." The video, directed by Dominic De Joseph, combines the band's performance, shot on the Chaplin Soundstage on the A&M Records lot in Hollywood,

California, with a spoof of an Italian movie. De Joseph and Stipe spent a night in Rome, Italy, following the Patti Smith tour. "We sat with a bottle of red wine and watched really bad Italian television and that's where the idea came from," Stipe said during a radio interview. The faux movie sports the title *Stanco E Nudo*, Italian for "tired and naked," a phrase pulled from the song's chorus. Before the music kicks in the video clip, an actor and actress exchange some dialog —"He's a navel gazer" and "He's all static and desire"—dubbed in English. Those phrases are also culled from Stipe's lyrics.

'Bittersweet Me,' as the second single from *New Adventures In Hi-Fi*, includes alternate versions of 'Undertow' and 'New Test Leper,' as well as a cover of the Jimmy Webb-penned Glen Campbell hit 'Wichita Lineman.'

Be Mine

'Be Mine' is another love song, but this one originated with Mills. "We had one version that I recorded by myself on the bus that will probably turn up somewhere as a B-side or maybe in the future on a boxed set, but we couldn't make it work," said Mills, who initially had envisioned the song as an instrumental.

"We actually did get a take when Mike played it on the bus and overdubbed it, but it felt a little too rigid," Buck added. So the band recut the entire track in the studio in Seattle with Mills on guitar and overdubbed keyboard parts, and Buck on bass and guitar.

For lyrical inspiration, Stipe initially turned to Valentine's candies and greeting cards. "Originally, I think the idea was to have a collection of clichés from greeting cards and candies," Buck explained. "Somewhere between that idea and the end it kind of mutated into something else that feels more meaningful."

Stipe concurred with that thought. "I'm showing something that's a little bit more full-spectrum, which is that even the most intense love probably has some weird little angles to it that you might either gloss over or ignore or forget about or not prioritize," he told Chris Heath in *Rolling Stone*.

Co-producer Scott Litt believed the song was highly commercial. "We could have made it like Whitney Houston, a power ballad," Buck said to Heath. "Scott Litt said, 'You know, if we produce this the right way, it'll be just like 'I Will Always Love You,' and it will be No. 1 for 16 weeks, and we said, 'Yeah… let's not produce it the right way.'"

To that end, the track opens with a snatch of the original demo Mills recorded on the tour bus. "The thing we kept from the bus version was the sound of the CB coming on," Buck explained. "That's Mike's bus driver saying something about speed ahead or cops ahead, or something. I said even if we don't use that take, we have to keep that talking."

Binky The Doormat

"This is called everything you wanted to know about sex but were afraid to ask," Stipe once said as an introduction to 'Binky The Doormat,' a particularly nasty song. Mills has said that the song is "about a person who is submissive and likes it." All of the band members will probably agree with Stipe's assertion that the song has "by far the worst title of any song that we've ever written."

That title comes from the Bobcat Goldthwait movie *Shakes The Clown*. "For some reason, Michael got really obsessed with that movie when we were making this record," Buck explained. In the film, Buck explained, "clowns are cool guys who snort cocaine, drink, and get laid all the time. One of the clowns is kind of evil and he does tons of blow and his name's Binky and he says something like, 'Everyone walks all over me, Binky the doormat, that's me.' Michael just liked the title. [The song] is about a character that feels that he has been done wrong, but I can't help but think of the movie."

Recorded live in Phoenix, Arizona, on November 4, 1995, with the audience noise removed, the song features Mills on fuzz bass and overdubbed keyboards, McCaughey on Farfisa organ, and Buck and December on some particularly vicious guitar interplay that is unleashed after a howl from Stipe.

Zither

'Zither' is another number in R.E.M.'s growing collection of instrumental tracks. It follows the tradition of *Automatic For The People*'s 'New Orleans Instrumental No. 1' and several B-sides. "It was recorded in a dressing room," Mills explained. "We like to do instrumentals. Michael had or has words for it, but we wanted to keep it an instrumental."

The song was recorded an hour before showtime in the visiting hockey team's dressing room at the CoreStates

Philadelphia Inquirer. "We had a guitar amp in the shower stall, the tambourine in the bathroom itself, the autoharp in the hallway, and the organ was in the [dressing] room. The bass went directly into the [mixing board]."

On the track, Berry plays bass, Mills organ, and December shook a tambourine. "We set up a DAT with a little mixing board and four mics," Buck recalled. "We spent an hour trying to record it, and we got a kind of cool

The restroom at the CoreStates Spectrum where the band recorded 'Zither.'

serviceable little take. Theoretically, it fits into the body of the record, and it really is the most road-tested, recorded in a bathroom, live with no overdubs… it also fits the mood of the record. We wanted something of that type near the end of the record. Since it's a long record, we thought it would give it a little breathing space about three-quarters of the way through. We didn't want it to turn into just a rock album."

Instrumentals are a natural result of the R.E.M. songwriting process, Buck explained. "What happens is we write a huge amount of songs for any given record. When you are writing a bunch of different stuff, you are eventually going to write something that is purely an instrumental. They are good for B-sides, but every now and then you capture something that is right for the mood of the record."

Spectrum during the band's October 12–14, 1995, stint in Philadelphia. Buck has claimed that it was actually written as "an instrumental specifically" to be recorded "in the bathroom at the show."

"We knew we'd be there for a few nights, so we could set up the room and leave it," Buck told Tom Moon of the

So Fast, So Numb

Recorded on November 15, 1995, at a soundcheck in Orlando, Florida, this song begins with a machine-gun drumbeat courtesy of Berry and features a particularly vicious Stipe vocal and lyric. The standard line-up is enhanced by Mills's overdubbed organ, and piano played by McCaughey.

"Someone said, 'Is that a drug song?' and I never have thought about that," Buck said. "That is something that doesn't occur around us a whole lot, but it seems

like it is a warning to someone for behavior, maybe just emotional behavior."

The song, a play on the old rock'n'roll cliché "live fast, die young," seems to be a wake-up call, with Stipe warning someone that they're "moving so hard, so fast, so numb" that they "can't even feel." Two of Stipe's close friends, River Phoenix and Kurt Cobain, lost their lives due to drug abuse and their loss was reflected in the songs of *Monster*.

Low Desert

This song was recorded at the soundcheck of the November 21, 1995, Atlanta show, the last day of the *Monster* tour. "It's simultaneously as loose and as tight as anything we've recorded," Buck boasted in the liner notes of the collector's edition of *New Adventures In Hi-Fi*.

The instrumental track had been kicking around since the *Monster* sessions. As the tentative title 'Swamp,' it is included on a list of potential song titles that was included in the *Monster* liner notes.

Buck said, "It's definitely a road song, because it's so scenic. It was called 'Swamp,' and toward the end of the tour, Michael said, 'It wasn't a swamp song, I wrote the words and said it was a desert song. It's about the dislocation of travel…'" Buck added, "I love the line 'ashtray cities.'"

The desert also featured prominently in the imaging of the album. A photo of a desert landscape and skyline that Stipe shot from the tour bus graces the cover of the album. Similar road photos were chosen for the covers of the singles.

'Low Desert' is another song that was road-tested during soundchecks. It features the band's core line-up complimented by Mills' overdubbed organ, McCaughey on piano, and December on slide guitar.

Working with December and McCaughey was rewarding for Buck. "I loved it," he said. "I like to write songs and hear them as close as possible to what they'll sound like when they are on the record while we're making it. Being that there are three instrumentalists in the band, it doesn't happen that way very much, so it's really nice to work things out with four of us and go over to Nathan and say, 'Play this here,' or Scott, 'play organ or do that.' It was a good thing. They added enough input that it sounds different than it would have had I done it myself. Even though I told Nathan kind of what to do, he has a different style than me, so it would come out differently and Scott doesn't play organ very much like Mike. It was a good thing. I think it broadened us out a little."

Stipe may have had a desert scene like this one in mind when he transformed 'Swamp' to 'Low Desert.'

Electrolite

'Electrolite' is the album finale and, in the tradition of 'Nightswimming' and '(Don't Go Back To) Rockville,' is driven by Mills' piano. "It was written on piano, so it has a different feel," Mills explained. "I learned how to play keyboards, piano, before anything else. It adds a nice dimension to the band when some songs get written on keyboards. It adds a whole different facet to the music."

Contributing to the atmosphere is banjo played by Buck, violin by guest musician Andy Carlson, and December on the guiro, an instrument that is called "the ultimate in musical usefulness" in the liner notes.

In the song, another one of Stipe's favorites, he drops the names of actors Martin Sheen, Steve McQueen, and Jimmy Dean. In the 'Man On The Moon' video, Stipe appropriated the look the latter sported in the film *Giant*.

The lyrics also include repeated mentions of Mulholland Drive, a hilltop canyon road that separates Bell Air from the San Fernando Valley. "It's hard to drive over Mulholland Drive and not feel like a movie star, but I don't know what you feel like when you hit bottom and go down the bottom of the hill." Buck quipped, "I guess we're going to have Charlie and Martin Sheen showing up at every show from now on."

The video for the track "involved dune buggies, crazy costumes, and rubber reindeer," Buck said. Despite the frivolous nature of the clip, Stipe, or at least his protagonist, is exhibiting a new-found courage. While his character in 'You Are The Everything' is "very scared of this world," his protagonist in 'Electrolite' is "not scared" of the future and confidently leaves listeners by singing *a cappella* "I'm outta here," signaling the end of *New Adventures In Hi-Fi*.

The view from Mulholland Drive at night, below, was featured prominently in the lyrics of 'Electrolite.'

James Dean—mentioned in the lyrics of 'Electrolite'— along with Martin Sheen and Steve McQueen.

October 30, 1997 is a day that will live in infamy for R.E.M. fans. It was the end of R.E.M. as we knew it, and undoubtedly a lot of people didn't feel fine. It was the day that Bill Berry officially announced he was leaving R.E.M.

Softening the blow was the announcement that R.E.M. would continue as a trio, contradicting earlier vows that promised if one member left, the band would cease to exist.

Berry's brush with death, when he suffered a brain aneurysm on the *Monster* tour, likely played into this decision to leave the band. "I'm at a point in my life where some of my priorities have shifted," he said in a statement. "I loved my seventeen years with R.E.M. but I'm ready to reflect, assess, and move on to a different phase of my life. The four of us will

UP

continue our close friendship and I look forward to hearing their future efforts as the world's biggest R.E.M. fan."

Mills, who has known Berry since junior high school, hinted at the gravity of Berry's situation. "As sad as this is the fact that Bill is still around to be my friend puts everything in perspective," he said. "I look forward to playing golf with Bill, and music with Michael and Peter."

The announcement came as the band was writing and preparing to record its eleventh album of new material. It would profoundly affect that set as well as the band's future.

Stipe compared R.E.M. to a "three-legged dog" after the departure of Bill Berry.

"It's the end of an era for us – Berry, Buck, Mills, Stipe – and that's sad," Stipe said. "I'm happy for Bill; it's what he really wants and I think it's a courageous decision. For me, Mike and Peter, as R.E.M., are we still R.E.M.? I guess a three-legged dog is still a dog. It just has to learn how to run differently."

And at first the new three-legged R.E.M. limped and turned on itself, making *Up* the most unpleasant recording experience in the band's history. "Making a record is hard enough as it is, and when you're trying to make a record at the same time you're trying to figure out how to be a three-piece band instead of a four piece, which you've been for seventeen years, we had no idea how hard that would be," Mills told me. "In retrospect, the smart thing to do would have been to take a few months off, play together, see how it felt, but everything was set up, the schedule was ready, everything was timed to go, so we went ahead and forged through it."

R.E.M.'s longtime drummer wasn't the only fixture missing when the band began recording its eleventh album. Just over a month before Berry's announcement, word leaked out that Scott Litt, who had produced every R.E.M. album for the past decade, wouldn't be on board for the band's latest effort. Litt's success with R.E.M. was undoubtedly instrumental in landing the producer his own label, Outpost, a subsidiary of Geffen Records.

Pat McCarthy, Litt's replacement, was hardly an unfamiliar face. He served as an engineer on the band's previous two albums and his credits also included work with U2, Patti Smith and Madonna. As it turned out, McCarthy's promotion into the producer's chair was a godsend. "Our secret weapon was Pat McCarthy," Stipe told LAUNCH's Dave DiMartino. "He'd just come off a Madonna record; he had a lot of ideas and they were really meshing well or interfering with the ideas we had in a really interesting way. He was the mortar that kept us together as this skewered unit, moving forward through the record-making process."

Those who assume that *Up*'s radical rethink of the R.E.M. sound was a result of Berry's departure are mistaken. "We got together in March 1997 in Hawaii and put down about 40 odd songs on tape, all using drum machines and most written without guitar," Stipe told DiMartino. "So we'd already embarked on what would be a very experimental record. Seven months later we got back together in the studio, [Berry] said he was ready to retire and didn't want to do it any more."

After Berry's announcement, R.E.M. did bring in another drummer, former Screaming Trees member Barrett Martin, who was already working with Buck in the instrumental side-project Tuatara. While Martin is best known as a drummer, he ended up playing vibes during much of the sessions, while Buck switched to bass and Mills played keyboards.

With Stipe facing a bout of writer's block and Buck growing impatient with the slow progress, the sessions at Toast studios in San Francisco were the most arduous of the band's career, with the group nearly packing it in. Berry's departure shifted the band dynamic to such an extent that the remaining members of R.E.M. were having trouble communicating. At one point, things got so bad that manager Bertie Downs called a summit for the trio to thrash out their differences at a remote lodge in Idaho. Somehow, the three-legged dog known as R.E.M. relearned how to walk unafraid into the future.

Bill Berry: "the World's Biggest R.E.M. fan" and only former member.

Airportman

If anyone had any illusions that the departure of Bill Berry would not radically reshape R.E.M., those beliefs fell by the wayside with the opening strains of 'Airportman.' While R.E.M. had opened albums with subdued tracks before (*Automatic*'s 'Drive,' *New Adventures*' 'How The West Was Won'), this was a completely different animal.

With a robotic machine rhythm, synthesized bass throbs, squalls of feedback, vibes, piano and a nearly whispered spoken vocal by Stipe, 'Airportman' captures the otherworldliness of an airport, but it certainly didn't sound like R.E.M. And that was the point.

"That's a song clearly that was a great experiment but it probably shouldn't have been on the record. It certainly shouldn't have opened it," Stipe told me. "But with the fragile state that we were in, it did feel like we were kind of throwing down the gauntlet, 'This is very different, so don't expect the same thing.'"

Incredibley, that gauntlet was also thrown down during R.E.M.'s first post-Berry live performance, and like the *Up* sessions, that too, didn't come easy. The band was set to play the annual Tibetan Freedom Concert on June 13, 1998 in Washington, D.C., but severe weather halted the show early, forcing R.E.M. to make up its set on the second day of the fest.

The new R.E.M. made its debut with Stipe wearing a belly shirt and sarong, backed by Mills and Buck, and additional musicians Scott McCaughey, plus newcomers to the R.E.M. camp Barrett Martin on vibes and Joey Waronker, known for his work with Beck, on drums. The first song they played to fans that filled RFK Stadium was 'Airportman.'

"I guess in retrospect, we didn't do what was expected of us," Stipe told LAUNCH's Dave DiMartino. "We opened with 'Airportman,' which is a slow, quiet song even though everyone was in rah-rah mode. We walked out and did what we do. It's not the Beastie Boys."

Listening to 'Airportman' after the 9/11 terrorist attacks, the song takes on an eerie new meaning, particularly the opening lines, "He moves efficiently / beyond security / great opportunity awaits."

"I wouldn't go there," Stipe cautioned. "To me it's just those guys that travel so much. They kind of become automaton. To me, I'm not so destination focused as a businessman is on his trip. To me, it's really about the journey."

Musically, the song is a homage of sorts to avant-garde pioneer Brian Eno, who in 1978 released *Ambient 1: Music For Airports*.

Lotus

Up's second track, 'Lotus,' also didn't sound like run-of-the-mill R.E.M., but it did possess some of the swagger, strut and spirit of past rockers. It too seems to be under the influence of Eno, but the glam-rock sounds of his early-seventies solo work, rather than the ambient sounds of his *Music For* instrumentals.

The band's initial plan for *Up* included a heavy promotional push in lieu of a tour. As part of that plan, the band made unprecedented appearances on the *Late Show with David Letterman* on consecutive nights. On the second night, R.E.M. unveiled 'Lotus,' with Buck wearing his trademark Rickenbacker, but playing the song's spacey intro on a keyboard before launching into the tune's guitar riff. Stipe was in his familiar spot front and center with Mills to his right on bass. Support musicians McCaughey and newcomer Ken Stringfellow of the Posies also manned keyboards, while Waronker played drums.

"Everything from the new record for us is kind of thrilling," Buck said at the time. "On 'Lotus' I get to play keyboards, which always excites me, even if it's only with one finger."

"But it's a big finger," added Mills. "It's just great."

As for the lyric, even Stipe is at a loss. "The whole language of that song is skewed and cartoonish," he told me. In an earlier interview, he told *Addicted to Noise*, "I think it's about someone who found a good place, lost it, and is trying to regain it. Floundering around a bit."

For the record, a lotus is an edible, aquatic plant that grows in Asia and Australia. A lotus-eater in Greek mythology was a person who lived in a drugged state from eating the lotus.

If the album version of 'Lotus' isn't strange enough, look for 'Lotus (Weird Mix),' which is coupled with the original on a CD single.

Suspicion

This seductive, down-tempo number, which R.E.M. covered on the *Monster* tour and released on a Christmas fan club single, bears some resemblance to Chris Isaak's 1991 hit 'Wicked Game.' Stipe took the comparison as a compliment, before revealing the inspiration for the lyric. "I actually thought about clubs that I've been to in Los Angeles and things that I had seen in clubs."

During the *VH1 Storytellers* taping, Stipe referred to the song as "'Everybody Hurts' with a hard-on". Later, he added, "I always loved 'Suspicious Minds' by Elvis Presley... I wanted to do a song that was somewhat reminiscent of that great, great American song and so we wrote this to be our version of that."

'Suspicion' was another track included in the band's set at the Tibetan Freedom Concert, months before it was officially released on *Up*.

Hope

R.E.M. continued its turn into relativity uncharted territory with 'Hope', a song credited to Leonard Cohen, Buck, Mills and Stipe. "We had to," Stipe told me, "because the melody was so lifted from 'Suzanne' without me knowing."

While Stipe may claim that the lifting of Cohen's melody was unintentional, it's not the first time he turned to the legendary singer-songwriter for inspiration. Stipe told me that *Monster*'s 'King Of Comedy' was his "Leonard Cohen rip-off". The band also covered 'First We Take Manhattan' on the 1991 tribute album *I'm Your Fan.*

Cohen, however, wasn't the only influence. The band was also inspired by New York punk duo Suicide, whose 1977 song 'Ghost Rider' R.E.M. covered as the B-side to 'Orange Crush.'

When asked about 'Hope,' Stipe told LAUNCH's DiMartino, "If I were to project one of these songs backwards to 1983 when we were recording our first record, the first song I just couldn't fathom that we'd ever put down on tape would be 'Hope.' That being said, a lot of what influenced *Murmur* – this might be a real stretch to imagine that it was an influence on the album – was the first Suicide album, the one Peter and I thought was just remarkable. 'Hope', to me, many years later, reflects that."

"I just remember when I first went to New York and rode the subway, I finally understood Suicide, the band," he added. "The sound of the subway was exactly the sound of their music, and it made such sense."

Lyrically, the song covers a favourite Stipe topic – "Belief systems, and science, discovery and science and evolution." Stipe told me he was proud about one part of the lyric in particular. "I found the word 'schism' because it rhymed. I didn't know what 'schism' meant. I guess somewhere deep in my unconscious I did. But I threw it into the lyric and then I looked it up, and it described exactly what the song is about, which shocked me. I remember going to Peter and Mike, 'You won't believe what I just did.' Somewhere inside my brain I guess I knew what that word meant and it just happened to rhyme with 'mechanism'."

Other parts of the lyric, such as "you want to cross your DNA / to cross your DNA with something reptile", might sound like something from *The X Files*. Stipe

admitted that not everyone understood his message loud and clear. Stipe shared two interpretations of a line from 'Hope' with *Rolling Stone*'s Chris Heath, but didn't reveal which one he intended when he wrote the line. "'You want to go out Friday, and you want to go forever.' And some people took that as: You want to go out and have a beer with your friends and not think about all the problems that are present in the rest of the song. The other interpretation is that you're planning the moment of your death, and you want it to be on a particular day."

'Hope,' Stipe said, reflects the influence of New York punk duo Suicide.

At My Most Beautiful

This is R.E.M.'s most direct love song to date and that fact made it a particular challenge for Stipe as a lyricist. "The body of the lyric, which is the verse, was a year in coming," he told me. "It took me that long to find non-cliché love song examples of what it was that I had found that would make you smile...I'm projecting myself into the character, of course. I wanted it to be something that really challenged and took that genre, which is so hackneyed at this point, to another place by not going to the easy examples."

Stipe came up with the idea for the song while driving on Santa Monica Boulevard in Los Angeles on the way to the offices of *Raygun* magazine, where he was working on

a book about Patti Smith – *Two Times Intro: On the Road with Patti Smith*. "I was stuck in traffic every day," he told *Addicted to Noise*'s Michael Goldberg. "And that's when I first wrote 'I found a way to make you smile.'"

For a moment, Stipe second-guessed himself when he realized that the title *Smile* was associated with the Beach Boys. "I never listened to their stuff that much. So I decided, well, that will be my gift to those guys 'cause they love the Beach Boys so much...Initially, I called the song 'Smile.' Peter thought it was too much, and so we changed the title...So that was my little paean to the Beach Boys, and my gift to Peter and Mike, and, at the time, Bill, to finish that song."

R.E.M. treated fans to a gift when they taped a performance of the song for a scene on the Fox TV series *Party of Five* on February 17, 1999 by performing a surprise hour-long preview of its upcoming tour at the Palace Theater in Hollywood, California. The crowd – consisting of actors, fan-club members, and radio-contest winners – were exclusively witness to six takes of 'At My Most Beautiful.'

Six months later, during the first show of the band's three-night stand at the Chastain Park Amphitheater in Atlanta, Berry walked onstage to embrace his former bandmates. Stipe was so moved by Berry's presence that he dedicated 'At My Most Beautifu' to the band's former drummer.

The Apologist

Following the sincere exquisiteness of 'At My Most Beautiful,' *Up* takes a downward turn with 'The Apologist.' With a sinister backing track, Stipe's protagonist tries to make good on past mistakes, but the apology rings hollow.

"I can't remember if it's the protagonist or the person they're talking to, but one of them has been through a 12-step program and is going back to make reparations to the people that he had fucked over, but it's not very believable," Stipe told me. "The apology is 'I'm sorry for the person that I was, this is the new me,' but it's not very believable at all. That's the germ of the idea."

Longtime R.E.M. fans will note the chorus of "I'm sorry" is familiar, but it was employed with much more sweetness and sincerity fourteen years earlier in 'So. Central Rain.' That fact was not lost on Stipe. After R.E.M. played 'The Apologist' at an October 21, 1998 MTV concert at New York's Bowery Ballroom, Stipe quipped, "Proving now that we're as sorry now as we always have been here's a song called 'So. Central Rain.' We hope you like it."

Stipe wrote 'At My Most Beautiful' as a tribute of sorts to the Beach Boys.

Sad Professor

Continuing *Up*'s downward emotional spiral is 'Sad Professor,' a song about regret and alcoholism. "It's about an emotional state in most of these songs and whomever the protagonist is, like in 'Sad Professor' pulling themselves from a place where they've been maybe for a long time to another place," Stipe told me, adding specifics about the song. "The guy was a drunk and now he's realized, at the age of 65, his life is empty and hollow and he wants to change that. That's the only glimmer of hope at the end of 'Sad Professor' but it's there. It's a little epiphany."

In a nice bit of word play, Stipe sings, "This may be a lit invention," which can be interpreted as either an abbreviation for "literary" or a reference to being drunk.

You're In The Air

With its spacey atmospheric mix of squealing guitars, keyboards, unusual percussion and the return of Buck's mandolin, 'You're In The Air' didn't sound like anything R.E.M. had done before.

In fact, Buck may have had this track in mind when he told LAUNCH's DiMartino, "If somebody played me *anything* on this record eighteen years ago, I would have thought, Jeez, I'm gonna go insane when I get older! Because this is really nutty! So much of the vocabulary of this record is so far away from what we were doing fifteen years ago that I doubt very much I would recognize it."

Likely adding to that perspective was that fact that Buck didn't hear the song's lyrics "until the day before it was mastered". Those lyrics appear to be about lust and obsession, leading some R.E.M. fans to theorize it's about oral sex. Stipe is remaining mum. "I barely remember writing it and haven't thought about it much since then," he told me. "It's a beautiful song, but I don't really listen to it. I'm not sure what it means. I'm not sure I can illuminate anything about that song."

Walk Unafraid

The inspiration for one of R.E.M.'s most powerful anthems came from a familiar source – Stipe's longtime heroine, Patti Smith. "She gave me the advice and that became a song title," he told me. "That was awesome and it was at a time when I really needed it. We were working in New York. It was just a horrible, horrible dark period. A lot of stuff going on."

In an interview with *Addicted to Noise*'s Michael Goldberg, he further explained, "I wanted the song to be more universal than just me having to embark on the writing of an album. That's a little too specific and not that interesting, so I wrote this song. And hopefully, I succeeded.

I wrote this song in the same voice I tried to write 'Losing My Religion' and 'Everybody Hurts,' so there's a kind of universality to it. Specific enough that it doesn't seem like just a bundle of clichés tied together. But unspecific enough that pretty much anyone could listen to the song and apply it to themselves and to their own situation and their own life and take from it what they need to. That was pretty much the idea behind that song."

Musically, the mix of Buck's slash-and-burn guitar with Mills' chaotic keyboards makes it the most potent track in the post-Berry R.E.M. catalog.

Why Not Smile

This was the first new R.E.M. recording since the departure of Berry and the first song released from *Up*, albeit in an unconventional form. 'Why Not Smile' initially appeared as the final track on *The Oxford American Southern Sampler 1998*, which was available with the Oxford, Mississippi-based literary magazine's second annual issue on Southern music. The track is a slow, mostly acoustic number that would not be out of place on *Out Of Time* or *Automatic For The People*. When the song appeared on *Up*, it was enhanced with additional keyboards, vibes, and Stipe adding some electric guitar noise.

While the song appears to be in the vein of 'Everybody

Hurts,' with Stipe's protagonist offering words of encouragement to a friend who is down in the dumps, it might not be that simple.

"Peter and I have argued about this, because he thinks it's a really sweet, loving song about pulling someone out of a really dark place," Stipe told me. "To me, it was someone who was taking a very easy route and not recognizing depression and not realizing that someone might have a chemical imbalance that makes them impossible to reach on that level. To just say, 'Why not smile,' you want to say that to people who might be slightly depressed, but that's not quite enough. You kind of have to tackle a little more than, 'Come on, pull yourself up by the bootstraps and let's get on with our day.' That doesn't work with people who are chronically depressed or who have genetic or chemical imbalances whether it's a bipolar disorder, chronic depression or schizophrenia or whatever. I felt like it was a very naïve brushing off of a very serious condition. Peter thinks the opposite. He thinks it's a very sweet and beautiful song. There's two ways to look at it.

"That's Peter's interpretation and he's one of the songwriters," he added. "That's the funny thing. Sometimes we don't completely agree on the intent of the song and the level to which it works or doesn't work. How other people interpret it is up to them."

Daysleeper

More than any other song on *Up*, 'Daysleeper' sounds like the old R.E.M. and for good reason. The instrumental track actually dated back to the *New Adventures in Hi-Fi* sessions, but Stipe didn't have lyrics completed at the time.

Those lyrics came a few years later when Stipe was in New York working on the collaborative book called *The Haiku Year*. Stipe recalled visiting one particular building that left an impression on him. "I'm stomping down the stairs, it's 4 o'clock in the afternoon, and I come to a door, it's apartment 3D or something and there's a sign on it that says 'daysleeper'," he explained on *VH1 Storytellers*. "And I walked a lot more carefully, quietly, down the steps thinking about that poor person that was trying to sleep in that room and me and my big ol' boots interrupting her sleep. So I wrote this song about a daysleeper that's working an 11 to 7 shift and how furious that balance is between the life that you live and the work that you have to do in order to support the life that you live. That's what the song is."

The fact that 'Daysleeper' sounded so much like the R.E.M. of the past made it easy for Warner Bros. Records executives to latch on to for the first single from *Up*.

Musically, the song's seesaw tempo recalls *Automatic for the People*'s 'Try Not to Breathe.' As for the female-sounding backing vocal toward the end of that track, it's not a woman. "That's Mike," Stipe revealed. "Singing in his real voice. No computers."

Diminished

Up again takes a dark turn with 'Diminished,' a moody crime story that could have been culled from newspaper headlines about a celebrity-related killing, with Stipe taking on the voice of the accused.

"It's about a guy who is on trial for murder and isn't sure if he did it or not and he's trying to figure out how to get out, and at the same time, questioning, 'Did I actually do it?'"

I'm Not Over You

This brief acoustic track, performed solo by Stipe, is a hidden track not listed on the back of the CD jewel box, but lyrics are included in the CD booklet. It's another one of Stipe's brutal, obsessive love songs that dovetails nicely with the dementia of "Diminished".

'I'm Not Over You,' which runs just over a minute, was actually part of another, longer song that didn't make the cut. "There was a whole song – it was really over the top, just this idea of a relationship gone bad," Stipe told *Rolling Stone*'s Heath. "Typical R.E.M. stuff, which I didn't really want on this record; there's too much of that stuff on the past couple of records. It ends with an atomic explosion that nullifies the world as we know it. And the song sucked. But what started it was the little part that made the record – that was the immediate and beautiful part."

Stipe also admitted the song was an expression of something in his life. "Directly," he admitted. "The title is what it is."

Parakeet

An elegant piano-driven song, 'Parakeet' is a song about a person escaping from a bad situation. "It was someone that was in a really bad relationship and pulled out of it," Stipe told me. "I think it was a woman who was being beaten and she went to a place where mean cats can't climb trees in Brisbane and something about how the flashes fly off the sun and how they effect electronics on earth. It's actually true. It's in the lyric. There is an effect that occurs on electronics when there is a solar flare."

During *VH1 Storytellers*, Stipe gave a less direct and rambling account of the song's inspirations, citing a voicemail message from a friend who had moved to Australia. "The desert sand speaks to me. The flowers speak to me. And so my name now is Parakeetio. I hope to hear from you soon," Stipe said. "I played that message 30 times trying to figure out who left it. And the closest I could get was Parakeetio, which inspired this next song, which is called 'Parakeet.'"

To confuse matters more, he added an anecdote about a trip to an outback petting zoo in Australia where he held a koala bear and decided that they are "the highest deified life form on earth."

Falls To Climb

Up, which began with the dreamlike optimism of 'Airportman,' comes to a close with the fatalistic, sacrificial hymn 'Falls To Climb.' Because of the difficulty R.E.M. had recovering from the loss of Berry and inter-band disharmony during the *Up* sessions, some speculated that when Stipe sang "Gentleman mark your opponents / Fire into your own ranks," he was addressing Buck and Mills.

"I thought you were going to make the AIDS analogy, because that has been proposed," Stipe fired back when asked about such speculation, before clarifying his intent.

"It's a rewriting of the short story called 'The Lottery,' which Marilyn Manson turned into a video for one of his songs where someone has taken a villager and stoned them to death. Seeing that video reminded me of the story, and the power of that story and I simply rewrote it. It's a great story."

Stipe is referring to Shirley Jackson's tale of an "average" New England village with "average" citizens who hold an annual selection of a sacrificial victim via a lottery. Not until the tail end of the story, does Jackson reveal the villagers will stone the lottery winner to death.

'The Lottery,' published in the June 28, 1948 issue of the *New Yorker* prompted hundreds of letters of complaint. It's no surprise that noted nineties rock provocateur Marilyn Manson would use 'The Lottery' for the inspiration for his 1997 'Man That You Fear' video, but many R.E.M. fans might be surprised to learn that Stipe would find inspiration through Manson.

Despite the grisly subject matter, intensified by military-type snare drum patterns, like most of R.E.M. album closers, *Up* somehow ends on an optimistic note, with Stipe's human sacrifice crying repeatedly, "I am free" at the song's conclusion.

Stipe ended *Up* with the cry of "I am free" on 'Falls To Climb.'

With its Western-flavoured guitar riffs and '70s flashbacks of the game of Life, Monopoly, and Andy Kaufman, 'Man On The Moon' is one of R.E.M.'s most cinematic songs. The band's video clip, directed by Peter Care, with Stipe parading around the desert in a cowboy hat, only furthered that notion. Still, the members of R.E.M. could never have predicted that 'Man On The Moon' would inspire and serve as the title for a Kaufman biopic and the band would be commissioned to write the score, but that's what happened in 1999.

"There was a television documentary in 1994 using our song, footage from the video, conversations and interviews with people who knew Andy through his life, and select clips of his work," Stipe told MTV. "Some people saw it, and I think they thought 'This is a brilliant, exciting idea to write a script around,' and they named the script *Man on the Moon*. When Danny DeVito got it, he handed it over to Milos Forman, who read it, called me on the phone right away,

and said, 'I'm going to make a movie about Andy Kaufman called *Man on the Moon*, and I want your band to score it.'"

Those plans were somewhat complicated by the fact that R.E.M. belatedly decided to tour in support of *Up*. With the tour dates already set, the band had to shoehorn in the sessions to record the music for the film. "Essentially we toured the summer of '99 and the three months prior to that we worked on *Man on the Moon*," Buck told me. "We really wanted to be involved in the movie, but unfortunately they didn't have an edit of the movie when we went on tour so it was really haphazard, but I'm happy with the movie, and was proud to work on it."

Aside from the original recording of 'Man On The Moon' and an orchestral version of the song, the album featured 'Tony Thrown Out,' 'Miracle,' 'Lynne & Andy,' 'Milk & Cookies,' all instrumental score numbers composed and performed by R.E.M., and two new recordings featuring Stipe's vocals.

The Great Beyond

Writing a sequel to a hit may prove fairly easy for Hollywood screenwriters, but that was not the case for Stipe, who was asked by the director Milos Forman to write a new song for the film. "I thought it would be a piece of cake, but it's really hard to write a sequel to a song that was in my opinion a really great prequel song," Stipe told me.

In an interview with MTV, Stipe provided further insight into the song. "I pulled lyrical elements into 'The Great Beyond' so that it can be a companion piece without diminishing the original, and at the same time stand alone as a really good pop song. I took the third verse of 'Man On The Moon' and made it a background vocal in the final choruses, just because those were my favorite lyrics from 'Man on the Moon', so I wanted to bring them back around. And there are other little easy references, like 'having something up your sleeve,' which is *Rocky & Bullwinkle*, we all know that. 'The Great Beyond,' in a way, is about someone who's trying to achieve the impossible. Pushing the elephant up the stairs. Andy's whole thing was breaking down the fourth wall to such a degree that the audience never really knew whether he was for real or not. And I wanted to capture a little bit of that in the song."

MAN ON THE MOON

Tony Clifton, heard on 'This Friendly World,' gets escorted away.

This Friendly World

This duet remake of a hit by 1950s teen idol Fabian features Stipe trading verses and, later, every second word, with *Man on the Moon* star Jim Carrey doubling up in the role of Andy Kaufman and Kaufman's evil alter ego Tony Clifton.

Although Stipe never met Kaufman, he did record with Carrey, who assumed the persona of his idol. "He was in character and he attacked me," Stipe told me, adding that the experience was "wild," but Carrey was a "really good guy".

R.E.M.'s association with *Man on the Moon* continued long after the release of the film. When R.E.M. played the Hollywood Bowl on September 10, 2003, the mysterious Tony Clifton bumrushed the stage during the band's performance of 'Man On The Moon' and traded verses with Stipe before becoming involved in an on-stage scuffle that had him dousing Stipe with a cup of water before he was dragged from the stage. In an interview posted on the R.E.M.hq website a few days later, the Clifton character (whoever he was) claimed that R.E.M. was "riding my coattails to get places". He also said that if Stipe "wants to ever succeed in showbiz, he needs a hairpiece. Like me."

not only did R.E.M. survive the turmoil of *Up*, it thrived, choosing to tour belatedly in support of the album, and embracing its reincarnation as a trio, injected with new life by touring musician Scott McCaughey, and newcomers Ken Stringfellow, and Joey Waronker.

"Mike and Michael were playing at the peak of their game, and then everyone – Scott, Ken Stringfellow, and Joey Waronker – have melded us all into a band again," Buck said of the band's forthcoming album. "Unlike the last record where it was kind of me and Mike and a drum machine, this is a real band record."

For the first time since the harrowing *Fables Of The Reconstruction* sessions in London, R.E.M. chose to record

REVEAL

its twelfth album out of the U.S. "Where I heard the record going sonically, it felt to me like the United States might not be the best place to work on it. I feel like the music that you hear on the streets or in the cafes, in bars, in restaurants, and in taxi cabs is a little stuck in a groove in the U.S., there's not a lot of variety," Stipe told me. "Whereas in Europe or in Vancouver, Canada, you hear a lot of different types of music."

"We kind of were working with two very disparate music styles and trying to combine them, trying to cross-graft them into something that represented our interests and where we were musically in 2001," Stipe continued. "And one being, of course, acoustic – real instruments performed by real people, and the other being very mechanical and very much coming out of machines. And fusing those together in a way that what you wound up with was something very warm and analog and acoustic sounding and incredibly subtle, but doesn't sound like someone's trying to fit a square peg into a round hole. I think we did it."

It also served as a method for Stipe to fend off the writer's block that plagued him during much of the *Up* sessions. "I thought if I can put myself in a place that's easy to access other places from, like Dublin, if I got stuck I could very easily remove myself from the place that I was and move someplace else," he told me. "It's a real dumb obvious

solution but it worked. I went to Israel and I went to France, I went to Italy and I went to Copenhagen and London, and I kind of flew my ass all over Europe for the summer. And a lot of it was actually escaping the bad weather – if it got rainy or cold or kind of crappy for the week, I'd just go where the sun was. We were writing a summer record, a record that maybe tries to capture the promise of summer and present it as a soundtrack to your summer or my summer. It made sense that I would go off kind of chasing the sun."

Buoyed by the upbeat first single 'Imitation Of Life,' some speculated that *Reveal* was a return to form following the mostly downbeat and experimental meandering of *Up*. Mills did not take kindly to such talk. "Yeah, well they can kiss my ass whoever they are," he told me. "It's not a return to anything. This is the record we made because of the space we're in right now."

Stipe concurred. "Every record that we make, Peter always says, is like a photograph of where we were as a group when we made it. And this record is that," Stipe told me. "But also for me, just on a personal level, it makes good on the promise that *Up* made – that we, as a trio, can be a force to rival or match a four-piece R.E.M. with Bill Berry."

The glowing reviews weren't just coming from within the band. R.E.M. friend and rival Bono called the album "extraordinary," prior to its release adding, "I know it's extraordinary because I felt ill when I heard it. It's a very beautiful, awe-inspiring record."

However, R.E.M.'s upward swing took a detour on April 21, 2001, less than a month before the release of *Reveal*. Buck, who is generally known for his good-natured demeanor, was arrested and charged for allegedly assaulting two members of a flight crew in the first-class section of a flight from Seattle to London. Buck took the flight from his home in Seattle to join Stipe and Mills in promotional activities surrounding the release of *Reveal*. On April 29, R.E.M. was set to play to an expected crowd of 20,000 at a South Africa Freedom Day Concert in Trafalgar Square, London. That show went on as scheduled, as did a promotional tour in support of *Reveal*.

During that trek, Buck was forbidden to speak about the specifics of the incident, but he told me, "I can say, I'm kind of embarrassed and sorry that it all happened and it's just something that I have to deal with."

Nearly a year later, he was cleared of the charges, following testimony from Stipe, Mills, and Bono. Buck's defense claimed that a combination of a sleeping pill and wine caused a reaction called "non-insane automatism" and that he had not consciously intended to cause a disturbance.

Ken Stringfellow of the Posies. One of the musicians that helped R.E.M. feel like a band again.

"I'm grateful to the court, the jury and my lawyers, to my family, friends, and supporters who have stood by me throughout this experience," said Buck in a statement read by his lawyer outside the courtroom. "I am obviously relieved to be finished here and I look forward to returning my attention to my family, my band, and my music."

183

The Lifting

With its spacey intro and layered instrumentation, *Reveal*'s first track wasn't a dramatic departure from the moody *Up*, but even the most astute R.E.M. fan would be unlikely to have guessed that lyrically Stipe conceived that song as a sequel to *Up*'s 'Daysleeper.'

"For me, it's the same character," he told me. "The character is a woman, which really challenged me as a writer, because I was like, 'Why have I chosen this character to be a woman? Am I not the feminist that I think I am?' It turned out that it's a woman that is working in a very male-dominated business and is challenged by her gender so it was OK for what I had done."

Like 'Daysleeper,' 'The Lifting' involves sleep, or lack thereof. "Someone is suffering from insomnia, probably worried about their job or their situation, and the ceiling represents those concrete thoughts and the ability to go beyond that," Stipe explained to me.

"This woman goes to a self-help group, a fairly fascist self-help group called The Lifting and for several hundred dollars this woman sits in a room with several other people who are not able to dream beyond the concrete and she fakes it, because that's what's expected of her, because she's in the terrible situation where you can't pee, you have to eat what they give you, and she's trapped in this horrible place in Los Angeles, where she lives, and she finally fakes it.

"She says to her counsellor, 'Yes, I can see beyond the concrete. Yes, I can dream. In my dreams I'm visiting places that don't exist in real life.' And the beauty of the song of course is the coda. She has seen these things. Not during 'The Lifting,' the little self-help course, but in real life she's been to those places, but she's forgotten about them, so the realization for her might come a little bit later."

Musically, R.E.M. allowed fans to get a glimpse into the making of 'The Lifting' by releasing the demo version included on the special edition of *In Time: The Best of R.E.M. 1998–2003*.

'The Lifting' was one of two new songs R.E.M. revealed for the first time at the Rock In Rio festival in Brazil on January 13, 2001.

I've Been High

Another track that wouldn't have been out of place on *Up* given its drum-machine-like backing. The rhythm track was actually constructed at Dalkey Lodge in Dublin, Ireland, by producer Pat McCarthy from beats played by Joey Waronker in Vancouver.

Lyrically Stipe told me that the song is rather straightforward. "It's probably pretty literal to the line, thinking what does that mean to you, you want to live your life to its fullest," he explained. "We all want the peaks without the valleys, the flow without the ebb, but that's not how life works."

Reveal's title was culled from the song's lyric "Have I missed the big reveal?" by the band manager Bertis Downs.

'I've Been High' was previewed live prior to the release of *Reveal*, but on a much different stage than Rock In Rio. On October 22, 2000, at the Land Aid festival in the band's hometown of Athens, Georgia, Stipe performed the song accompanied by a boom box.

All The Way To Reno (You're Gonna Be A Star)

The early incarnations of 'The Lifting' and 'All The Way to Reno' were similar in tempo, but those similarities had virtually disappeared by the time the songs turned up on *Reveal*.

'Reno' began as an instrumental called 'Glockenspiel,' named for an instrument Buck found in a Seattle music shop. "It's kind of like a vibraphone, it looks like an old-fashioned lyre, and you play it with little sticks. It was a marching band glockenspiel, and I bought it and put it on every demo I did for about six weeks, and it drove everyone completely batshit. It was completely insane," Buck said in an interview with Virgin Radio. "In 'Reno,' I wanted the riff to be beautiful and to have that high chiming thing, then we put the six string

Singer-songwriter Jimmy Webb, below, influenced the sound of 'All The Way To Reno,'

Filmmaker Michael Moore, above, gave cameras to the kids of the 'Reno' video.

bass on to ameliorate the fairy dust kind of feel of the glockenspiel. The record sounds exactly like the demo."

Another influence on 'Reno' was Jimmy Webb, the noted singer-songwriter who composed Glen Campbell's 1968 country hit, 'Wichita Lineman,' which R.E.M. covered and released as the B-side of 'Bittersweet Me.'

"His songwriting is just so lush, and he used the major seventh chords and the harmonies," Buck said of Webb. "I guess the little guitar solo in the entry definitely has a 'Wichita Lineman' feel."

Lyrically, Stipe sings of an aspiring performer who is so naive that they travel to Reno, of all places, to seek stardom. Perhaps in a nod to the anyone-can-be-a-star hopefulness of the song, R.E.M. worked with director Michael Moore on a video clip for the song. "We kind of gave him free reign on it and we shot for a day in a high school in Brooklyn," Stipe told me. "He [Moore] would give cameras to the high-school kids, the youngest being thirteen-year-olds, who were interested in film or in some kind of television and were thinking of pursuing something like that as part of their schooling. And they shot the whole video."

185

She Just Wants To Be

"We're going to play a new song. We've been working for about a year-and-half on a record. It's going to come out in May sometime. That doesn't really matter. What matters is we've never played this song before in front of anyone, and so we want to play it for you tonight." That's how Stipe introduced 'She Just Wants To Be' to the largest crowd that the band had performed in front of in its career, on January 13, 2001 at the Rock In Rio festival in Brazil.

In the song, a rocker that features a Neil Young & Crazy Horse-like guitar jam, Stipe name drops jazz greats Chet Baker and Charles Mingus as a soundtrack for 'pomegranate afternoons.' Stipe told me the lyrics came "flying out of me," but rather than speak specifically about the lyrics he chose to discuss how the song has become a staple of the band's live set.

"The interesting thing is what a song is in the studio versus what it becomes live," Stipe told me. "There is a demarcation in this band in the way that we interpret our own music. We don't interpret our music like some people do, like Dylan, certainly. Maybe the Pixies would be in line with R.E.M.... The interpretation of the music of the song is that it is pretty as it is, but the energy that you have in live performance is very different from the energy you have in the studio. This would be an interesting song to study in that regard."

Jazz greats Chet Baker, opposite page, and Charles Mingus, left, were namedropped by Stipe on 'She Just Wants To Be.'

Disappear

This track, initially known as 'Underwater Acoustic,' begins with a chaotic, psychedelic introduction, and for good reason. After all, the band – with McCaughey and Stringfellow – recorded the basic track in one take. After that, they employed a technique called a "group overdub," in which each member of the band grabbed a different instrument, in an effort to keep the proceedings fresh and interesting.

"Since you picked a different instrument, you really didn't have the time to figure out a part to play," McCaughey told Q's David Cavanagh. "The first take of the group overdub was always eccentric. I think we almost always used the first ones, because you'd get much odder stuff."

Lyrically, Stipe initially feared he performed a psychic overdub of lyrics penned by his pal Thom Yorke of Radiohead.

"I was at this all-night dance party in Tel Aviv with a bunch of Israeli friends and this kid came up to me and he just said, 'Why are you here?' It was the most unobvious place that anyone would expect me to be. I said, 'I came to disappear.' And I thought, 'Wow that's a pretty good line,' so I wrote a song about it, not about myself but about someone who's searching for something," he told me.

Stipe was happy with his lyric, but had a nagging concern. "In the back of my head I was thinking, 'God, it seems like I read about a song called 'Disappear.' When I got back to Dublin, I said, 'Have you guys heard about this song 'Disappear' by some other band – Depeche Mode or somebody?' And Pat McCarthy said well Radiohead have that song 'How to Disappear Completely.' And I was like, 'Ah fuck, I'm such an idiot, I can't believe it.' I loved the song at that point. I wasn't about to let go of it. And that line is very crucial to the whole storyline, the narrative of the song."

That prompted Stipe to leave Yorke a voicemail about the dilemma. When Yorke called back and Stipe explained his quandary, Yorke laughed, and said that Stipe had influenced the Radiohead song

"He said the chorus of that song is something that he had taken from a conversation we'd had a year and a half earlier," Stipe recalled. "And the words of that chorus are something that I had said to him in the form of advice, and so it kind of brought the whole thing full circle and everything was OK. And they're very different songs."

Saturn Return

The instrumental experimentation continued on 'Saturn Return,' a song Stipe is still impressed with. "The music was incredible, when it comes out, the box set or on a B-side some day, the original demo of that song is just mind-blowing. And it changed because it went through the R.E.M. machine and each of us did our things to it," Stipe told me. "But I love that song. I love the melody and the tension in that song. I was able to build this narrative that felt very now, but set in the future."

Stipe further explained the lyrics, making it sound like something from a lost episode of The X-Files. "This girl climbs up on to the roof of a 7-11 she works at in the middle of the desert, and makes this monumental discovery that changes the way we look at the heavens," he told me. "It's in the lyric. It's all there. She works the nightshift and she climbs up on the roof, it's a clear night, and she sees something that is monumental in the sky that changes the trajectory of science. Her discovery."

Beat A Drum

This song, once described as "summer on a stick" by Stipe, further explores the Beach Boys influence the band experimented with on *Up*'s 'At My Most Beautiful.' As Buck explained, "Mike and myself are both Beach Boys fans, Michael wasn't that knowledgeable about them," he told me. "I think when you start using the keyboards and drum machines and harmonies you're kind of reminded of those late sixties, early seventies Beach Boys records, and I know the influence is there, but it's not super conscious."

The intent behind the song's lyrics is even a mystery to Stipe. "I remember rehearsing the song for a tour," he told me. "I don't go back and listen to the stuff. The band is playing it, they've been rehearsing it, I've got the words written down and I'm singing it and I'm going, 'What the fuck is this song about? What the fuck am I going on about?' And then there is something at the very end that makes sense.

"I think it's the 'half way to coal'. That's just about creation, how far along we think we are and how far along we are, which is not very."

Imitation Of Life

With its jangling guitar and upbeat synthesizer riff, 'Imitation Of Life' was the first single released for *Reveal*, and in some quarters, prompted talk of the band's return to form.

"To me, that indicates something that's come before is now being presented again in a different way," Stipe said to me. "And OK, maybe that's the case. We're the same people that we were with every record that we've made but things have changed dramatically in our little universe and hopefully this reflects that."

The origins of 'Imitation Of Life' date back to the *Up* tour, during which the band recorded it backstage. "Like all demos, it was about six minutes long," Buck told Virgin Radio. "It had these really bad synth trumpets on it, and this big hammering drum machine. To tell the truth, that demo was really draggy."

For *Reveal*, the band opted to tighten and speed it up, transforming it into a pop song. "It almost got left off the album because, although we were very happy with the song, we were not really concentrating on it until some people from the record company said, 'You know, we love that song.' Everyone seemed to like it, so we said, 'OK, we'll just buckle down and work on a chorus and come up with something.'"

After several revisions, Stipe came up with a new chorus when he and Buck were driving to dinner one night. "Michael said, 'Oh, I've got the chorus' so we put the tape on in the car. He started singing along to it and we said, 'That's great! We gotta do that tomorrow!'"

The video clip for the song is also memorable. Directed by Garth Jennings, the shoot – on location in a backyard in the San Fernando Valley – included 75 cast members and a monkey. "I got to co-star with a monkey," said Buck at the time, "and I must admit I was out-acted by about ten to one."

Summer Turns To High

This Beach Boys-influenced summer song was originally so complex that Stipe had to deconstruct it in order to construct a melody and lyrics for the track.

"We called the song '32 Chord Change' because the band laughingly had 32 chords in it, and I had to strip that song down to a synthesizer and a beat box in order to find a melody. I couldn't find anything over the music they created and then we built it back up."

Like 'Beat a Drum,' 'Summer Turns To High' makes reference to dragonflies. "The interesting thing about that song is people thought I was using dragonflies as some metaphor for something else," Stipe told me. "It was only when the third or fourth person asked me about it that I thought I must have a lot of dragonflies in my life, and I do. In Georgia they hover over the backyard. If you wear metallic fingernail polish they come and sit right on your fingers or your toes confused about what this thing is. They come and hover right in front of you and it looks like they just look at you and then they fly off. It's like that movie *Minority Report*, like one of those futuristic bugs that you find in [David] Cronenberg movies or something set in the future. I found it funny that people thought the dragonflies represented something and they actually don't. They're just dragonflies."

Chorus And The Ring

This song, which wouldn't be out of place on *Automatic For The People*, was inspired in part by two pop-culture icons that had figured in R.E.M.'s past – Nirvana's Kurt Cobain, who inspired Stipe's *Monster* plea "Let Me In", and Beat writer William Burroughs, who added his vocals to a version of 'Star Me Kitten.'

"That song is about a conversation I had with William Burroughs about Kurt Cobain," Stipe told me. But that was just the starting point. "There's the *Deus ex machina* in Greek tragedies and plays," he continued. "P.T. Anderson uses this to some effect in his movies: God descending by machine from the ceiling of the theater, because the plot has become so complicated and convoluted, and the characters have worked their way into these corners, the only way to end play is for God to descend and strike everyone dead...It's a narrative trick that is not often used because it makes no sense and leaves people very angry, especially when something ends very, very suddenly and then it's over."

Musically, too, the song seemed to be touched by the hand of God, or at least Peter Buck. The song was recorded spontaneously in a single take. "Peter just started playing it and we all joined in," McCaughy told *Q*'s Cavanagh. "Mike came into the room literally just in time to pick up his bass. None of us had any idea what this song was!" McCaughy followed Buck's hands, while the guitar players barked out the chord changes to Mills. Legend has it that Buck's instructions were picked up by Waronker's drum mics.

I'll Take The Rain

Dating back to 1984's 'So. Central Rain' to 1986's 'Fall On Me.' rain has, at least indirectly, inspired some of R.E.M.'s most memorable songs. This song was released as a single, but failed to connect, peaking at Number 44 in the U.K. "It was a little too slow and too long to be a hit," Stipe told me, "but it's a beautiful song."

The song began life as an instrumental known as 'Pedal Steel.' which first started taking shape on the *Up* tour, with McCaughey playing the instrument for which it was named. Initially, the song was slated to close the album, but it was moved up a track, because the band opted to go with the more upbeat closer 'Beachball.'

Peter Buck, left, plays sideman for Scott McCaughey at a Minus Five gig.

Beachball

"It was Peter's sequence," Stipe told me of the decision to end *Reveal* with the encouraging words of "you'll do fine,' which close 'Beachball.'

While the summery feel led some to assume the Beach Boys also inspired this track, Stipe has a different take on it. "It was taken from a real place in Vancouver that I would go to," he told me. "It was right on the seashore, which was the whole idea, kind of a 'Girl From Ipanema' song."

When the news broke that R.E.M. would release a greatest-hits set and support it with a tour, more cynical individuals assumed it was a move to make good on the band's reported $80 million deal with Warner Bros. Since signing the mega-deal, R.E.M.'s sales fell south in the U.S. and now it was time to pay the piper.

For R.E.M., however, there were other motives. "There are several different reasons," Mills told me prior to the album's release. "Mainly because when Bill left the band in '97, it turned everything on its head and it's taken us this long to get back to our highest confidence level. We feel good about where we've been, but feel even better about where we're going, so it seemed right to put a little retrospective together. Remind people that we've done a lot of good work and we've got a lot more coming."

Stipe concurred. "We've always looked forward, we've never looked back to such a degree that in 23 years we never put out a greatest hits. It kind of felt like a good time to close that chapter of R.E.M. After two albums as a trio, I feel like we are at a confidence peak right now as songwriters, as friends, as cohorts in this thing that we now call R.E.M. as a trio. By putting out the greatest hits, in a way it closes that chapter and opens the next one."

IN TIME THE BEST OF R.E.M. 1988-2003

While there is no doubt that the timing was right, at least in R.E.M.'s mind, to release a *Best Of*, Stipe's contention that it was the band's first greatest hits collection is debatable. When the band ended its relationship with IRS, the label issued *Eponymous* in 1988, featuring the band's best-known songs from its first five albums along with some rarities. An album released a decade later, but not in the U.S., featured nearly an identical track listing, minus the rarities, and was even called *The Best of R.E.M.* It could be argued that the band hadn't really had too many hits at that point in its career, since 'The One I Love' was its only single to break into the top 10 of the U.S. pop singles chart.

Whatever the case, the album did allow fans to get *most* of the band's best-known songs from its Warner Bros. era on a single disc. Notably absent was the U.S. top 10 hit 'Shiny Happy People,' one of the songs that Stipe now calls part of the "R.E.M. kids collection."

"There was a point where [the band] gave me really fruity songs and I wrote really fruity lyrics to go with them," he told me. "And those are what I consider our kids collection. The kids collection includes 'Stand,' 'Sidewinder Sleeps Tonite,' 'Shiny Happy People,' 'Pop Song 89,' and 'Get Up.' We put 'Stand' and 'The Sidewinder Sleeps Tonite' on the *Best Of* because of all the people we went to, asking people what do you think? What songs are very popular? What songs do people want to hear? A lot of people said those two. It was a concession." Or as Buck put it to Virgin Radio, "We ignored anyone who asked for 'Shiny Happy People,' put together a list of things ... they weren't all exactly hit singles, because we haven't had that many hit singles, but it is a good overview."

As for the title, R.E.M. once again didn't take the task of naming the album lightly. "There's two ways you can go when you do one of these compilations, you can have in

Stipe on the *In Time* album and tour: "It felt like a good time to close that chapter."

193

big golden letters, 'Greatest hits of all time as seen on TV.' We're not that much of a huge hit-making machine. *Best Of* sounded good and since our big record was called *Out Of Time*, who knows, maybe we're back in time again? *In Time* being the title. It's a little bit of a pun and maybe it's a little optimistic statement. Also, it's a title and that's the hardest thing to come up with ever."

As an added bonus, there was also a deluxe package available featuring a second disc with rarities and B-Sides, a sort of *Dead Letter Office 2*. "Kind of like that, except the songs are better. *Dead Letter* was really just a bunch of mongrels," Mills explained. "A lot of these things

---

On 'Bad Day,' Michael Stipe was "sick of being jerked around."

---

on the rarities are really good songs. We look at them and go, 'Why didn't we put that on the record that came out then?' But for one reason or another we left them off." (See the B-Sides section for information on songs that don't appear on another R.E.M. album.)

Yet, even the standard issue of *In Time* included something new for the fans, the previously unreleased recordings 'Bad Day' and 'Animal.'

Bad Day

If 'Bad Day' sounded like the R.E.M. of the past, it was for good reason. The song actually dates back to the *Lifes Rich Pageant* sessions. One of the band's best-known tracks, 'It's The End Of The World As We Know It (And I Feel Fine),' spun out of the song that was shelved for nearly two decades before it was unearthed and released.

"If we finished the song then, it would have been a track on *Lifes Rich Pageant*. I don't know why we didn't," Buck told me. "We were on the road so much, it was just hard to finish things. Whatever was ready, we'd record it and go back out. We thought, theoretically, it might be interesting to do something a little bit older [and] lyrically, finish it up now. It kind of bookends the record – we've got "Animal", which is brand new and 'Bad Day,' which is 17 years old."

At that time, Ronald Reagan, whose policies the band despised, was President of the U.S. But the original unreleased version of 'Bad Day,' then known as 'PSA,' was

more an indictment on the media than the President. In fact, it was reportedly inspired by the time a video camera crew knocked on Stipe's front door with cameras rolling. The revised 'Bad Day' took on another Republican administration years later, with Stipe taking aim at "whitewashed presidency" and railing, "We're sick of being jerked around."

"I didn't set out to write a political song at all," Stipe told me. "In fact, the songs that I think are our best songs, the ones that I look back on and say, 'I'm really proud of that,' are the ones I didn't think too much about. They just came out of me. I have no desire to write political songs, however, I'm a U.S. citizen and it's a little hard to breathe right now without breathing politics, so it works its way into music."

'Bad Day' is also notable as the first release featuring new drummer Bill Reiflin, known for his work with such industrial acts as Ministry and the Revolting Cocks.

Animal

While "Bad Day" was the look back, "Animal" was included on *In Time* to give fans a glimpse into the future. The only problem is that it ended up being a bit misleading, given the softer and sombre turn that *Around the Sun* eventually took.

Buck gave Virgin Radio the lowdown on "Animal", a track that wouldn't have been out of place on *Monster*. "It's a super-high-octane rock song with really weird, discordant

background vocals and strange guitar textures. It's real spontaneous. We listened to the demo tape once, played it through three times, and the track just sounded great. There isn't much overdubbing on it except the vocals and the guitar solo. It sounded like a real track immediately. It's really fun to play, so we were playing it live every night on the last tour [Europe, summer 2003]."

following the release of 'Animal' and statements the band made around the time of the release of *In Time*, speculation was that R.E.M.'s thirteenth effort would be a more rocking affair compared to the relatively subdued *Reveal* and *Up*. Yet even before 'Animal' hit the streets there were hints that R.E.M. was not in a raucous mood and that would be reflected on its forthcoming album.

In late March 2003, R.E.M. released 'Final Straw' free via its website. The traditional acoustic folk protest song took direct aim at the Bush administration and its decision to launch a pre-emptive strike against Iraq. It was the first hint that the next R.E.M. album would be the band's most politically minded work since *Document*, but, rather than that rock-oriented effort, it would be subtle and subdued.

"I'm sure that when I said, 'Things are either very loud and chaotic or so quiet you can barely hear them,' we were mixing 'Bad Day' and 'Animal' and about to go on a tour behind the *Best Of* and a lot of the material we had was really loud, but that was the stuff that kind of took a backseat," Stipe told me.

"We had so much material for the record. And I had a very clear idea of the kind of record I wanted to make. Among other things, I wanted a record you could put on and serve as almost background noise without any real interruption in flow…I wanted it to be around 55 minutes long and we made that. [We were] just responding to how people listen to music now, which is very different from the way we listen to music because we're huge music fans or the way casual music fans listened to music ten years ago or fifteen years ago, which was you sat down and you listened to it. You didn't have the Xbox going and CNN with the crawl and the captioning and checking out the Internet at the same time to see what's going on there while listening to music at the same time."

Around The Sun was recorded at a leisurely pace, giving the band plenty of time to ponder the political situation and that was reflected on the album. The sessions began in Vancouver. Following the *In Time* tour, the band reconvened in the Bahamas in winter and mixed the album in Miami.

Rather than simply promote the album with the usual tour,

R.E.M. signed on for the Vote For Change trek with Bruce Springsteen and Bright Eyes in support of presidential candidate Senator John F. Kerry.

Even after the band finished the all-star fundraising trek of swing-states, R.E.M. seemed more concerned about the presidential election than promoting *Around The Sun*, which had the dubious distinction of being the band's lowest charting debut of the SoundScan era, when it bowed in at Number 13. When the band kicked off its own North American tour, on

October 13 at the Greek Theater in Los Angeles, the set leaned heavily on politically driven album cuts. Before ending the set with 'Man on the Moon,' Stipe still had one order of business to complete. Emerging shirtless, he pulled on a Kerry T-shirt, making it clear that R.E.M. had its eye on something bigger than chart positions.

Leaving New York

The song that served as *Around The Sun*'s opening track and first single is Stipe's love letter to his second home, and was inspired not so much by the events of September 11, but the recovery and healing.

"I wanted to write a song to the city and it took the form of a love song not specific to any one person," he told me. "It just felt like the time was right to move on and to celebrate what New York is now, which is very different from what it

AROUND THE SUN

was before 9/11." The inspiration came as Stipe was sitting on a plane. "I was leaving New York," he recalled, "looking out the window and down at the city and the words just kind of fell out of me."

Additional inspiration came on another flight after the 9/11 attacks. "I remember flying into New York within a year that it happened – and I was there when it happened – looking at the skyline and for the first time it looked OK to me," he said.

"That to me was a very profound moment as someone who has been infatuated with New York since the seventies and I finally made it my second home after Athens. To fly in to the airport there and see Manhattan, the side without the Trade Center, and just go, 'That's New York now,' was for me a big kind of personal moment, a profound moment for me."

In the song, Stipe sings, "leaving was never my proud," a turn of phrase that he acknowledged is not grammatically cor- rect. "One of Mike's pet peeves is people who use words incorrectly," he told me. "We had a discussion when I said, 'Yeah, I know it's ungrammatical,' but yet that's what I felt, it was part of the unconscious. And we agreed that there wasn't really a word to change it to that would work. We tried, but there wasn't anything there that felt as real."

Muiscally, 'Leaving New York' is a ballad with a meditative mix of guitar and piano, a sweeping chorus, and layered vocals.

Electron Blue

This synth-laden track, which was slated to open *Around the Sun* before "Leaving New York" took off, is what Stipe calls one of his "future songs."

"These are songs that the band present to me. A lot of material for *Up,* but certainly 'Electron Blue', and certainly 'The Outsiders,' feels like the soundtrack to my dreams, not to right now, but somewhere in the near or distant future," Stipe told me. "Typically it's the near future and that's where the lyric usu- ally goes. 'Electron Blue,'" Stipe explained, is "a song about a drug made out of light that this guy is looking very hard for."

The politics of U.S. President George W. Bush, left, influenced *Around The Sun*.

Like most of the songs on *Around The Sun*, 'Electron Blue' was written from what Stipe calls his "unconscious voice. I'm really proud of that. I feel like I finally reached something as a writer, being able to pull that out of myself and turn off my thinking brain and not focus on the craftsmanship of songwriting or the tricks, but rather allow some-thing else to come through. And then my job is really to try to edit that stuff and try to make it make sense."

Musically, Stipe compares 'Electron Blue' to "the best of Eno, circa early seventies," adding: "If you want to look at just the surface of it, it's using instrumentation that we usually don't use. Connor Oberst [Bright Eyes] just did the same thing with his EP [*Take It Easy (Love Nothing)*]...It sounds Eno-esque because he's using electronic drumming and syn-thesizers."

The Outsiders

With its trip-hop beat and guest appearance by a rap artist, 'The Outsiders' is a bit like a mix of *New Adventures in Hi-Fi*'s 'How The West Was Won' with *Out Of Time*'s 'Radio Song.'

As Stipe noted at a press conference in Milan, it's one of the few tracks in the R.E.M. catalog to sport a prominent guest vocalist. In this case, it's the former Tribe Called Quest member Q-Tip, who raps the song's final verses.

"There are only four times in 24 years where we wrote a song and I heard a voice that wasn't my voice or Mike Mills' voice, it was someone else," Stipe said. "For 'The Outsiders' it was Q-Tip. ...The first time was KRS-One, the second time was Kate Pierson, the third time was Patti Smith. Now we have Q-Tip. They are all people with very unique voices. I think that's why he was chosen. What hap-pened was, I wrote the lyric, it fell out of me without me trying. I found some music that these two [Buck and Mills] had written, in this case I think it was a Mike song, and I put the two together and I instantly heard a voice that wasn't either one of us."

The inspiration for the song came during a Radiohead show at the Beacon Theater in New York. "I was there with Q-Tip and other friends," he told *Mojo*. "There was complete silence during the songs until 'No Surprises,' then Thom [Yorke] sang the line: 'Bring down the government/They don't, they don't speak for us', and the entire audience shouted it out. It was like, 'Did that just fucking happen?'"

He explained further in another interview. "I felt that the tipping point had occurred. For me in New York, with New Yorkers who, having been through 9/11, having felt what I call The Great Quiet, with this administration and the choic-es that they made, where people couldn't raise their voices

Q-Tip was the voice Stipe heard for the final verses of 'The Outsiders.'

– at that moment, that changed for me," he told the *Independent*'s Craig McLean. "I realized it was shifting rapidly. And I see the result of that now. I see the ripple effect is moving through the country..."

An interesting musical footnote, Buck plays drums on the track.

Make It All Okay

A ballad in the vein of 'Everybody Hurts' and 'Why Not Smile,' 'Make It All Okay' is clearly a song about a relationship gone bad, but like much of *Around The Sun*, there are also political overtones to the song.

"Politics to me is not limited to policy makers or government," he told me. "I have to be careful how I use that word, particularly in an election year. But the politics of the song 'Make It All Okay,' which is a clear-cut, straight-out love song.

You know someone's been spurned and then they're asked to come back, and they're like, 'No, fuck you. I found my own feet, thank you.' And yet that thing has challenged their own faith in the process, but they're not going to go back. There's a beauty there, there's a moving on. That's as political as 'Final Straw' in its way. It's the politics of emotion and relationships, and because of the Jesus lines in the song, the politics of belief and belief systems."

Final Straw

Possibly R.E.M.'s most overtly political song was initially released via the Internet at the onset of the U.S. invasion of Iraq.

"We didn't do that because we're big Hollywood pop stars, we did that because we're people and I have family members in the armed forces and I don't want them going to Iraq, and as it turns out one of them is," Stipe told *NME*.

The song's lyric "Who died and lifted you up to perfec-tion?" was aimed squarely at President George W. Bush and his cronies. "There's a whole group of men around Bush who believe it's America's duty to spread our greater morality to the rest of the world," Mills told the *Independent*'s McLean. "America is, if not the most decadent country in the world, certainly up there! But, yeah, these guys think it's our job to spread our morality around the Middle East."

I Wanted To Be Wrong

Around the Sun continues its political bent with "I Wanted to be Wrong", a sweet acoustic-sounding track that wouldn't be out of place on *Automatic For The People*. Despite the reference to the 1973 sci-fi classic *Westworld* and its star Yul Brenner, Stipe told me that the song is not a "future song," but set in the here and now. "It's just the idea of this robotic cowboy and the comparisons are obvious," he said of the *Westworld* reference.

Elsewhere the song takes aim at the Bush administration's decision to invade Iraq with the lyric, "We can't approach the Allies 'cause they seem a little peeved and speak a language we don't understand."

There are also pop-cultural references. The line "rattle jewelry seats" approximates John Lennon's famous quote, "Will the people in the cheaper seats clap your hands? And the rest of you, if you'll just rattle your jewellery." Lennon delivered the line in 1963 during the Beatles' set at the Royal Variety Performance in front of

members of the British Royal Family.

'I Wanted To Be Wrong' is also notable for its use of what Stipe calls "ghost lyrics," which appear on the lyric sheet in parenthesis, but aren't heard on the record. "There's another line that didn't make it in, which is about the *Omega Man*," Stipe told me, referencing another seventies sci-fi film. "The idea of the ghost lyric came in on this record because there were lyrics that I thought were significant to the arc of the story and the narrative, but did not make it into the song. If you read the lyrics on 'I Wanted To Be Wrong' there's a whole verse that didn't make it in. Those references I think balance the *Westworld* reference, the Apollo 13 reference, and the John Lennon reference with the 'children of the free' riding in T-Birds with the top down, which is the 1979 Patti Smith reference."

When I admitted to Stipe that I didn't catch the Patti Smith reference, he quipped, "Nobody did, but that's OK. That's what these kind of books are for, I think."

Wanderlust

The most upbeat and poppy song on *Around The Sun* chugs along with a sixties-style guitar riff and some of Stipe's most animated singing, particularly on the lines, "I want to kiss the astronauts/When they salute to me me me me."

"I have no idea where it came from," he told me. "It just came." Some critics assumed that Stipe was working some wordplay in by interchanging the "wander" with "wonder" at some points in the song, but that's simply not the case. "It's 'w*ander*lust'. It's in the lyric. My pronunciation in singing might get carried away," he explained. "Or there might be a little bit of Texas, a little bit of Georgia or Alabama in there."

Boy In The Wall

Following the upbeat 'Wanderlust,' *Around The Sun* heads south with 'Boy In The Well.' As Stipe told me, it's a song about leaving. "It's someone who is really trapped in a place where they don't belong and even though it's everything they know, they know that they have to leave," he explained. "That's what that song is."

Stipe said that it only makes sense that he writes about leaving. "It's partly about velocity, and being in motion and moving and travelling, the whole thing," he explained. "My peripatetic lifestyle – and our peripatetic lifestyle as a band that travels and tours and does promo and what have you – obviously would be an influence, but for me it's more than that. It's about an emotional state in most of these songs and whoever the protagonist is, like in 'Sad Professor' pulling themself from a place where they've been maybe for a long time, where they find themselves, to another place. Typically, it's emotional."

Musically, Buck has said the song features the band performing live, with minimal overdubs.

Aftermath

With its title and reference to "when London falls," 'Aftermath' could be another one of Stipe's future songs. "My dreams always take place in the future," he told me. "It's a decrepit, post-apocalyptic, for lack of a better term, existence and yet everything is OK there. Everyone's getting by, it's just like now, but it's very, very, very different. That's where my dreams are set. And they always have been since I was a kid."

Despite the apocalyptic vision, 'Aftermath' is one of *Around The Sun*'s more upbeat songs. In fact, at one point Buck had hoped the album would be even slower and 'Aftermath' was one of the song's he would have dropped.

Since R.E.M. was on tour in the U.S. when the video for the song was shot, director Peter Care shot the band in front of a green screen and superimposed them on images of London, chosen to match the song's lyrical references.

High Speed Train

Another Stipe "future song" that is light years away from 'Driver 8,' R.E.M.'s most famous train song. "Yeah," Stipe agreed, "I was 24 when I wrote that song."

As Stipe explained, 'High Speed Train' is more about a relationship than a train, with the vehicle merely serving as a form of transportation for one of the song's characters. "They're going to meet the love of their life and just wondering if this is what they want," he said. "And in the end, the whole sleeping bag thing, that kind of says it all."

The song was a favourite of Buck's on the 2004 tour. "Just on a sonic level, it's so great for us to play," he told Gene Stout of the *Seattle Post-Intelligencer*. "It's a really powerful sounding song. When we started the tour, I thought we might play it once a week. But we've been playing it every night and just loving it."

The Worst Joke Ever

To R.E.M.'s dismay, this song was mistakenly listed as 'The Worst Joke Over' on advance CDs distributed to the press, but by the time the official album was released, the mistake was corrected.

Stipe explained the intent of the song: "It's the idea of pulling this really bad kind of late fifties early sixties *Playboy* joke cartoon character out of the past. This guy has been telling the same joke his whole life and the joke in fact is his inability to change his attitude or recognize that a joke that might have been funny in the late sixties is no longer applicable to the world that he has moved into.

"At the age of 44, and being somewhat utopian as a youngster and reading comic books and looking at the world and seeing the opportunity for us to move into a better place as people, as individuals, as a culture, I look at this sort of mid-century attitude and it seems so tired to me and so twentieth century, and so stuck in this kind of Cold War, post-war, pre-Cold War mentality that to me is just suffocating," he told me. "Rather than leaping forward, we are just being dragged back by these ideas and some of the reasons for this are cultural and social and others are people digging their heels in and refusing to change or recognize that the world is not what they thought it might be then, and in fact it might have never been."

The Ascent Of Man

This soulful song is another track that Buck would have left off in his effort to make *Around The Sun* even slower. The song undoubtedly has the most "yeahs" of any R.E.M. track to date, something that Stipe does not regret. "It just came out of me," he told me. "I love it."

Again, pop cultural references abound. The lyrics include the line, "I try to float like a telegram sam," a nod to a song by seventies glam-rockers T. Rex. "I love Marc Bolan," Stipe said.

There's also the line "but I am what I am." Is Stipe borrowing from the great philosopher Popeye? "I think it might be," he laughed. "I'm sure Popeye's famous proclamation came from somewhere else, but I quote that because Popeye is probably where I heard it the first time."

In the song, Stipe also sings, "my book is called 'The Ascent of Man.'" For the record, *The Ascent of Man* is the title of a book by noted polymath Jacob Bronowski, based on the TV series of the same name, which is said to have inspired Carl Sagan's *Cosmos*. In the series, Bronowski traced the development of society through its understanding of science. Less than a year after the series aired, Bronowski died.

Around The Sun

After 23 years of recording, this song has the distinction of being R.E.M.'s first title track. It was more a result of desperation than design. "We couldn't find a title," Stipe told me. "I finally, frustratedly, just went on vacation to a place where my cell phone didn't work and I didn't have Internet access. I kind of left it to the band. Find some lyric in the record and let's just go with that. It was our ongoing issue with titling things. It's always a problem. Peter came up with *Around The Sun*."

Stipe gave me his take on the song. "Simply, it opens with an almost childish innocence about a better world and it becomes a little more complicated with each line. That to me is the progression of the song. The idea behind the song was to write a song that wasn't actually in the structure of a song, but was parts of music that were put together and worked as a song. I think it works well that way. It's a little bit of an experiment on our part."

As is the case with most R.E.M. albums, *Around The Sun* ends on an upbeat note thanks to the optimistic title track. Stipe again gives credit to Buck. "I'm not the one who sequences, but I thought it was a great idea to end up on a positive note. If there are melancholic songs on a record, we always try to end on a little bit of an up note."

B-SIDES, ETC.

After the release of *Dead Letter Office*, previously unreleased R.E.M. material has continued to crop up on the B-sides of singles and the reissues of the band's I.R.S. albums. What follows is a rundown of the post-1987 bonus tracks that have been released on singles or compilations. Live versions of tracks already featured on albums, and songs available only on fan club singles and promotional items, are not included.

TIGHTEN UP
The R&B roots of Mills and Berry shine through on this fun and loose cover of Archie Bell & The Drells's 1968 U.S. Number One hit. Over Mills' thumping bass, Stipe's soul-man goofing is particularly amusing. Easter—a "special guest" —is featured playing an impressive solo on the vibes.

Initially, R.E.M.'s rendition of 'Tighten Up' was only available on a flexi-disc included in the February 1985 issue of *Bucketful Of Brains*. I.R.S. opted to include it when it released the expanded edition of Reckoning in 1992.

MOON RIVER
Although the band occasionally covered it live, R.E.M.'s recording of this classic by Henry Mancini and Johnny Mercer was previously unreleased until the 1992 expanded edition of Reckoning was issued.

Stipe, who would later profess his fondness of Mancini when the band recorded 'Endgame' for *Out Of Time*, once claimed that he loved 'Moon River' not because of its association with the film classic *Breakfast At Tiffany's*, but because he thought the line "my huckleberry friend" was a reference to Huckleberry Hound, a favorite cartoon character. R.E.M.'s version, recorded live on February 17, 1983, is heartfelt. Stipe's voice cracks with emotion at points, and Mills plays a beautiful piano.

TIRED OF SINGING TROUBLE
In concert, R.E.M. often used this foot-stomping gospel traditional as a lead-in to 'I Believe.' This version, an outtake from the *Fables Of The Reconstruction* sessions, didn't surface until the 1993 expanded edition of *Lifes Rich Pageant*.

DREAM (ALL I HAVE TO DO)
R.E.M. recorded this cover of the 1958 Everly Brothers hit for the soundtrack to *Athens, Ga—Inside/Out* and were featured performing the song in the film. It showed that R.E.M. was not only capable of covering obscure Velvet Underground gems, but could cover pop classics. The band's harmonies are notably effective. R.E.M.'s cover was recorded during an acoustic performance on February 3, 1986, at the Lucy Cobb Chapel in Athens and mistitled '(All I've Got To Do Is) Dream.' It later resurfaced on the 1993 expanded edition of *Lifes Rich Pageant* under the title 'Dream (All I Have To Do).'

LAST DATE
Floyd Cramer's 1960 instrumental hit first appeared on 'The One I Love' single and was later included on the expanded edition of *Document*.

In 1993, R.E.M.'s version of the song was given new life when former Blondie frontwoman Deborah Harry recorded a new version. Her version, with lyrics, was titled 'My Late Date (With You).' The song appeared as a bonus track on Harry's album *Debravation*.

RED RAIN
R.E.M.'s interpretation of this 1986 Peter Gabriel track from the album So was included on the band's 'Time After Time Etc.' live medley, as a bridge between the two R.E.M. originals 'Time After Time' and 'So. Central Rain.'

Buck claimed that R.E.M. was thinking of his hit 'Sledgehammer,' also included on So, when it wrote *Document*'s 'Finest Worksong.'

ROMANCE
This song wasn't released until 1987—on the soundtrack to *Made In Heaven*, a film starring Timothy Hutton and Kelly McGillis—it was written and initially recorded at the time the band cut the 'Radio Free Europe' Hib-Tone single.

The final version of the song marked the band's first collaboration with longtime producer Scott Litt.

Aside from its appearance on the soundtrack, the song did turn up on the 1988 "best of" album *Eponymous*. Stipe wasn't necessarily fond of the album, although he did contribute a photo of himself from high school, with the words "They airbrushed my face" written across it, for the back cover.

MEMPHIS TRAIN BLUES
After the band tired of playing the repetitious chords of Green's 'Hairshirt,' they broke into this instrumental, recorded at Ardent Studios in Memphis, Tennessee.

"I started playing this bass riff, it was like a boogie bass riff and Bill started soloing on mandolin," Buck recalled. "That turned out to be a B-side, 'Memphis Train Blues.' If you actually listen to the take, 'Hairshirt' is just fading out and then we start that."

GHOST RIDER
Suicide, a '70s New York underground act, wouldn't on the surface seem to be an R.E.M. influence, given the duo's reliance on synthesizers. R.E.M. managed to record a convincing cover of this song, which was originally featured on Suicide's self-titled 1977 album.

DARK GLOBE
The song was written and originally recorded by Pink Floyd-founder Syd Barrett. Stipe's vocal on this track, sung in his higher voice, is particularly delicate and vulnerable. Produced by former Pink Floyd mates Roger Waters and Dave Gilmour in 1969, Barrett's version, titled 'Wouldn't You Miss Me (Dark Globe),' is available on the odds-and-ends collection *Opel*.

SKIN TIGHT
Berry and Mills's R&B cover band roots show up again on this version of the 1974 Ohio Players hit, recorded in Orlando, Florida, on April 30, 1989, during the *Green* tour.

FUNTIME
R.E.M. learned how to play this 1977 Iggy Pop classic while on the road. "Someone gave us a video of Iggy doing 'Funtime' on Dinah Shore, and we just learned it from the video," Buck explained. The band's version, according to the sleeve, was recorded and mixed in four minutes at John Keane's studio in Athens, Georgia—an amazing feat considering that the recording is two minutes and 14 seconds long.

Not only did R.E.M. cover 'Funtime,' but in *Monster*'s 'I Took Your Name,' Stipe saw fit to include a mention of Iggy.

ROTARY ELEVEN
This instrumental is the sequel of sorts to an earlier R.E.M. track. "'Rotary Ten' is the real good one," Buck explained. "'Rotary Eleven' is like a soft shoe shuffle. Any time we do demos, before we go in to record before a record, we all bring in a bunch of a songs, and I'll go, 'I've got an instrumental,' and every-one goes, 'Oh God,' and rolls their eyes, but then we do it and knock it out and it's kind of fun and ends up on a B-side."

AFTER HOURS
This is the fourth Velvet Under-ground cover to be officially released by the band. This is an extremely loose live version featuring a brief Berry drum solo, and Stipe hamming it up.

The original version of 'After Hours,' sung by drummer Moe Tucker and included on the 1967 album *The Velvet Underground & Nico*, effectively showed off the band's light-hearted side. R.E.M.'s take, recorded during the Green tour had a similar effect.

FORTY SECOND SONG
With its baroque mix of keyboards, guitar, and Stipe's wordless vocals, this rarity covers roughly the same territory of *Out Of Time*'s 'Endgame.' The song actually runs one minute and 21 seconds.

TOM'S DINER
As part of the band's promotional efforts for *Out Of Time*, R.E.M. played several intimate and secret gigs in the UK, many of which were taped for radio broadcast.

On March 15, 1991, the band performed under the pseudonym of Bingo Hand Job, with Peter Holsapple and special guest Billy Bragg, and offered up this hilarious cover of Suzanne Vega's 1987 song 'Tom's Diner.' Stipe took a co-writing credit on R.E.M.'s version, which begins as an a cappella number, with Stipe's improvised lyrics. Bragg provided human beatbox percussion and shouts of "baggy trousers" and "unbelievable."

This track first appeared as 'Tom's ?,' on the 1991 album *Tom's Album*, a collection of 13 different versions of 'Tom's Diner.'

I WALKED WITH A ZOMBIE
This marked the first of several R.E.M. appearances on tribute albums. The band's decision to contribute to the 1990 album *Where The Pyramid Meets The Eye: A Tribute To Roky Erickson* only made sense. Erickson made his name as the singer of legendary Texas '60s combo 13th Floor Elevators, a band that was right up Buck's alley. R.E.M.'s version of the song, produced by the band and John Keane, features a guitar solo by Keane.

LOVE IS ALL AROUND (live)
'Love Is All Around' showed off the Trogg's gentler side and is well suited to R.E.M.'s style.

This live version, recorded on April 1, 1991, on the syndicated radio program *Rockline*, features Mills on lead vocals with Stipe adding sweet harmonies. Another version appeared on the 1996 soundtrack *I Shot Andy Warhol*.

Buck, Mills, Berry, Holsapple, and Keane were featured on a 1992 Troggs comeback album titled *Athens Andover*, named after the two group's respective hometowns.

IT'S A FREE WORLD BABY
After first turning up as the B-side to 'Drive,' this *Out Of Time*-era track, which includes strings, was in addition included on the 1993 soundtrack to Coneheads.

"That should probably have gone on *Out Of Time*," Buck said. "We really liked the song, but we didn't think it fit in very well. I'm not sure that the song is really about anything. That's probably why we never used it on the album. It's just there, but it sounds really good."

WINGED MAMMAL THEME
Prince and U2 aren't the only superstar attractions to contribute music to the *Batman* films. R.E.M. did as well, only its contribution didn't make the films or the soundtracks.

"We had just started recording at Woodstock and Tim Burton knows Michael and he said, 'Do you have anything?' Michael told him we had this one thing, so we just dubbed the vocals 'Batman' on it and mailed it to him. It was just something we did, it was kind of stupid. None of us have any feeling about it as a song. He just said no thanks. He had said, 'Send anything, send an instrumental.' After we dubbed 'Batman' on it, it came back with a note, no thank you, but return post. And it's funny, Batman is a Warner Bros. movie, but they wouldn't let us use the word *Batman*. Are they going to get confused and sue themselves or something?"

FIRST WE TAKE MANHATTAN
This track, which opened the 1991 album *I'm Your Fan—The Songs Of Leonard Cohen*, was R.E.M.'s second venture into the tribute album field, and a stunning one at that.

Recorded at John Keane's studio in Athens, the song features Mills doubling on bass and organ, and Stipe delivering a searing vocal. Cohen's original appears on the 1988 album *I'm Your Man*.

ARMS OF LOVE
Over the years, Buck has played on several tracks by Robyn Hitchcock and Stipe once provided backing vocals. It only seemed logical that R.E.M. would record one of his songs.

R.E.M.'s folky, confessional version turned up on the B-side of 'Man On The Moon' in 1992. Another version of the song, attributed to Stipe as a solo artist, turned up on the 1993 album *In Defense Of Animals: A Benefit Compilation*. That substitutes R.E.M.'s folk-rock strains for a popping bass, strings, and percussion effects.

ORGAN SONG
This instrumental sounds like something you might hear in church, and for a good reason. "We actually have a demo of Michael singing that song, which is kind of cool," Buck said. "It has tremolo guitar on it. I don't know why we didn't ever work on that. We just kind of gave up. We thought the track was cool, so Mike went to a church in Minneapolis with this huge pipe organ and taped it."

FRUITY ORGAN
This upbeat instrumental is the polar opposite of the somber 'Organ Song.' "We write so much, we just did it in an afternoon," Buck explained.

NEW ORLEANS INSTRUMENTAL NO. 2
This sequel was recorded on the same night as the similarly titled 'New Orleans Instrumental No. 1,' but is sweeter than that tune, yet not nearly so sugary as 'Fruity Organ.'

"It sounded like a Juicy Fruit gum commercial," Buck said. "I was playing stand-up bass, Michael was playing this chiming omni-chord thing. It was kind of jolly, but there was no way we were going to use it on the album."

THE LION SLEEPS TONIGHT
Being the fine outstanding men that they are, when the members of R.E.M. lift from a song they admit it and agree to cover the classic they've borrowed from in return. That was the case with *Automatic For The People*'s 'The Sidewinder Sleeps Tonite,' which borrowed part of its title and melody from this 1961 hit by the Tokens.

FRETLESS
As chilling and discomforting as Green's 'The Wrong Child,' this

track landed on the 1993 soundtrack to *Until The End Of The World*, a film by Wim Wenders. "We're all huge fans of his and really pleased to be able to work with him," Stipe said on *Rockline*. Added Buck, "I would love to work with him, even if it is only by mail." The B-52's Kate Pierson is featured as a backing vocalist , reportedly named after the type of bass Mills used when writing it.

MANDOLIN STRUM
On Sam Phillips's 1996 album *Ominipop*, R.E.M. received a co-writing credit on a song called 'Slapstick Heart.' "They sent one of their B-sides...for a movie," Phillips said. "The movie came and went. Then I was listening to it one day, and I came up with a melody and an idea and then put it together with another piece of the song I had, and I sent it to them. They said, 'Yeah, OK. That's all right. You can do that."

The song that R.E.M. sent Phillips was 'Mandolin Strum,' but you need a keen ear to hear it in 'Slapstick Heart.' "It's kind of funny," Buck said. "I could tell the chord changes, but the melody is totally different. When I played it on mandolin for Michael, it was a really long-winded whiny thing, and he said, 'I can't sing that.' It's a nice B-side, because it has a nice melody and good chord changes. I was really flattered when Sam put it on her record, because I love her work and like that record." Buck played guitar on Sam's 1994 album *Martinis & Bikinis*.

CHANCE (DUB)
Over a robotic drumbeat, Stipe rambles in a monotone, before confessing, "This is very tedious."

"Michael was just reading, I think one of the local papers, and he thought this would be kind of cool to take some of these personal columns and just read them," Buck explained. "I'm not even sure if I was there. Scott and Mike came up with the drum beat and just kind of played along and it had all these synthesizer sounds. It was incredibly stupid, but it was fun. It was one of those things that we're not going to stick on the record, but a B-side is a good place for it."

PHOTOGRAPH
A rare collaboration with former 10,000 Maniacs vocalist Natalie Merchant, which was included on the 1993 album *Born To Choose*. Merchant co-wrote the song and contributes vocals. Stipe lent vocal support to 10,000 Maniacs's 'Campfire Song,' from the band's 1987 album *In My Tribe*.

"Michael had a good portion of the melody and he was about halfway through the lyrics and he was just totally lost," Buck explained. "A lot of times if he isn't inspired, he will just throw something away, which could be frustrating for us, but he always comes up with good stuff, so we just kind of let it go. We got an invitation to do something for the benefit thing, *Born To Choose*, and we all wanted to be involved and I suggested why don't we just

give it to someone we know and let them finish it and we can do it as a duet. Natalie came up with great stuff. I think she changed most of the lyrics."

The track was completed in an afternoon. "We recorded it in one or two takes" Buck added, "and I went in and overdubbed a guitar when they sang it, so I've maybe heard it 10 times in my life, so it's still kind of fresh."

WALL OF DEATH
One reason R.E.M. hired Joe Boyd to produce *Fables Of The Reconstruction* was because of his work with Fairport Convention, the folk-rock group that featured Richard Thompson. R.E.M. tipped their hats to Thompson by contributing 'Wall Of Death' to the 1994 album *Beat The Retreat – Songs By Richard Thompson*.

R.E.M.'s cover features Mills on bass and piano, and John Keane on pedal steel guitar. Thompson's original can be found on the 1982 album *Shoot Out The Lights*, recorded with his then-wife Linda.

TRICYCLE
Recorded on September 22, 1995, at a soundcheck in St. Louis on the Monster tour, this is an addition to R.E.M.'s canon of instrumental work.

"I write hundreds and hundreds of songs, and we can only use X amount in a year," Buck explained. "I end up writing a lot of instrumentals. Sometimes it is trying to figure out a key or go from one place to another.

"We had this series of unlikely notes that was really chromatic and weird," Buck added. "Mike started playing the verse with all these weird harmonies and it just got funnier and funnier and stupider and stupider. We played it for a couple of weeks at soundcheck. To us, it was just kind of a musical joke. It's not really in a key and it has all these kind of half-step walks-ups that are kind of stupid. But I love that kind of music. Once we finally learned to play it all the way through, we just stopped playing it. Luckily we captured it on tape. I like it, it's a cool little thing. It's a good B-side, but in a way I think we should have stuck everything from this tour on this new record and have an 80-minute album. 'Revolution' didn't make it and 'Tricycle' would have been good."

As for the title, "At first I thought it was a really dumb hot rod song, so it should be called 'Four Wheels To Hell,' but we've never been that kind of melodramatic band. So I said, how about 'Tricycle.' I was going to call it, 'Laika Cosmonaut' after that Swedish band I really like, Laika & The Cosmonauts, but I was afraid they would sue us."

SPONGE
Like 'Tricycle,' this song was recorded on the *Monster* tour—in a Chicago dressing room with instrumental support from Scott McCaughey and Nathan December. Like 'Wall Of Death,' it is another contribution to a tribute album—in this case *Sweet Relief II: Gravity Of The*

Situation—The Songs Of Vic Chesnutt.

"That version of 'Sponge,' that Vic Chesnutt song that we did in the dressing room, that to me is part of the *Hi-Fi-Adventure-Tour* thing, because it was recorded on tour," Buck explained.

R.E.M.'s decision to pay tribute to Chesnutt, a wheelchair-bound singer-songwriter and fellow Athenian, was a natural. Stipe worked on some of Chesnutt's albums, and Chesnutt contributed a loopy version of 'It's The End Of The World As We Know It (And I Feel Fine),' featuring a sample of Stipe saying "alright," on the R.E.M. tribute album *Surprise Your Pig*.

REVOLUTION
This rocker was played nightly on the Monster tour, but didn't make *New Adventures In Hi-Fi*. "It was the oldest song of the batch of new songs," Buck explained. "We actually almost finished it when we made *Monster*. We had a demo and thought it was a great first track for the record, but as the tour went on, it didn't fit in with the other new songs, but it fit perfectly in the live set."

WICHITA LINEMAN
This cover of the Jimmy Webb-penned classic, a hit for Glen Campbell in 1968, was recorded live on September 15, 1995, in Houston with McCaughey and December. The band got the idea working on *Monster*. "We were in Miami and we had a night off and I know this really, really, really tacky bar," Buck said in the 1996 documentary *Rough Cut*. "It's at the bottom of a hotel and it's totally Miami. They had Karaoke night and Michael got up and just blew away all these people by doing Jimmy Webb songs. I was like, 'We really ought to do one of those on the road,' and he was like, 'Sure, no problem.'"

DRAGGIN' THE LINE
The bubble gum influence displayed in such R.E.M. songs as 'Stand' can be traced to such '60s artists as Tommy James & The Shondells, known for such hits as 'Mony Mony' and 'I Think We're Alone Now.' This song was a hit for James in 1971 after he split from the Shondells. R.E.M.'s version was included on the soundtrack to *Austin Powers: The Spy Who Shagged Me*. "Just a great song," Stipe told me.

EMPHYSEMA
A lounge-y, bass-heavy instrumental track that has left fans divided with some calling it a "silly song" and others proclaiming it "the best instrumental ever". Named after a lung condition that results in laboured breathing.

SURFING THE GANGES
As the titled suggests, this is a surf-style instrumental in the vein of the *Ventures*. The Ganges is a sacred river to Hindus, which runs through northern India and Bangladesh rising in the Himalaya Mountains through a vast plain to the Bay of Bengal.

PASSENGER
The second Iggy Pop cover version released by R.E.M., following 'Funtime.' This version was recorded during the band's appearance on the BBC's *Later With Jools Holland*. While Iggy has been cited as an influence and even namedropped in *Monster*'s 'I Took Your Name,' apparently he is not too pleased with R.E.M.'s remarks about the use of his songs in TV commercials. "Hell, if I was R.E.M., I sure as hell wouldn't let my songs be used for an ad either," he told *Blender* in September 2003. "Their songs already sound so fucking prissy."

2JN
As Buck revealed in the liner notes of the *In Time: The Best of R.E.M. 1988–2003* special edition, this track is a tribute to composer/songwriter/producer/arranger/studio musician Jack Nitzsche and was written the week that he died – on August 20, 2001 – of cardiac arrest due to a bronchial infection at the age of 63. Although Nitzsche is probably best known for his work with the Rolling Stones and Neil Young, as well as penning the Jackie DeShannon hit 'Needles And Pins' with Sonny Bono, he was also a recording artist. His only hit single, 'The Lonely Surfer,' peaked at Number 39 in 1963. "I think we captured a bit of the 'Lonely Surfer' vibe on this one," Buck wrote. "So long, Jack."

ALL THE RIGHT FRIENDS
This oldie, which dates back to the band's earliest days, was dug out and recorded for the soundtrack to Cameron Crowe's *Vanilla Sky*, which also included *Automatic For The People*'s 'Sweetness Follows.'

YELLOW RIVER
Mills sings lead on this cover of British band Christie's upbeat 1970 hit 'Yellow River.' The original version was a huge hit in the U.K. and several other countries, but only reached Number 23 in the U.S. While R.E.M.'s version mostly flew below the radar, one fan not only heard it, he was inspired to write a long and convoluted story, posted on the Christie/'Yellow River' website (www.yellowriver.com) about how the band's update led to world peace. If only.

165 HILLCREST
A surf-style instrumental named after the address of John Keane Studios, which is located on 165 Hillcrest Ave., in a historic district of R.E.M.'s hometown of Athens, Georgia. R.E.M. has worked at the studio, which resides inside a 1920s-era home, since the Document-era B-side 'Last Date.' Several subsequent B-sides have been produced at the studio, which the band has also used to cut instrumental performances and engineer portions of its Warner Bros. album.

FAVORITE WRITER
The 'Bad Day' single was a virtual bonanza for R.E.M. fans, who of late had to settle for B-sides featuring either live versions of earlier hits or instru-

mentals. On 'Bad Day' they were treated to three previously unreleased recordings: two cover versions with vocals as well as one new instrumental. 'Favorite Writer' is a cover originally recorded by Athens, Georgia-based quartet *Magnapop* whose singer, Linda Hopper, and guitarist, Ruthie Morris, wrote the song. Stipe produced the band's demos, which ended up being released as a self-titled effort in 1992. *Magnapop*'s version of 'Favorite Writer' was included on a re-released version of that album, which featured bonus tracks.

Hopper's relationship with Stipe actually predates his involvement with Magnapop. In the early '80s Hopper was a member of Oh-OK with future Magnapop drummer David McNair, Matthew Sweet, and Stipe's sister, Lynda. Michael Stipe shot the cover photo of the band's 1983 EP and another one of his sisters, Cyndy, is credited with backup vocals on 'Choukoutien.'

Hopper told Jason Gross about her relationship with Michael Stipe, who she met in art school. "We had grown to be quite good friends," she said. "He would be like, 'I want you to be in a band with my sister.' We went to a party one night and he brought Lynda. She was sixteen and still in high school. I just remember that I loved her from the moment that we met each other. We became close friends. She was like an older sister for me in Athens where everybody hung out together. Lynda wanted to be in a group and that's when it hit me. 'I love music and I love going to see R.E.M. so let's be in a group!'"

OUT IN THE COUNTRY
Mills sings lead on this cover of the 1970 *Three Dog Night* hit. This song was written by Roger Nichols and Paul Williams, the songwriters that wrote such Carpenters hits as 'We've Only Just Begun' and 'Rainy Days And Mondays.'

ADAGIO
The final track on the ''Bad Day' single is a dreamy R.E.M. instrumental that wouldn't be out of place on the *Man On The Moon* soundtrack. The title of the track is a word of Italian origin that means a slow piece of music.

PERMANENT VACATION
This rocking oldie was finally released as a live recording featured on the *Perfect Square* DVD and later as part of the band's *iTunes Originals* session. "'Permanent Vacation' was one of a whole batch of songs we wrote during the first year of our existence," Mills said in the iTunes interview. "Those gradually took over [and] forced all the covers from the set and they were all pretty much gone by 1982 in favour of the stuff that later came out on *Murmur and Chronic Town*." As Buck explained, the band "rediscovered" the song in 2003 and once again added it to its live set.

CHRONOLOGY

1956
December 6: Peter Lawrence Buck born in Oakland, California.

1958
July 31: William Thomas Berry born in Duluth, Minnesota.
December 17: Michael Edward Mills born in Orange County, California.

1960
December 4: John Michael Stipe born in Decatur, Georgia.

1977
December: Buck helps organize a free show by the B-52's at Emory University in Atlanta, Georgia.

December: Buck takes a job as a clerk at Wuxtry Records in Athens, Georgia, near the University of Georgia.

1978
January 5: Buck had reserved a ticket to see the Sex Pistols at the Great Southwest Music Hall, but upon his arrival finds the show oversold. He bum rushes the door with friends, but is thrown out and beaten by a bouncer after one-and-a-half songs.

Winter: Buck meets a mysterious teenager who frequently visits Wuxtry with two pretty girls. The teenager is Michael Stipe. The girls are Stipe's sisters Lynda and Cyndy. Buck and Stipe find they share a love of Patti Smith and the Velvet Underground.

1979
January: Best friends Mills and Berry, who had performed together in a number of cover groups, move to Athens.

1980
January: Kathleen O'Brien, who roomed with Buck and Stipe at an old Episcopal church on Oconee Street in Athens, Georgia, introduces Buck to Berry.

April 5: R.E.M., then unnamed or going by the name of Twisted Kites, makes its first public appearance playing at O'Brien's birthday party at the church on Oconee Street.

May 9: The 40 Watt Club opens with a show by the Side Effects. R.E.M. would frequently gig at the small club, which charged only $1 for admission.

May 12: R.E.M. makes it first headline appearance at Tyrone's in Athens, Georgia.

July 18-19: R.E.M. fills in for Pylon for two dates at the Station in Carrboro, North Carolina.

December: R.E.M. support the Police at the Fox Theatre in Atlanta.

1981
Winter: R.E.M. writes 'Radio Free Europe.'

April: R.E.M. records 'Radio Free Europe,' 'Sitting Still' and 'White Tornado' during its first session with Mitch Easter at the Drive-In Studio in Winston-Salem, North Carolina.

June: The band makes its first trip to New York to play at the Ritz as the opening act for Gang Of Four.

July: The 'Radio Free Europe' single, with 'Sitting Still' on the flipside, is released on the independent Hib-Tone label.

October: R.E.M. returns to the Drive-In to record new songs for an EP.

1982
February 1-2: The band records seven songs at RCA studios in New York.

February: R.E.M. returns to the Drive-In to finish EP.

March 12: The band plays at the Beat Exchange in New Orleans. I.R.S. Records VP Jay Boberg attends and is impressed.

May 31: R.E.M. signs with I.R.S. Records.

August 19: Band makes Los Angeles debut at the Music Machine.

August 24: *Chronic Town* EP is released.

1983
January: R.E.M. records demos with producer Stephen Hague in Atlanta. Unhappy with the results, they reunite with Easter and Don Dixon at Reflection Studios in Charlotte, North Carolina to record Murmur.

February: Chronic Town is named the second best EP of 1982 in the prestigious Village Voice Pazz & Job critics poll.

April 12: *Murmur*, which climbed to No. 36 in a 30-week run on the *Billboard* album chart, is released. Stipe's close friend Carol Levy dies in a car accident.

April: Band tours in support of *Murmur*.

July: A re-recorded version of 'Radio Free Europe' reaches No. 73 on *Billboard*'s Hot 100.

August: The band supports the Police on five shows on the East Coast, including an August 18 date at Shea Stadium. They call the experience one of the worst of their lives.

October 6: R.E.M. makes its U.S. national TV debut on *Late Night With David Letterman* performing 'Radio Free Europe' and a song "too new to be named," later titled 'So. Central Rain.'

November 18: R.E.M. makes its U.K. TV debut on *The Tube*.

November 19: Band makes its U.K. concert debut at Dingwalls, Camden, London, England.

December: The band returns to Reflection Studios to record with Easter and Dixon.

Also in 1983: Stipe makes guest appearance on Jason and the Nashville Scorchers' Fervor EP, co-writing 'Both Sides Of The Line' and singing backing vocals on 'Hot Nights In Georgia.'

1984
January: *Murmur* is named Album Of The Year, beating Michael Jackson's *Thriller*, the Police's *Synchronicity*, and U2's *War* by Rolling Stone, which also calls R.E.M. the best new artist and third best band. The *Village Voice* Pazz & Job critics poll calls *Murmur* the second best album of the year.

January: Side project the Hindu Love Gods, featuring R.E.M. with Bryan Cook on vocals instead of Stipe, plays the 40 Watt Club. Warren Zevon, who the group records demos with, joins the group.

April 16: *Reckoning* is released. It peaks at No. 27 in the U.S. and spends more than a year on the chart.

December: Outtake 'Windout' appears in the film and on the soundtrack to *Bachelor Party*.

1985
January: R.E.M. travels to London to record its third album with veteran producer Joe Boyd.

March: Jay Boberg is appointed president of I.R.S. Records.

March 4: Buck joins the Fleshtones on stage in Paris on 'When The Night Falls' and R.E.M.'s 'Windout.' The results are preserved on the Fleshtones' Speed Connection II.'

June: Buck joins Fleshtones Keith Streng in a side project known as the Full Time Men. Buck plays guitar, banjo, and produces self-titled EP. Mills guests on organ.

June 10: Fables Of The Reconstruction is released to mixed reviews. The album peaks at No. 28 in the U.S.

June 22: R.E.M. supports U2 at the Milton Keynes Bowl. The band was not well-received.

Also in 1985: Buck makes an appearance on 'The Party,' featured on the self-titled debut by U.K. band the Dream Academy.

1986
Winter: A film crew from Los Angeles descends on Athens to film the documentary titled *Athens Ga—Inside/Out*.

Summer: R.E.M. hires Don Gehman, best known for his work with John Cougar Mellencamp, to produce its fourth album at Mellencamp's Bloomington, Indiana studio.

July: *Lifes Rich Pageant* is released. It will reach No. 21 on the U.S. album chart.

September 5: R.E.M. embarks on Pageantry tour in support of *Lifes Rich Pageant* in Birmingham, Alabama.

November: Gehman isn't available to produce 'Romance' for the *Made In Heaven* soundtrack, so he recommends Scott Litt. The band and Litt forge a long relationship.

1987
Spring: R.E.M. begins recording its fifth album at Sound Emporium with Litt producing.

May: *Dead Letter Office*, a collection of B-sides, is released.

May 24: Stipe and Buck make a surprise appearance at a benefit concert, held at McCabe's Guitar Shop in Santa Monica, California and perform new songs in an acoustic set.

August: *Murmur* is named the 58th best album of all time by Rolling Stone.

August 31: *Document* is released on the same day as Michael Jackson's *Bad*. R.E.M.'s album will reach the top 10.

September 12: R.E.M. begin the Work Tour, in support of *Document*, at Hammersmith Odeon in London, England.

December: 'The One I Love' becomes the band's first hit single, peaking at No. 9 in the US.

December: R.E.M. is called "America's Best Rock'n'Roll Band" by Rolling Stone, which features the group on the cover.

1988
June: After completing its obligation to I.R.S., R.E.M. signs a five-album deal, reportedly worth $10 million, with Warner Bros.

Summer: R.E.M. records Green with Litt producing, at Ardent Studios in Memphis, Tennessee and Bearsville Studio near Woodstock, New York.

October 2: I.R.S. releases the "best of" collection Eponymous, which features the Hib-Tone version of 'Radio Free Europe' and an alternate take of Gardening At Night.'

October: Stipe takes ads out in college newspapers supporting Democratic presidential candidate Michael Dukakis.

November 8: To the dismay of R.E.M., George Bush is elected President of the United States of America. *Green*, which peaks at No. 12 on the charts, is released.

1989
January 26: R.E.M. begin the Green World Tour at MZA Stadium in Tokyo, Japan.

March 1: The band launches the U.S. leg of its first arena trek.

April 8: 'Stand' becomes the band's second top 10 hit. It peaks at No. 6 on the Hot 100 and will be given new life a few years later as the theme to the Chris Elliot sit-com *Get A Life*.

April: Berry falls victim to Rocky Mountain spotted fever in Munich, Germany, forcing band to cancel German tour.

August: Green tour documentary Tourfilm is released.

1990
Summer: R.E.M. begins recording Out Of Time at Bearsville Studios in Woodstock, New York with Litt again producing.

1991
Winter: R.E.M., without Berry, previews 'Losing My Religion' at the 40 Watt Club in Athens, Georgia.

March 12: *Out Of Time* is released on would have been Jack Kerouac's 69th birthday.

April: The 'Losing My Religion' video is banned in Ireland because of its use of religious imagery.

May 18: R.E.M. scores its first No. 1 album, as *Out Of Time* tops the Billboard 200 in its eighth week on the chart. 'Losing My Religion' becomes the band's biggest hit single, reaching No. 4 on the Hot 100.

September 5: R.E.M. wins six trophies at the eighth annual MTV Video Music Awards, including the best video of the year. In addition to best video of the year, 'Losing My Religion' also wins best group video, breakthrough video, best direction in a video (Tarsem), best art direction (Jose Montana), and best editing (Robert Duffy).

1992
February 25: After seven nominations, R.E.M. wins three Grammy Awards: best pop performance by a duo or group with vocal, best video for 'Losing My Religion,' and best alternative album for Out Of Time.

February: The readers and critics of *Rolling Stone* name R.E.M. the best band, Out Of Time best album, and 'Losing My Religion' best single and video. *Rolling Stone* readers also name R.E.M. artist of the year and Stipe best singer, and best songwriter.

Spring: R.E.M. begins recording follow-up to *Out Of Time* in New Orleans.

Summer: *Surprise Your Pig: A Tribute to R.E.M.* is released. Contributors include Mitch Easter and Vic Chesnutt.

September 2: R.E.M. performs 'Everybody Hurts' and a funk version of 'Drive' at the MTV Video Music Awards.

October 6: *Automatic For The People* is released. It debuts and peaks at No. 2 in America. It is the second consecutive album released by R.E.M. without the support of a tour.

November 19: R.E.M. makes a surprise appearance at the 40 Watt Club in Athens as a benefit for Greenpeace. The concert is recorded on a solar-powered mobile studio.

1993

January 20: Stipe and Mills join U2's Larry Mullen Jr. and Adam Clayton as Automatic Baby and perform U2's 'One' at MTV's Rock'n'roll Inaugural Ball in honor of newly elected President Bill Clinton. Stipe also joins 10,000 Maniacs on a cover of 'To Sir With Love' and 'Candy Everybody Wants.'

February: *Automatic For The People* is named best album, R.E.M. best band, and Stipe best male singer by critics in *Rolling Stone*'s 1993 Music Awards.

1994

March: R.E.M. begins recording *Monster* at studios in New Orleans, Miami, Atlanta, and Los Angeles, "and a couple of parking lots." During the sessions, Buck became a father of twin girls, and Mills had an emergency appendectomy.

April: Nirvana frontman Kurt Cobain, who had planned to collaborate with Stipe, is found dead from a self-inflicted gunshot to the head.

September 27: *Monster* is released and debuts at No. 1 on The Billboard 200.

October: Stipe forms Single Cell Pictures, a film production company, with New Line Cinema.

1995

January 13: R.E.M. launches its first tour in five years in Perth, Australia.

March 1: Berry has to leave the stage during a show in Lausanne, Switzerland, but the show goes on as Joey Peters from opening act Grant Lee Buffalo sits in. Later Berry is rushed to the hospital where he undergoes brain surgery for two ruptured blood vessels.

May 15: With Berry recovered, R.E.M. resumes the Monster tour at the Shoreline Amphitheatre near San Francisco, California.

July: Mills becomes ill in Cologne, Germany and has to be operated on for an adhesion in his abdominal tract.

August: Stipe has surgery for a hernia. No dates are canceled, but he admits having trouble with the high notes.

November 21: The Monster tour wraps with three concerts in Atlanta.

1996

May 13: R.E.M. splits with manager Jefferson Holt. The *Los Angeles Times* reported that Holt allegedly sexually harassed an employee at the band's Athens, Georgia headquarters. Attorney Bertis Downs assumes the role of manager.

August 24: R.E.M. signs a new five-album deal with Warner Bros. reportedly worth $80 million. The new deal is announced at the WEA convention in Anaheim, California. Some Warner Bros. employees cry tears of joy.

September 10: *New Adventures In Hi-Fi*, recorded on the road during the Monster tour, is released. It debuts and peaks at No. 2.

October 1: *Road Movie*, documenting the final nights of the Monster tour, is released.

1997

April: R.E.M. begins writing songs for a follow-up to *New Adventures In Hi-Fi*.

June 6: Pearl Jam's Eddie Vedder and Mike McCready turn up on stage during the Tibetan Freedom Concert, joining R.E.M.'s Michael Stipe and Mike Mills for a performance.

October 30: R.E.M. officially announces that Bill Berry is leaving the band, but vows to carry on as a trio.

November 18: R.E.M. contributes a version of 'Crush With Eyeliner' to *Live On Letterman: Music from the Late Show*.

December: 'Live For Today,' R.E.M.'s last recorded performance with Bill Berry is released as part of a split single with Pearl Jam, which serves as a holiday fan club single for both bands.

1998

May 26: Tuatara's *Trading With the Enemy*, is released.

June 14: R.E.M. makes its first live performance without Berry at the annual Tibetan Freedom Concert in Washington, D.C.

July: The first new R.E.M. recording since the departure of Berry is released. The song, 'Why Not Smile,' is the final track on The Oxford American Southern Sampler 1998, which is available with the Oxford, Miss.-based literary magazine's "second annual double issue on Southern music".

November: *Velvet Goldmine*, a film loosely based on the glam-rock era exploits of David Bowie and Iggy Pop, opens. Stipe

serves as the film's executive producer.

October 17–18: R.E.M. plays 12th Annual Bridge School Benefit Concert, organized by Neil Young.

October 27: *Up*, R.E.M.'s eleventh album is released and debuts at No. 3 in the U.S.

1999

February: R.E.M. appears on *Sesame Street* performing 'Furry Happy Monsters' with the Muppets and tapes a segment for Party of Five performing 'At My Most Beautiful.' *Up* is certified gold for sales of 500,000 copies in the U.S.

June 1: The *Austin Powers: The Spy Who Shagged Me* soundtrack, featuring R.E.M. covering Tommy James' 1971 hit 'Draggin' The Line,' is released.

August 9: R.E.M. opens first U.S. tour without Berry at the Greek Theatre in Los Angeles

August 29: Berry walks onstage to embrace his former bandmates during the first show of the band's three-night stand at the Chastain Park Amphitheater in Atlanta.

September: *The Royal Philharmonic Orchestra Plays the Music of R.E.M.* is released.

October 29: *Being John Malkovich* is released. Stipe serves as one of the film's producers.
November 23: The soundtrack to *Man on the Moon*, featuring a score by R.E.M. and the new song 'The Great Beyond,' is released.

2000

April: R.E.M. confirms it will start recording the follow-up to *Up* in May with Pat McCarthy in Vancouver, Canada.

July: The railroad trestle featured on the back cover of *Murmur* is given a stay of execution from a wrecking ball after fans rally against its demise.

August: R.E.M. continues work on the follow-up to *Up* in Dublin, Ireland.

October: Atlanta radio station 99X (WNNX-FM) releases *Walk Unafraid*, a multi-artist charity CD. R.E.M. contributes a live version of the title track.

October 22: R.E.M. makes a surprise appearance at the Land Aid festival in its hometown of Athens, Georgia, with Stipe performing a new song 'I've Been High' accompanied by a boom box.

2001

January 13: R.E.M. plays *Rock In Rio*, one of the largest gatherings for live music ever, in Rio de Janeiro.

April 21: Buck, who is generally known for his good-natured

demeanor, is arrested and charged for allegedly assaulting two members of a flight crew in the first-class section of a flight from Seattle to London.

April 29: R.E.M. headlines the South Africa Freedom Day Concert in London's Trafalgar Square.

May 8: 'Imitation of Life,' the first single from *Reveal*, is released.

May 15: *Reveal*, R.E.M.'s twelfth album is released and debuts at No. 6 in the U.S. Stipe admits he's gay in an interview with Time magazine, saying, "I was being made to be a coward about it rather than someone who felt like it really was a very private thing."

July: *Reveal* is certified gold for sales of 500,000 in the U.S.

July 31: Buck pleads not guilty to assault and other charges stemming from an alleged air-rage incident that occurred during an April flight from Seattle to London.

September: 'Everybody Hurts' receives airplay as programmers attempt to comfort listeners in wake of the September 11 terrorist attacks on America.

October 20–21: R.E.M. plays the 15th Annual Bridge School Benefit Concert.

November 18: Stipe, Buck, and Mills appear as special guests on The Simpsons' *Thanksgiving* episode.

December 4: The soundtrack to Cameron Crowe's *Vanilla Sky*, featuring R.E.M.'s 'All The Right Friends' and 'Sweetness Follows,' is released.

2002

February 14: R.E.M. honours Bono at The Love Rocks event in Hollywood. The band plays 'I Got You Babe' with Cher, and U2's 'One' with Bono joining on vocals.

March 26: Bono testifies at Buck's air-rage trial in a London court, calling him a "quiet" and "peaceful" man.

March 27: Stipe and Mills testify at Buck's air-rage trial in a London court, with Stipe describing Buck as a "gentle and polite" person who is "just not...rude to anyone."

April 5: Buck is cleared of all charges of physical and verbal attacks against a British Airways crew in London.

May: R.E.M. puts an album's worth of remixes of tracks from *Reveal* on its official website (remhq.com).

2003

January 28: 1987's *Document* is released as a DVD-Audio disc mixed in 5.1 surround sound.

March: A new anti-war song, titled 'Final Straw', is posted on the band's official website (remhq.com).

June 27: R.E.M. plays the Glastonbury Festival in the U.K.

August 29: A six-week North American tour begins at Thunderbird Stadium in Vancouver – where the trio has been working on its next studio album.

September 1: On the heels of a summer European jaunt, R.E.M. kicks off its first American tour in four years at Seattle's Bumbershoot Festival.

October 11: R.E.M. wraps its fall North American tour with a show at Atlanta's Phillips Arena. The night before in Raleigh, N.C., Berry made a surprise appearance, drumming on 'Permanent Vacation' and offering backing vocals on 'Radio Free Europe.'

October 28: In Time: The Best of R.E.M. 1988–2003 is released, bowing at Number 8 in the U.S. A two-CD deluxe version enters at Number 16. In the U.K., the album becomes the group's sixth chart-topper.

2004

March 16: Perfect Square, a DVD of R.E.M.'s July 29, 2003 concert at Bowling Green in Weisbaden, Germany, is released.

August 10: 'Final Straw (MoveOn Mix)' is featured on the benefit album Future Soundtrack for America.

September 15: R.E.M. unveils several songs from *Around The Sun* at a secret gig in a London church, recorded for broadcast by BBC Radio 2. Radiohead vocalist Thom Yorke makes a surprise appearance.

October 1: The *Vote for Change* tour opens in Philadelphia with R.E.M. playing five shows with Bruce Springsteen, John Fogerty and Bright Eyes. During the tour, Springsteen joins R.E.M. on 'Man On The Moon,' while Stipe returns the favour on Because the Night,' and Buck and Mills join the E Street Band on 'Born to Run.'

October 5: *Around The Sun*, R.E.M.'s thirteenth album, is released. It debuts at No. 13 in the U.S., but becomes the band's seventh chart-topping album in the U.K.

October 13: R.E.M. opens its most intimate North American tour in 15 years at Los Angeles' Greek Theater.

October 26: A live version of 'Drive' is included on For The Lady, a benefit album for imprisoned Burmese peace activist Aung San Suu Kyi.

2005

January 7: R.E.M. kicks off 2005 World Tour in Lisbon

February 15: The band's entire Warner Bros. catalog is reissued as two-disc CD/DVD combo package.

DISCOGRAPHY

(Chart peaks refer to *Billboard*'s album chart and Hot 100 singles chart in the US.)

ALBUMS

Murmur

Release date: April 1983

Catalog number: IRS SP7064

Producers: Mitch Easter and Don Dixon

Tracks: Radio Free Europe / Pilgrimage / Laughing / Talk About The Passion / Moral Kiosk / Perfect Circle / Catapult / Sitting Still / 9-9 / Shaking Through / We Walk / West Of The Fields

[1992 UK expanded version includes: There She Goes Again / 9-9 (live) / Gardening At Night (live) / Catapult (live)]

Chart peak: 36

Reckoning

Release date: April 1984

Catalog number: IRS SP70044

Producers: Mitch Easter and Don Dixon

Tracks: Harborcoat / 7 Chinese Bros. / So. Central Rain / Pretty Persuasion / Time After Time (Annelise) / Second Guessing / Letter Never Sent / Camera / (Don't Go Back To) Rockville / Little America

[1993 UK expanded version includes: Windout (with friends) / Pretty Persuasion (live in studio) / White Tornado (live in studio) / Tighten Up / Moon River]

Chart peak: 27

Fables Of The Reconstruction

Release date: June 1985

Catalog number: IRS IRS5592

Producer: Joe Boyd

Tracks: Feeling Gravitys Pull / Maps And Legends / Driver 8 / Life And How To Live It / Old Man Kensey / Cant Get There From Here / Green Grows The Rushes / Kohoutek / Auctioneer (Another Engine) / Good Advices / Wendell Gee

[1992 UK expanded version includes: Crazy / Burning Hell / Bandwagon / Driver 8 (live) / Maps And Legends (live)]

Chart peak: 28

Lifes Rich Pageant

Release date: July 1986

Catalog number: IRS IRS5783

Producer: Don Gehman

Tracks: Begin The Begin / These Days / Fall On Me / Cuyahoga / Hyena / Underneath The Bunker / The Flowers Of Guatemala / I Believe / What If We Give It Away? / Just A Touch / Swan Swan H / Superman

[1993 UK expanded version includes: Tired Of Singing Trouble / Rotary Ten / Toys In The Attic / Just A Touch (live in the studio) / Dream (All I Have To Do) / Swan

Swan H (acoustic)

Chart peak: 21

Dead Letter Office

Release date: April 1987

Catalog number: IRS SP70054

Producer: various

Tracks: Crazy / There She Goes Again / Burning Down / Voice Of Harold / Burning Hell / White Tornado / Toys In The Attic / Windout / Ages Of You / Pale Blue Eyes / Rotary Ten / Bandwagon / Femme Fatale / Walter's Theme / King Of The Road

(CD includes *Chronic Town* EP)

Chart peak: 52

Document

Release date: September 1987

Catalog number: IRS IRS42059

Producers: Scott Litt and R.E.M.

Tracks: Finest Worksong / Welcome To The Occupation / Exhuming McCarthy / Disturbance At The Heron House / Strange / It's The End Of The World As We Know It (And I Feel Fine) / The One I Love / Fireplace / Lightnin' Hopkins / King Of Birds / Oddfellows Local 151

[1993 UK expanded version includes: Finest Worksong (other mix) / Last Date / The One I Love (live) / Time After Time Etc. (live) / Disturbance At The Heron House (live) / Finest Worksong (lengthy club mix)]

Chart peak: 10

Eponymous

Release date: October 1988

Catalog number: IRS IRS6262

Producers: various

Tracks: Radio Free Europe (original Hib-Tone single) / Gardening At Night (different vocal mix) / Talk About The Passion / So. Central Rain / (Don't Go Back To) Rockville) / Cant Get There From Here / Driver 8 / Romance / Fall On Me / The One I Love / Finest Worksong (mutual drum horn mix) / Its The End Of The World As We Know It (And I Feel Fine)

Chart peak: 44

Green

Release date: November 1988

Catalog number: Warner Bros. 25795

Producers: Scott Litt and R.E.M.

Tracks: Pop Song 89 / Get Up / You Are The Everything / Stand / World Leader Pretend / The Wrong Child / Orange Crush / Turn You Inside-Out / Hairshirt / I Remember California / (untitled track)

Chart peak: 12

Out Of Time

Release date: March 1991

Catalog number: Warner Bros. 26496

Producers: Scott Litt and R.E.M.

Tracks: Radio Song / Losing My Religion / Low / Near Wild Heaven / Endgame / Shiny Happy People / Belong / Half A World Away / Texarkana / Country Feedback / Me In Honey

Chart peak: 1

Automatic For The People

Release date: October 1992

Catalog number: Warner Bros. 45138

Producers: Scott Litt and R.E.M.

Tracks: Drive / Try Not To Breathe / The Sidewinder Sleeps Tonite / Everybody Hurts / New Orleans Instrumental No. 1 / Sweetness Follows / Monty Got A Raw Deal / Ignoreland / Star Me Kitten / Man On The Moon / Nightswimming / Find

The River

Chart peak: 2

Monster

Release date: September 1994

Catalog number: Warner Bros. 45740

Producers: Scott Litt and R.E.M.

Tracks: What's The Frequency, Kenneth? / Crush With Eyeliner / King Of Comedy / I Don't Sleep, I Dream / Star 69 / Strange Currencies / Tongue / Bang And Blame / I Took Your Name / Let Me In / Circus Envy / You

Chart peak: 1

New Adventures In Hi-Fi

Release date: September 1996

Catalog number: Warner Bros. 46320

Producers: Scott Litt and R.E.M.

Tracks: How The West Was Won And Where It Got Us / The Wake-Up Bomb / New Test Leper / Undertow / E-Bow The Letter / Leave / Departure / Bittersweet Me / Be Mine / Binky The Doormat / Zither / So Fast, So Numb / Low Desert / Electrolite

Chart peak: 2

Up

Release date: October 1998

Catalog number: Warner Bros. 47112

Producers: Pat McCarthy and R.E.M.

Tracks: Airportman / Lotus / Suspicion / Hope / At My Most Beautiful / Apologist / Sad Professor / You're in the Air / Walk Unafraid / Why Not Smile / Daysleeper / Diminished / Parakeet / Falls to Climb

Chart peak: 3

Reveal

Release date: May 2001

Catalog number: Warner Bros. 47946

Producers: Pat McCarthy and R.E.M.

Tracks: The Lifting / I've Been High / All the Way to Reno (You're Gonna Be A Star) / She Just Wants To Be / Disappear / Saturn Return / Beat a Drum / Imitation of Life / Summer Turns to High / Chorus and the Ring / I'll Take the Rain /

Beachball

Chart peak: 6

In Time: The Best of R.E.M. 1988–2003

Release date: October 2003

Catalog number: Warner Bros. 48381

Producers: Scott Litt, Pat McCarthy and R.E.M.

Tracks: Man on the Moon / The Great Beyond / Bad Day / What's the Frequency, Kenneth? / All The Way to Reno / Losing My Religion / E-Bow The Letter / Orange Crush / Imitation of Life / Daysleeper / Animal / The Sidewinder Sleeps Tonite / Stand / Electrolite / All the Right Friends / Everybody Hurts / At My Most Beautiful / Nightswimming

Special Edition Bonus Disc: Pop Song '89 (Acoustic) / Turn You Inside-Out (Live) / Fretless / Chance (Dub) / It's A Free World Baby / Drive / Star Me Kitten (feat. W.S. Burroughs) / Revolution / Leave (alt. version) / Why Not Smile (alt. version) / The Lifting (demo) / Beat A Drum (demo) / 2JN / The One I Love (live) / Country Feedback (live)

Chart peak: 8

Around The Sun

Release date: October 2004

Catalog number: Warner Bros. 48894

Producers: Pat McCarthy and R.E.M.

Tracks: Leaving New York / Electron Blue / The Outsiders (feat. Q-Tip) / Make It All Okay / Final Straw / I Wanted to be Wrong / Wanderlust / Boy in the Well / Aftermath / High Speed Train / The Worst Joke Ever / The Ascent of Man / Around the Sun

Chart peak: 13

SINGLES AND EPs

(This is a combination of US and UK releases. Some titles were omitted to avoid duplication. If a release was only issued in one country, it is noted. Two-part singles are listed in one entry.)

Radio Free Europe

Release date: July 1981

(US)

Catalog number: HTOOO1

Producers: Mitch Easter and R.E.M.

Tracks: Radio Free Europe / Sitting Still

Chronic Town

Release date: August 1982

(US)

Catalog number: IRS SP7052

Producers: Mitch Easter and R.E.M.

Tracks: Wolves, Lower / Gardening At Night / Carnival Of Sorts (Box Cars) / 1,000,000 / Stumble

Radio Free Europe

Release date: May 1983

Catalog number: IRS IR9916

Producers: Mitch Easter and Don Dixon

Tracks: Radio Free Europe / There She Goes Again

Chart peak: 78

Talk About The Passion

Release date: November 1983 (UK)

Catalog number: IRS PFSX 1026

Producers: Mitch Easter and Don Dixon/R.E.M.

Tracks: Talk About The Passion / Shaking Through / Carnival Of Sorts (Box Cars)/ 1,000,000

So. Central Rain (I'm Sorry) (UK)

Release date: March 1984

Catalog number: IRS IRSX105

Producers: Mitch Easter and Don Dixon

Tracks: So. Central Rain (I'm Sorry) / Voice Of Harold / Pale Blue Eyes

So. Central Rain (I'm Sorry)

Release date: May 1984

Catalog number: IRS IR 9927

Producers: Mitch Easter, Don Dixon

Tracks: So. Central Rain (I'm Sorry) / King Of The Road

Chart peak: 85

(Don't Go Back To) Rockville (UK)

Release date: June 1984

Catalog number: IRS IRSX107

Producers: Mitch Easter/Don Dixon

Tracks: (Don't Go Back To) Rockville / Wolves / 9-9 (live) / Gardening At Night (live)

(Don't Go Back To) Rockville

Release date: August 1984

Catalog number: IRS IR9931

Producers: Mitch Easter/Don Dixon

Tracks: (Don't Go Back To) Rockville / Catapult (live)

Cant Get There From Here

Release date: June 1985

Catalog number: IRS 52642

Producer: Joe Boyd

Tracks: Cant Get There From Here / Bandwagon

Cant Get There From Here (UK)

Release date: July 1985

Catalog number: IRS IRT102

Producer: Joe Boyd

Tracks: Cant Get There From Here / Bandwagon / Burning Hell

Driver 8 (US)

Release date: September 1985

Catalog number: IRS IRS52678

Producer: Joe Boyd

Tracks: Driver 8 / Crazy

Wendell Gee (UK)

Release date: October 1985

Catalog number: IRS IRMD105

Producers: Joe Boyd / Mitch Easter and Don Dixon

Tracks: Wendell Gee / Crazy / Ages Of You / Burning Down

Wendell Gee

Release date: October 1985

Catalog number: IRS IRT105

Producer: Joe Boyd

Tracks: Wendell Gee / Crazy / Driver 8 (live)

Fall On Me

Release date: August 1986

Catalog number: IRS IRS52882

Producer: Don Gehman

Tracks: Fall On Me / Rotary Ten

Chart peak: 94

Fall On Me (UK)

Release date: September 1986

Catalog number: IRS IRMT121

Producer: Don Gehman

Tracks: Fall On Me / Rotary Ten / Toys In The Attic

Superman

Release date: November 1986

Catalog number: IRS IRS52971

Producer: Don Gehman/Mitch Easter

Tracks: Superman / White Tornado

Superman (UK)

Release date: March 1987

Catalog number: IRS IRMT128

Producer: Don Gehman

Tracks: Superman / White Tornado / Femme Fatale

The One I Love (US)

Release date: August 1987

Catalog number: IRS IRS23792

Producers: Scott Litt and R.E.M.

Tracks: The One I Love/ The One I Love (live)/ Maps And Legends (live)

Chart peak: 9

It's The End Of The World As We Know It (And I Feel Fine) (UK)

Release date: August 1987

Catalog number: IRS IRM145

Producers: Scott Litt and R.E.M.

Tracks: It's The End Of The World As We Know It (And I Feel Fine) / This One Goes Out (live) / Maps And Legends (live)

The One I Love (UK)

Release date: November 1987

Catalog number: IRS IRMT146

Producers: Scott Litt and R.E.M.

Tracks: The One I Love / Last Date / Disturbance At The Heron House

It's The End Of The World As We Know It (And I Feel Fine) (US)

Release date: January 1988

Catalog number: IRS IRS53220

Producers: Scott Litt and R.E.M.

Tracks: It's The End Of The World As We Know It (And I Feel Fine) / Last Date

Chart peak: 69

Finest Worksong

Release date: March 1988

Catalog number: IRS IRS23850

Producers: Scott Litt and R.E.M.

Tracks: Finest Worksong (Lengthy Club Mix) / Finest Worksong (Other Mix) / Time After Time Etc. (live)

Stand (UK)

Release date: January 1989

Catalog number: Warner Bros. W7577

Producers: Scott Litt and R.E.M.

Tracks: Stand / Memphis Train Blues / (untitled)

Chart peak: 6

Orange Crush (UK)

Release date: May 1989

Catalog number: Warner Bros. W2690

Producers: Scott Litt and R.E.M.

Tracks: Orange Crush / Ghost Riders / Dark Globe

Stand (UK)

Release date: August 1989

Catalog number: Warner Bros. W2833

Producers: Scott Litt and R.E.M.

Tracks: Stand / Pop Song 89 (acoustic version) / Skin Tight

Pop Song 89 (US)

Release date: June 1989

Catalog number: Warner Bros. 27640

Producers: Scott Litt and R.E.M.

Tracks: Pop Song 89 / Pop Song 89 (acoustic)

Chart peak: 86

Get Up (US)

Release date: 1989

Catalog number: Warner Bros. 22791

Producers: Scott Litt and R.E.M.

Tracks: Get Up / Funtime

Losing My Religion

Release date: February 1991

Catalog number: Warner Bros. W0015

Producers: Scott Litt and R.E.M.

Tracks: Losing My Religion / Rotary Eleven / After Hours (live) / Stand (live) / Turn You Inside-Out (live) / World Leader Pretend (live)

Chart peak: 4

Shiny Happy People

Release date: May 1991

Catalog number: Warner Bros. WOO27

Producers: Scott Litt and R.E.M.

Tracks: Shiny Happy People / Forty Second Song / Losing My Religion (live acoustic) / I Remember California (live) / Get Up (live) / Pop Song 89 (live)

Chart peak: 10

Near Wild Heaven

Release date: August 1991

Catalog number: Warner Bros. W055

Producer: Scott Litt and R.E.M.

Tracks: Near Wild Heaven / Pop Song '89 (live acoustic) / Half A World Away (live) / Tom's Diner (live)/ Low (live) / Endgame (live)

Radio Song

Release date: November 1991

Catalog number: Warner Bros. WOO72

Producers: Scott Litt and R.E.M.

Tracks: Radio Song / Love Is All Around (live) / Shiny Happy People (Music Mix) / You Are The Everything (live) / Orange Crush (live) / Belong (live)

Drive

Release date: September 1992

Catalog number: Warner Bros. WO136

Producers: Scott Litt and R.E.M.

Tracks: Drive / It's A Free World, Baby / Winged Mammal Theme / First We Take Manhattan

Chart peak: 28

Man On The Moon

Release date: November 1992

Catalog number: Warner Bros. W0143

Producers: Scott Litt and R.E.M.

Tracks: Man On The Moon / Turn You Inside-Out / Arms Of Love / Fruity Organ / New Orleans Instrumental No. 2

Chart peak: 30

The Sidewinder Sleeps Tonite

Release date: February 1993

Catalog number: Warner Bros. W0152

Producers: Scott Litt and R.E.M.

Tracks: The Sidewinder Sleeps Tonite / The Lion Sleeps Tonight / Fretless / Organ Song / Star Me Kitten

Everybody Hurts

Release date: March 1993

Catalog number: Warner Bros. W0169

Producers: Scott Litt and R.E.M.

Tracks: Everybody Hurts / New Orleans Instrumental No. 1 (Long Version) / Mandolin Strum / Chance (Dub) / Dark Globe

Everybody Hurts (US)

Release date: 1993

Catalog number: Warner Bros. 40442

Producers: Scott Litt and R.E.M.

Tracks: Everybody Hurts/ Mandolin Strum / Belong (live) / Orange Crush (live) / Star Me Kitten (Demo) / Losing My Religion (live) / Fruity Organ

Chart peak: 29

Nightswimming (UK)

Release date: July 1993

Catalog number: Warner Bros. W0184

Producers: Scott Litt and R.E.M.

Tracks: Nightswimming / Losing My Religion (live) / World Leader Pretend (live) / Belong (live) / Low (live)

Find The River

Release date: November 1993

Catalog number: Warner Bros. W021

Producers: Scott Litt and R.E.M.

Tracks: Find The River / Everybody Hurts (live) / World Leader Pretend (live) / Orange Crush (Instrumental)

What's The Frequency, Kenneth?

Release date: September 1994

Catalog number: Warner Bros. 41760

Producers: Scott Litt and R.E.M.

Tracks: What's The Frequency, Kenneth? / Monty Got A Raw Deal (live) / Everybody Hurts (live) / Man On The Moon (live)

Chart peak: 21

Bang And Blame

Release date: October 1994

Catalog number: Warner Bros. W0275

Producers: Scott Litt and R.E.M.

Tracks: Bang And Blame / Losing My Religion (live) / Country Feedback (live) / Begin The Begin (live)

Chart peak: 19

Crush With Eyeliner

Release date: 1995

Catalog number: Warner Bros. WO281

Producers: Scott Litt and R.E.M.

Tracks: Crush With Eyeliner / Fall On Me (live) / Me In Honey (live) / Finest Worksong (live)

Strange Currencies

Release date: 1995

Catalog number: Warner Bros. W0290

Producers: Scott Litt and R.E.M.

Tracks: Strange Currencies / Drive (live) / Funtime (live) / Radio Free Europe (live)

Chart peak: 47

E-Bow The Letter

Release date: August 1996

Catalog number: Warner Bros. 43763

Producers: Scott Litt and R.E.M.

Tracks: E-Bow The Letter / Tricycle / Departure (Rome soundcheck) / Wall Of Death

Chart peak: 49

Bittersweet Me

Release date: November 1996

Catalog number: Warner Bros. W0377

Producers: Scott Litt and R.E.M.

Tracks: Bittersweet Me / Undertow (live - Atlanta) / Wichita Lineman (live - Houston) / New Test Leper (acoustic)

Chart peak: 46

Electrolite

Release date: December 1996

Catalog number: Warner Bros. W0383

Producers: Scott Litt and R.E.M.

Tracks: Electrolite / The Wake-Up Bomb (live - Atlanta) / Binky The Doormat (live - Atlanta) / King Of Comedy (808 State remix)

How The West Was Won (Germany)

Release date: June 30, 1998

Catalog number: 43851

Producers: Scott Litt and R.E.M.

Tracks: How The West Was Won / Be Mine (Mike on Bus version) / Love Is all Around / Sponge

Daysleeper (U.K.)

Release date: October 1998

Catalog number: 455

Producers: Pat McCarthy and R.E.M.

Tracks: Daysleeper / Emphysema / Why Not Smile (Oxford American version)

Lotus (U.K.)

Release date: December 1998

Catalog number: 466

Producers: Pat McCarthy and R.E.M.

Tracks: Lotus / Surfing The Ganges / Suspicion (live in the studio) / Lotus (weird mix)

At My Most Beautiful (U.K.)

Release date: March 1999

Catalog number: 477

Producers: Pat McCarthy and R.E.M.

Tracks: At My Most Beautiful / Passenger (live) / Country Feedback (live)

Suspicion (U.K.)

Release date: June 1999

Catalog number: 488

Producers: Pat McCarthy and R.E.M.

Tracks: Suspicion / Electrolite (live) / Man on the Moon (live)

The Great Beyond (U.S.)

Release date: February 2000

Catalog number: 44816

Producers: Pat McCarthy and R.E.M.

Tracks: The Great Beyond (edit) / The One I Love (live) / Everybody Hurts (live) / Man on the Moon (live)

Imitation of Life (U.S.)

Release date: May 2001

Catalog number: 42363

Producers: Pat McCarthy and R.E.M.

Tracks: Imitation of Life / The Lifting (original version) / Beat a Drum (Dalkey Demo) / 2JN

All The Way To Reno (You're Gonna Be A Star) (U.K.)

Release date: August 2001

Catalog number: 42396

Producers: Pat McCarthy and R.E.M.

Tracks: All the Way to Reno (You're Gonna Be A Star) / Yellow River / 165 Hillcrest

I'll Take The Rain (U.K.)

Release date: November 2001

Catalog number: 42416

Producers: Pat McCarthy and R.E.M.

Tracks: I'll Take the Rain / Summer Turns to High (32 Chord Song Demo) / I've Been High (live) / She Just Wants to Be (live)

Bad Day (U.K.)

Release date: October 2003

Catalog number: 42668

Producers: Pat McCarthy and R.E.M.

Tracks: Bad Day / Favorite Writer / Out in the Country / Adagio

Animal (U.K.)

Release date: February 2004

Catalog number: 42699

Producers: Pat McCarthy and R.E.M.

Tracks: Animal / Pretty Persuasion (live) / Welcome to the Occupation (live) / So. Central Rain (live)

Leaving New York (U.K.)

Release date: September 2004

Catalog number: 42755

Producers: Pat McCarthy and R.E.M.

Tracks: Leaving New York / You Are the Everything (live) / These Days (live) / Don't Go Back To (Rockville) (live)

Aftermath (U.K.)

Release date: November 2004

Catalog number: 658

Producers: Pat McCarthy and R.E.M.

Tracks: Aftermath / So Fast So Numb (live) / All the Right Friends (live) / High-Speed Train (live)

R.E.M. WEB SITE LISTING

www.remhq.com
www.murmurs.com
www.retroweb.com/rem.html
http://orangefox.svs.com/rem/
www.remrock.com
www.remonline.co.uk
www.sweetnessfollows.co.uk
www.rem-fan.com/

INDEX

All numbers in italics refer to illustrations.

PICTURE CREDITS

The publishers would like to thank the following sources for their kind permission to reproduce the pictures in this book:

All Action 140, 164/James Young 6; Archive Photos 132/Fotos International 97; Courtesy Athens Daily Newspaper 55; Courtesy of Comcast Spectacor 166; Corbis Images/ Bettman187/ John Shults/Reuters 185/ Karen Mason Blair 183, 191;/Reuters 189, 196; Corbis-Bettman 82, 84, 92, 100, 131, 169/UPI 47, 60, 123, 129; Coward-McCann Inc., illustration by Kurt Weise from The Five Chinese Brothers by Claire Huchet Bishop © 1938, © 1965 reproduced by permission, Coward-McCann Inc. 36; Mary Evans Picture Library 16; Getty Images/Sion Touhi/ 179; Ronald Grant Archive 125, 156, 170t;

Robert Harding Picture Library/Robert Francis 168; Hulton Getty 25, 143; Image Select 66; Katz/ Frederick Reglain/Gamma 170/Jean-Marc Ayral/Gamma174 /Trevor Ray Hart 188; Dennis Keeley 14; Laura Levine 9, 12, 17, 20, 26, 27, 28, 30, 35, 39, 43, 49, 62, 68, 70t, 75, 116; London Features International 52, 136/Gregg Deguire 80/FGN 149/Simon Fowler 32, 83/L. Lawry 104/Kevin Mazur 74, 117, 134, 161/G. de Sota 72; Sandra-Lee Phipps 8, 15, 22, 24, 41, 42, 48, 51, 76, 78, 79, 87, 88, 111, 138, 170b; Pictor 167; Pictorial Press Ltd. 109, 112/Showtime 64/Strange Things 70b/Rob Verhorst 142; Picture Desk/ The Kobal Collection/Universal/Francois Duhamel 180; Redferns 58, 114/Mick Hutson 148, 150/Ebet Roberts 29, 171t, 176; Retna Pictures Ltd/Michael Benabib 107, 198/Jay Blakesberg 144/Adrian Boot 173;/Monica Dee 162/H. Diltz 94l/Steve Double 2/ Robin Francois 195/Jolt

192/Robin Kaplin 54/Walter McBride 38/Tony Mottram 10/Chris Taylor 185/ Luciano Viti 186/ 18/Photo Fest 65/Bob Ramirez 152, 158/Ronnie Randall 126/Chris Taylor 154/Chris v.d. Vooren 171b; Rex Features Ltd. 99; Courtesy of Rykodisc Ltd. 46; S.I.N. 44/Peter Anderson 56, 94r, 103/Steve Double 93, 146/Tony Mott 118/Leo Regan 90/Roy Tee 7, 102/Ian T.Tilton 141; Science Photo Library 53; Courtesy of Weaver D's Delicious Fine Foods 121.

Every effort has been made to acknowledge correctly and contact the source and/or copyright holder of each picture, and Carlton Books Limited apologises for any unintentional errors or omissions which will be corrected in future editions of this book.